Wine

maranGraphics™

&

THOMSON

COURSE TECHNOLOGY

Professional ■ Technical ■ Reference

MARAN ILLUSTRATED™ Wine

Distributed in the U.S. and Canada by Thomson Course Technology PTR. For enquiries about Maran Illustrated™ books outside the U.S. and Canada, please contact maranGraphics at international@maran.com

For U.S. orders and customer service, please contact Thomson Course Technology at 1-800-354-9706. For Canadian orders, please contact Thomson Course Technology at 1-800-268-2222 or 416-752-9448.

ISBN: 1-59863-318-X

Library of Congress Catalog Card Number: 2006906790

Printed in the United States of America

06 07 08 09 10 BU 10 9 8 7 6 5 4 3 2 1

Trademarks

Important

Copies

maranGraphics Inc.
Educational facilities, companies, and organizations located in the U.S. and Canada that are interested in multiple copies of this book should contact Thomson Course Technology PTR for quantity discount information. Training manuals, CD-ROMs, and portions of this book are also available individually or can be tailored for specific needs.

maranGraphics™

maranGraphics Inc.
5755 Coopers Avenue
Mississauga, Ontario
L4Z 1R9
www.maran.com

THOMSON

COURSE TECHNOLOGY
Professional ■ Technical ■ Reference

Thomson Course Technology PTR, a division of Thomson Course Technology
25 Thomson Place ■ Boston, MA 02210 ■ http://www.courseptr.com

maranGraphics is a family-run business

At **maranGraphics**, we believe in producing great books—one book at a time.

Each maranGraphics book uses the award-winning communication process that we have been developing over the last 30 years. Using this process, we organize photographs and text in a way that makes it easy for you to learn new concepts and tasks.

We spend hours deciding the best way to perform each task, so you don't have to! Our clear, easy-to-follow photographs and instructions walk you through each task from beginning to end.

We want to thank you for purchasing what we feel are the best books money can buy. We hope you enjoy using this book as much as we enjoyed creating it!

Sincerely,

The Maran Family

We would love to hear from you! Send your comments and feedback about our books to family@maran.com

To sign up for sneak peeks and news about our upcoming books, send an e-mail to newbooks@maran.com

Please visit us on the Web at:
www.maran.com

CREDITS

Author:
maranGraphics
Development Group

Content Architects:
Ruth Maran
Kelleigh Johnson
Andrew Wheeler

Technical Consultant:
Tonia Wilson

Project Manager:
Judy Maran-Tarnowski

Copy Development Director:
Jill Maran Dutfield

Copy Developers:
Andrew Wheeler
Dana Grimaldi

Editor:
Dana Grimaldi

**Layout Designers &
Photographic Retouching:**
Mark Porter
Sarah Kim

**Photographic Retouching &
Chart Design:**
Sam Lee

Photographers:
Sam Lee
Andrew Wheeler

Cartographer:
Bill Nelson

Indexer:
Kelleigh Johnson

Post Production:
Robert Maran

**Publisher and General Manager,
Thomson Course Technology PTR:**
Stacy L. Hiquet

**Associate Director of Marketing,
Thomson Course Technology PTR:**
Sarah O'Donnell

**Manager of Editorial Services,
Thomson Course Technology PTR:**
Heather Talbot

ACKNOWLEDGMENTS

Thanks to the dedicated staff of maranGraphics, including
Kelleigh Johnson, Sam Lee, Jill Maran Dutfield, Judy Maran-Tarnowski,
Robert Maran, Ruth Maran, Mark Porter and Andrew Wheeler.

Finally, to Richard Maran who originated the easy-to-use graphic
format of this guide. Thank you for your inspiration and guidance.

TONIA WILSON

When it comes to wine and food, Tonia Wilson has both sides covered—she is certified as both a Sommelier and a Chef. Tonia's love for wine began while completing her university degree in the Loire region of France; it was there that she first realized what wine could really be, and she then focused her efforts on increasing her wine knowledge and tasting experience.

Along the way, her culinary career took off and she found herself holding the position of Head Chef at the Canadian Embassy in Rome, Italy. During this period, she had the distinction of cooking for dignitaries such as the Queen of England. The greatest advantage, however, was having access to tasting some of the world's finest wines. While in Italy, Tonia attained her Sommelier Certification with the Italian Sommelier Guild (AIS) and spent much time visiting the vineyards of some of Europe's greatest wine regions.

Tonia's company, Savour (www.savourflavour.com), specializes in Taste Education with a focus on the dynamic relationship between wine and food. She has appeared on television networks in both Canada and Italy and has been featured internationally in magazines and newspapers.

A few words from Tonia:

My philosophy about wine is simple: wine is to be enjoyed, but simple, wine is not.

Wine envelops so many things; history, culture, geography and nature. In this book, we have simplified the wealth of information about the world of wine, enabling people to better understand and enjoy the wine they drink. This book makes wine knowledge accessible to everyone and is unlike any book of its genre.

In addition to giving a very heartfelt thanks to everyone at maranGraphics for their hard work and professionalism, I would like to make mention of those who are very dear to me. My parents and lovely Nan, for instilling in me that anything is possible. And both my Mikes, for being two of my most favorite and special people.

The following companies have allowed us to publish photos of their fine products and facilities.

Beringer Vineyards

We would like to thank Beringer Vineyards for their cooperation and photographic material. Established in 1876, Beringer Vineyards is the oldest continually operating winery in California's famed Napa Valley. Beringer produces a wide range of exceptional wines, from festive White Zinfandel to Private Reserve Cabernet Sauvignon. For more information, visit www.beringer.com for a full listing of Beringer's wine offerings as well as recipes and tips for pairing wine with food.

Hip Restaurants

A special thanks to Hip Restaurants, operator of *Ten Restaurant and Wine Bar* and *On The Curve Hot Stove and Wine Bar* in Mississauga, Ontario, for allowing us to use Ten Restaurant and Wine Bar as the setting for several of our photos. Hip Restaurants also provided us with several photos and allowed us to reproduce portions of their wine lists. For more information about Hip Restaurants, visit www.hiprestaurants.com.

Cork & Bottle

A special thanks to the Cork & Bottle wine and spirits shop in Miami for allowing us to use a number of photos of their store and its extensive selection of wines. For more information about Cork & Bottle, visit www.thecorkandbottle.com.

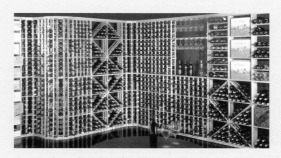

Vintage Keeper

We would like to thank Vintage Keeper for providing photos of their wine-storage equipment for use in this book. For more information about Vintage Keeper's range of products, visit www.vintagekeeper.com.

Henry of Pelham Family Estate

We would like to thank Henry of Pelham Family Estate for providing us with photos of their winemaking facilities. Producing wines in Canada's renowned Niagara Peninsula winemaking region, Henry of Pelham Family Estate helped to establish Ontario's appellation

system, the Vintners Quality Alliance (VQA). For more information about the full range of wines offered by Henry of Pelham, visit www.henryofpelham.com.

Gonzalez Byass

A special thanks to Gonzalez Byass for providing photographs that were included in this book. This family-run Spanish wine producer makes a wide range of products from sparkling wines to various types of Sherries. For more information about Gonzalez Byass, visit www.gonzalezbyass.com.

Individual Photo Credits

Page	Photo Number (left to right)	Photo Courtesy Of
Table of Contents, page 1	1	Beringer
Table of Contents, page 2	1	Cork & Bottle
14	1	Beringer
23	1	Beringer
44	1	Beringer
44	2	Beringer
45	1	Beringer
45	2	Beringer
46	1	Beringer
46	2	Beringer
47	1	Beringer
47	2	Beringer
48-49	n/a	Beringer
50	1	Henry of Pelham
51	1	Henry of Pelham
51	2	Valiant Vineyards
52	1	Beringer
53	1	Forgeron Cellars
54	1	Beringer
55	1	Beringer
55	2	Windy Ridge Vineyard & Winery
72	n/a	Cork & Bottle
74	2	Costco
75	1	Cork & Bottle
75	2	Berkeley Wine Co.
76	1	Beringer

Individual Photo Credits (cont.)

Page	Photo Number (left to right)	Photo Courtesy Of
77	1	Berkeley Wine Co.
78	1	Cork & Bottle
78	2	Cork & Bottle
79	1	Cork & Bottle
79	2	Cork & Bottle
81	1	Cork & Bottle
107	1	Vintage Keeper
107	2	L.A. Fine Arts & Wine Storage Co.
118	1	Hip Restaurants
120	1	Hip Restaurants
122	1	Hip Restaurants
126	n/a	Beringer
129	1	Cork & Bottle
240	1	Gonzalez Byass
240	2	Gonzalez Byass
241	1	Gonzalez Byass
241	2	Gonzalez Byass
258	n/a	Beringer
260	top photo	Beringer
260-261	photo along bottom	Beringer
261	logo	International Sommelier Guild
261	top photo	Beringer
264	1	Henry of Pelham
264	2	Beringer
265	1	Henry of Pelham
265	2	Beringer

Table of Contents

CHAPTER 1   Wine Basics

Did You Know? 16

Types of Wine 18

About Grape Varieties 22

Red Grape Varieties 24

White Grape Varieties 28

How Wines are Named 32

Understanding Terms on Wine Labels . . . 36

How European Wine is Classified 40

CHAPTER 2   How Wine is Made

How Grapes are Grown 44

How Climate Affects
   Developing Grapes 48

How Wine is Made 50

Making Wine with Oak Barrels 54

CHAPTER 3   Tasting Wine

Look at a Wine's Appearance 58

Smelling Wine 60

Tasting Wine 62

Writing Tasting Notes 68

Wine Tasting Tips 70

CHAPTER 4   Buying Wine

Where to Buy Wine 74

Choosing a Wine Shop 78

Strategies for Buying Wine 80

About Wine Ratings 82

CHAPTER 5   Serving Wine

Tools for Removing a Cork 86

Removing a Cork 88

Serving Wine at the
   Right Temperature 90

Types of Wine Glasses 92

Aerating Wine 94

Decanting Wine 96

Storing Leftover Wine 98

Entertaining with Wine 100

CHAPTER 6   Storing and Collecting Wine

How to Properly Store Wine 104

Where to Store Wine 106

How Long to Store and Age Wine 108

About Collecting Wine 110

Wine Collecting Strategies 112

CHAPTER 7   Selecting Wine in Restaurants

How Wine is Sold in Restaurants 118

How Wine Lists are Organized 120

Wine Service in Restaurants 122

CHAPTER 8   Matching Wine and Food

Combining Wine with Food 128

Suggested Wine-and-Food Pairings 132

Table of Contents

CHAPTER 9 French Wines

About French Wine 138
Bordeaux 140
Burgundy 144
Rhône 148
Loire 150
Alsace 152
Provence 154
Languedoc-Roussillon 155

CHAPTER 10 Italian Wines

About Italian Wine 158
Piedmont 160
Tuscany 164
Northeastern Italy 168
Other Important Italian Regions 170

CHAPTER 11 Other European Wines

Spanish Wines 174
Portuguese Wines 178
German Wines 180
Austrian Wines 184
Hungarian Wines 186
Greek Wines 188

CHAPTER 12 New World Wines

Australian Wines 192
New Zealand Wines 196
South African Wines 198
Chilean Wines 200
Argentinean Wines 202
American Wines 204
Canadian Wines 212

CHAPTER 13 Champagne and
                Sparkling Wines

About Champagne and
    Sparkling Wine 218

How Champagne is Made 222

Types of Champagne 224

Opening Champagne and
    Sparkling Wine 228

Serving and Storing Champagne 230

Evaluating Champagne and
    Sparkling Wine 232

Sparkling Wines from Around
    the World 234

CHAPTER 14 Fortified and Sweet Wines

About Sherry 238

About Port 244

About Madeira 250

About Sweet Wines 254

CHAPTER 15 Learning More About Wine

Wine-Education Classes 260

Participating in Wine Tastings 262

Visiting Wineries 264

CHAPTER 16 Glossary

Glossary 268

Wine Basics

Did You Know?

Types of Wine

About Grape Varieties

Red Grape Varieties

White Grape Varieties

How Wines are Named

Understanding Terms on Wine Labels

How European Wine is Classified

DID YOU KNOW?

Before you get started on your journey learning about wine, take a moment to browse through these commonly asked questions and answers. You may find some interesting facts to share with your friends!

How long can I store, or age, a wine?

You should drink most wines soon after bottling, while the wine's aromas and flavors are still fresh and vibrant. Most red wines should be consumed within two to five years of the vintage, or year, shown on the label, while most white wines should be consumed within one to three years of the vintage.

How long can I keep an opened bottle of wine?

An opened bottle of red wine that has been recorked and refrigerated will stay fresh for about three days. An opened bottle of white or rosé wine that has been recorked and refrigerated will stay fresh for about two days.

How many calories does a glass of wine have?

The good news is that wine contains no fat, but if you are counting calories, you should know that a 5-ounce glass of red wine has about 110 calories and a 5-ounce glass of white wine has about 100 calories. In general, the sweeter the wine, the higher the calories.

What are the main differences between red and white wines?

Red wine is made from only red grapes, but white wine can be made from white or red grapes. Red wine generally has a more complex flavor and comes in more styles than white wine. Red wine also contains tannin, which gives the wine its backbone and creates a dry, mouth-puckering sensation.

How are wines named?

Most European countries, including France and Italy, name their wines after the region, or appellation, where the grapes used to make the wine are grown. For example, wines produced in the Bordeaux region of France are named "Bordeaux." In most non-European countries, including the United States and Australia, wines are named after the primary type of grape used to make the wine. For example, Australian wines made from the Shiraz grape are named "Shiraz."

What is a vintage?

The vintage is the year the grapes for the wine were picked and the wine was made. The vintage of a wine is important as the quality of wine can change significantly from year to year due to weather conditions.

Is all Champagne the same?

Although many people describe all types of sparkling wine as "Champagne," true Champagne is produced only in the Champagne region of France. Many other countries in the world also produce sparkling wines of different styles and prices, which can be very interesting and of good value.

What is Old World wine and New World wine?

Old World wine refers to wines made in Europe, where tradition and old-fashioned methods are often the basis of winemaking. New World wine refers to wines that are made outside of Europe, such as in Australia, South Africa and North and South America, where technology and innovation are often the keys to making good wine.

TYPES OF WINE

When choosing wine for your next meal or special event, there are many different types of wine to choose from. Wine can be placed into one of four categories—table wine, sparkling wine, fortified wine and sweet wine. Table wine is generally available in three different styles—red, white and rosé. As the name implies, red wines are a shade of red. White wines, however, are closer to yellow or gold in color. Rosé wines, sometimes called blush wines, come in shades of pink.

Table Wine

- Table wine includes white, red and rosé wine.

- The color of a table wine depends on whether the juice from the grapes, which is pale in color, stays in contact with the skin of the grapes during the winemaking process.

Note: For more information on the color of table wines, see the top of page 19.

White Wine

- White wine is actually yellow or gold, not white in color, and is more refreshing than red wine.

- Chardonnay is one of the most popular white wines in the world. Other popular white wines include Riesling and Sauvignon Blanc.

- White wine is best served chilled.

TIP *Did you know?*

- Red wine can only be made from red grapes. The wine's color comes from the skins which are left in contact with the grape juice during the winemaking process.

- Most white wines are made from white grapes. However, white wine can also be made from red grapes.

- Rosé wines can only be made from red grapes. The grapes' skins are left in the grape juice for just a few hours, which gives the wine a pink color.

TIP *Are the grapes used to make wine actually white and red?*

Red grapes can be red, blue or purple in color. While red grapes used to produce wine are sometimes referred to as black grapes, none of them are actually black. Just as white wines are not truly white in color, white grapes are not actually white. White grapes range in color from green to yellow to a pinkish copper hue. As a general rule, any grape that is not a dark shade of red or blue is considered a white grape.

Red Wine

- Red wine generally has a more complex flavor and comes in more styles than white wine.

- Cabernet Sauvignon is considered to be one of the finest red wines in the world. Other popular red wines include Merlot and Pinot Noir.

- Red wine contains tannin, which comes from the skin and seeds of the grapes. Tannin gives red wine its backbone and creates a dry, mouth-puckering sensation.

- Most red wine is best served at room temperature.

Rosé Wine

- Rosé wine, also called blush wine, is pink in color and tastes more like white wine than red wine.

- White Zinfandel is one of the most popular types of rosé wine.

- Rosé wines are generally light and fruity tasting and can be sweet, which makes them a great introductory wine for people to try since they are easy to drink.

- Rosé wine is best served chilled.

CONTINUED

A special occasion is often celebrated with a glass of sparkling wine. This special type of wine is made all over the world, but it is the sparkling wine from France's Champagne region that is recognized as the best of the best.

Fortified wines are unique wines that have had an extra dose of alcohol, often brandy, added during the winemaking process. Sweet wines, also called dessert wines, contain a high amount of sugar and are often served alongside dessert or as a sweet treat by itself after a meal.

Sparkling Wine

- Sparkling wine is wine that contains carbon dioxide bubbles.

- Carbon dioxide, a natural byproduct of the winemaking process, is trapped in a sealed bottle or tank, where it dissolves into the wine instead of escaping into the air. Carbon dioxide can also be added artificially to wine.

- Sparkling wine is most often white or pink in color, but is sometimes red in color.

- Champagne is the most celebrated and one of the best types of sparkling wine. Champagne is made in Champagne, France.

- Only sparkling wine produced in Champagne, France can be properly labeled "Champagne." All other bubbly wines should be called sparkling wines.

What types of sweet wine are available?

Popular sweet wines include ice wine, late harvest wine and noble rot wine.

- Ice wine is made from grapes that have frozen on the vine.
- Late harvest wine is produced with grapes that have been left on the vine for an extended period of time.
- Noble rot wine is made from shriveled grapes that are affected by a beneficial mold called *botrytis cinerea*.

TIP *How long does wine last after it has been opened?*

If you refrigerate wine after opening, the wine will normally last at least a couple of days. The following gives you a general idea of how long your opened wines will keep in the refrigerator.

White wine—two days

Rosé wine—two days

Sparkling wine—two days

Red wine—three days

Fortified and sweet wines—a few days to a couple of months

Fortified and Sweet Wine

Fortified Wines

- Fortified wines are also known as liqueur wines. Popular types of fortified wines include Port, Vermouth and Sherry.
- Fortified wines can be sweet or dry tasting.
- To produce fortified wine, alcohol is added to the wine during or after the fermentation process. Adding alcohol to the wine stops the fermentation process and increases the alcohol content of the wine.

Sweet Wines

- Sweet wines are also known as dessert wines. A popular type of sweet wine is ice wine.
- To produce sweet wine, grapes with a higher concentration of sugar are used or sugar is added to the wine during or after the fermentation process.
- Sweet wine as well as fortified wine are generally served in small amounts after a meal, often with dessert or in place of dessert.

ABOUT GRAPE VARIETIES

Different types of wine are made in a wide variety of ways, but they all have one thing in common—grapes. While winemaking techniques, such as aging wine in oak barrels, can affect how a wine turns out, it is the grape itself that has the greatest effect on the wine. The traits of each grape variety used to create a wine give the wine its personality and much of its quality.

About Grape Varieties

- You can easily distinguish between different wines if you know the grape variety that was used to create each wine.

- A grape variety refers to the grapes of a certain type of grapevine. For example, the grapes of a Chardonnay grapevine make Chardonnay wine.

- Although there are thousands of wine grape varieties, you will likely encounter fewer than 50 different grape varieties in your lifetime.

- The grape variety used to make a wine primarily determines the appearance, aroma, flavor and other characteristics of a wine.

- A wine's color comes from the skins of the grapes used to make the wine. White wine is usually made from white grapes, while red wine is made from red grapes.

- A wine's aromas and flavors, which can include fruit, vegetable, herb, spice and floral scents, are also primarily determined by the grape variety used to make a wine.

TIP *What is phylloxera?*

Phylloxera are tiny, parasitic lice which infect the roots of the widely used *Vitis vinifera* grape vines. Fortunately, it was discovered that phylloxera will not attack the roots of the lesser *Vitis labrusca* varieties of grape vines. To prevent phylloxera infestation, most vineyards have now planted hearty *Vitis labrusca* roots and grafted *Vitis vinifera* vines to them. These hybrid plants produce the best grape varieties while remaining immune to phylloxera.

TIP *Do some grape varieties have more than one name?*

Yes. In fact, most grape varieties have a number of different names that change depending on the country and region in which they are grown. For example, the Primitivo grape from Italy is called Zinfandel in California. Another example is the Syrah grape from France. The same variety is known as Shiraz in other parts of the world, including Australia and the United States.

About Genus and Species

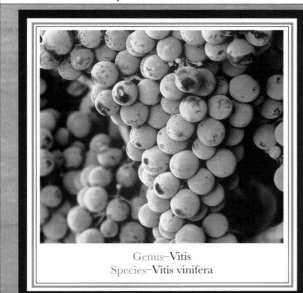

Genus—Vitis
Species—Vitis vinifera

About Noble Grapes

Noble Grape Variety	Best Regions
Cabernet Sauvignon	Bordeaux, France
Chardonnay	Burgundy, France
Chenin Blanc	Loire Valley, France
Nebbiolo	Piedmont, Italy
Pinot Noir	Burgundy, France
Riesling	Mosel and Rheingau regions, Germany
Sangiovese	Tuscany, Italy
Syrah	Northern Rhône Valley, France
Tempranillo	Rioja, Spain

- All wine grape varieties belong to the genus *Vitis*, which is the Latin term for vine.

- Most wine is made from grapes that belong to the species *Vitis vinifera*.

  Note: A genus is a classification of plants or animals. Each genus contains one or more closely related species.

- Wine can also be made from grapes that belong to other species, but these wines are not as popular. For example, the Concord grape, which is used to make wine as well as juice and jelly, belongs to the species *Vitis labrusca*.

- Grape varieties that produce the world's finest wines are called noble grape varieties.

- Noble grapes that produce white wines include Chardonnay, Chenin Blanc and Riesling. Noble grapes that produce red wines include Cabernet Sauvignon, Pinot Noir and Syrah.

- Each noble grape variety has a wine region where the best grapes are produced.

- The above chart shows some examples of noble grape varieties.

RED GRAPE VARIETIES

Red grapes are used to make red wines. The wide variety of red grapes, each with its own unique flavors, color and characteristics, provides wine drinkers with a vast array of red wines to choose from.

The eight most important red grape varieties used for making wine include Cabernet Sauvignon, Pinot Noir, Merlot, Syrah, Nebbiolo, Sangiovese, Zinfandel and Tempranillo. Whether they are made into wine alone or blended with other grapes, these eight types of red grapes produce some of the world's best red wines.

CABERNET SAUVIGNON

The Cabernet Sauvignon grape is one of the most popular red grapes. This grape is used to produce more wines than any other red grape and is often blended with other grape varieties, such as Merlot.

Flavors	Blackcurrant, plum, green pepper, mint or cocoa. Cabernet Sauvignon wines aged in oak barrels also have flavors of vanilla or cedar.
Oak	Usually aged in oak barrels.
Body	Medium to full body.
Acidity	High acidity.
Tannin	High tannin.
Color	Deep blue-purple.
Regions	Most popular in the Bordeaux region of France, Italy, Australia, South Africa, Chile, Argentina, California and Washington State.

PINOT NOIR

The Pinot Noir grape can be difficult to grow and needs very specific climatic conditions to produce good quality grapes. When the grapes do grow well, however, they can make some of the world's finest red wines.

Flavors	Red berries, baked cherry, plum, damp earth, mushroom or cedar.
Oak	Usually aged in oak barrels.
Body	Light to medium body.
Acidity	Medium to high acidity.
Tannin	Low to medium tannin.
Color	Transparent ruby.
Regions	Most popular in the Burgundy region of France, Australia, New Zealand and the states of Oregon and California.

MERLOT

Merlot is a grape that makes great wines on its own or blended with other red grapes. Merlot grapes are most often blended with Cabernet Sauvignon, Cabernet Franc or Malbec grapes.

Flavors	Plum, blackcurrant, blackberry, baked cherry, chocolate, mocha or leather.
Oak	Usually aged in oak barrels.
Body	Medium to full body.
Acidity	Medium acidity.
Tannin	Low to medium tannin.
Color	Deep red.
Regions	Most popular in the Bordeaux region of France, the Tuscany region of Italy, Australia, Chile and many winemaking regions in the United States.

SYRAH

The Syrah grape has a spicy quality that makes it unique from many other red grape varieties. The Syrah grape is also called the Shiraz grape in some parts of the world.

Flavors	Blackberry, blueberry, plum, black pepper, spices, smoke, tar or chocolate.
Oak	Usually aged in oak barrels.
Body	Medium to full body.
Acidity	Medium acidity.
Tannin	Medium to high tannin.
Color	Deep reddish purple.
Regions	Most popular in the Rhône and Languedoc-Roussillon regions of France, as well as Italy, Spain, Australia, South Africa, California and Washington State.

NEBBIOLO

The Nebbiolo grape is the grape used to produce some of Italy's best red wines—Barolo and Barbaresco. The Nebbiolo grape needs more aging than any other red grape variety to achieve its potential.

Flavors	Black plum, strawberry, lavender, roses, violets, earth or dried leaves.
Oak	Aged in oak barrels.
Body	Full body.
Acidity	High acidity.
Tannin	High tannin.
Color	Brick red.
Regions	Though it is found almost exclusively in the Piedmont region of Italy, Nebbiolo is now starting to be produced in North and South American winemaking regions.

CONTINUED

SANGIOVESE

The Sangiovese grape is the most widely planted red grape variety in Italy and produces some of Italy's best wines, such as Chianti, Vino Nobile di Montepulciano and Brunello di Montalcino.

Flavors	Sour cherry, plum, violets, dried herbs, orange zest, nuts, cedar or mocha.
Oak	Usually aged in oak barrels.
Body	Light to full body.
Acidity	Medium to high acidity.
Tannin	Medium tannin.
Color	Light reddish-purple to dark cherry.
Regions	Most popular in the Tuscany region of Italy, but also found in California.

ZINFANDEL

The Zinfandel grape is very versatile. It is often used to produce every style of wine, from white to rosé to red and even fortified, Port-style wines. The Zinfandel grape is called Primitivo in Italy.

Flavors	Blackberry, raspberry, plum, bitter cherry or spice.
Oak	Usually aged in oak barrels.
Body	Full body.
Acidity	Low to medium acidity.
Tannin	Medium to high tannin.
Color	Light pink to deep ruby red.
Regions	Most popular in California and southern Italy.

TEMPRANILLO

The Tempranillo grape originated in Spain. Tempranillo is often blended with other wines and is one of the important grape varieties used in the fortified wine, Port. The Tempranillo grape is also called Tinta Roriz in Portugal.

Flavors	Cherry, raspberry, strawberry, spice or vanilla.
Oak	Usually aged in oak barrels for at least 2 years.
Body	Medium body.
Acidity	Medium acidity.
Tannin	High tannin.
Color	Light brick red.
Regions	Most popular in Spain, the Douro region of Portugal and Argentina.

OTHER RED GRAPE VARIETIES

You may also want to sample some of the following red grape varieties.

GRENACHE

Flavors: Raspberry, strawberry or spices.

Body: Medium body.

Acidity: Medium acidity.

Tannin: Low to medium tannin.

Regions: Popular in Spain, southern France, Italy, Australia and California.

Note: Also called Garnacha or Cannonau.

AGLIANICO

Flavors: Dark cherry, earth or chocolate.

Body: Medium body.

Acidity: Medium to high acidity.

Tannin: High tannin.

Regions: Popular in southern Italy.

CABERNET FRANC

Flavors: Blackberry, red currant, sweet pepper, flowers or herbs.

Body: Medium to full body.

Acidity: Medium acidity.

Tannin: Medium tannin.

Regions: Popular in the Loire and Bordeaux regions of France, northeastern Italy and eastern Europe.

Note: Cabernet Franc is often blended with Cabernet Sauvignon.

MALBEC

Flavors: Blackberry, blackcurrant, black pepper or spice.

Body: Medium body.

Acidity: Medium acidity.

Tannin: High tannin.

Regions: Popular in Argentina and Chile, but also found in the Bordeaux region of France, Australia and South Africa.

Note: Usually blended with other red grape varieties. Also called Auxerrois or Cot.

TOURIGA NACIONAL

Flavors: Strawberry, raspberry, roses or violets.

Body: Medium to full body.

Acidity: Medium acidity.

Tannin: High tannin.

Regions: Popular in the Douro and Dão regions of Portugal.

Note: This grape is the basis of the best vintage Ports. Also called Mortágua or Touriga.

GAMAY

Flavors: Grape, strawberry, plum, peach or banana.

Body: Light to medium body.

Acidity: High acid.

Tannin: Low tannin.

Regions: Popular in the Burgundy region of France, but also found throughout Europe and in Ontario, Canada.

Note: Also called Gamay Noir, Bourguignon Noir and Petit Gamai.

WHITE GRAPE VARIETIES

White grapes are used to make white wines. White grapes are not truly white in color, but often have light skins in shades of green, yellow, copper or amber. Each type of white grape produces wines with unique flavors, colors and characteristics, depending on where the grapes are grown. Each type of grape also grows best under particular growing conditions.

The eight most important white grape varieties used for making wine include Chardonnay, Riesling, Sauvignon Blanc, Pinot Gris, Gewürztraminer, Albariño, Muscat and Chenin Blanc. These eight types of white grapes are often made into white wines on their own or may be blended with other grape varieties to produce wine.

CHARDONNAY

The Chardonnay grape is one of the most popular white grapes and is used to produce some of the best dry white wines in the world.

Flavors	Apple, pineapple, mango, mushroom or minerals. Chardonnay wines aged in oak barrels also have flavors of vanilla, butter or butterscotch.
Oak	Usually fermented or aged in oak barrels.
Body	Medium to full body.
Dry or Sweet	Dry.
Acidity	Medium to high acidity.
Color	Greenish, light straw to dark gold.
Regions	Most popular in the Burgundy and Champagne regions of France, Northeastern Italy, Australia and California.

RIESLING

The Riesling grape is a grape variety used to produce some of Germany's best white wines.

Note: Riesling is sometimes called Johannisberg Riesling or Rhine Riesling.

Flavors	Apple, floral, lime, melon or minerals.
Oak	Never fermented or aged in oak barrels.
Body	Light to medium body.
Dry or Sweet	Very dry to off-dry.
Acidity	High acidity.
Color	Very pale yellow.
Regions	Most popular in Germany, the Alsace region of France, Austria, the Niagara region of Canada and New York State.

SAUVIGNON BLANC

The Sauvignon Blanc grape is known for changing its character and flavor depending on where it is grown. White wines made from the Sauvignon Blanc grape are becoming more and more popular throughout the world.

Note: Sauvignon Blanc is sometimes called Fumé Blanc.

Flavors	Herbs, grass, green tea, lemon, lime, grapefruit, minerals, melon or passionfruit.
Oak	May or may not be fermented or aged in oak barrels.
Body	Light to medium body.
Dry or Sweet	Dry.
Acidity	High acidity.
Color	Pale, greenish straw.
Regions	Popular in the Bordeaux and Loire regions of France, Northeastern Italy, South Africa, New Zealand and California.

PINOT GRIS

The Pinot Gris grape, which is one of several varieties of the Pinot grape family, is becoming more and more popular with white wine drinkers.

Note: Pinot Gris is sometimes called Pinot Grigio and is called Ruländer in Germany.

Flavors	Peach, orange rind, almond, honey or spice.
Oak	May or may not be fermented or aged in oak barrels.
Body	Medium to full body.
Dry or Sweet	Dry.
Acidity	Low acidity.
Color	Deeper than other types of white wine.
Regions	Popular throughout Northeastern Italy and Germany, but also found in the Alsace region of France as well as Oregon and California.

GEWÜRZTRAMINER

The Gewürztraminer grape is distinctively exotic and spicy and can make fascinating wines.

Flavors	Lychee, rose, bitter almond or smoke.
Oak	May or may not be fermented or aged in oak barrels.
Body	Medium to full body.
Dry or Sweet	Dry to sweet.
Acidity	Low acidity.
Color	Amber.
Regions	Popular in the Alsace region of France, Austria, New Zealand and several winemaking regions of the United States, including Oregon, New York and California.

ALBARIÑO

The Albariño grape originated in Spain and is used to make good-quality white wines. White wines made from the Albariño grape are highly regarded by wine critics and experts.

Note: Albariño is called Alvarinho in Portugal.

Flavors	Peach, apple, spice or minerals.
Oak	May or may not be fermented or aged in oak barrels.
Body	Medium body.
Dry or Sweet	Dry.
Acidity	High acidity.
Color	Pale yellow to dark straw.
Regions	Popular in the northwestern area of Spain and Portugal's northern winemaking regions.

MUSCAT

The Muscat family of white grapes has hundreds of different varieties of grapes. The most highly regarded Muscat grape for making white wines is the Muscat Blanc à Petits Grains.

Flavors	Musk, melon, fresh grapes, spice or flowers.
Oak	May or may not be fermented or aged in oak barrels.
Body	Light to full body.
Dry or Sweet	Dry to sweet.
Acidity	Medium acidity.
Color	Very light straw to very dark copper.
Regions	Popular in the Alsace region of France, Austria and Hungary. Sweet Muscat wines are most commonly made in southern France and Italy as well as Australia.

CHENIN BLANC

The Chenin Blanc grape produces some incredible, complex wines, particularly in the Vouvray and Savennière winemaking regions of France.

Note: Chenin Blanc is called Steen in South Africa.

Flavors	Pear, melon, peach, apple, honey, lime, white flowers, spice, minerals or mushroom.
Oak	May or may not be fermented or aged in oak barrels.
Body	Medium to full body.
Dry or Sweet	Very dry to sweet.
Acidity	High acidity.
Color	Pale straw to dark gold.
Regions	Popular in the Loire region of France, as well as South Africa, California and Washington State.

OTHER WHITE GRAPE VARIETIES
The following are some other white grape varieties worth mentioning.

PINOT BLANC

Flavors: Apple, pear, melon, apricot, cream or smoke.

Body: Medium body.

Dry or Sweet: Dry.

Acidity: Medium acidity.

Regions: Popular in the Alsace region of France, northern Italy, Austria and Germany.

FURMINT

Flavors: Citrus fruit, nuts, spices or minerals.

Body: Medium body.

Dry or Sweet: Dry to sweet.

Acidity: High acidity.

Regions: Most popular in Hungary and Austria.

MARSANNE

Flavors: Almond, honey, honeysuckle flower or minerals.

Body: Full body.

Dry or Sweet: Dry.

Acidity: Low acidity.

Regions: Most popular in the Rhône region of France.

Note: This wine can become intriguing and excellent with aging.

VIOGNIER

Flavors: Apricot, flowers, minerals, spices, musk or smoke.

Body: Medium to full body.

Dry or Sweet: Dry.

Acidity: Low acidity.

Regions: Popular in the Rhône region of France as well as Australia and California.

SÉMILLON

Flavors: Honey, beeswax or dried apricots.

Body: Full body.

Dry or Sweet: Dry to sweet.

Acidity: Low acidity.

Regions: Popular in Australia and southwestern France, especially Bordeaux.

Note: This grape is often blended with Sauvignon Blanc grapes and is usually fermented or aged in oak barrels.

GRÜNER VELTLINER

Flavors: White pepper, pear, apple, spice or minerals.

Body: Medium body.

Dry or Sweet: Dry.

Acidity: High acidity.

Regions: Most popular in Austria, but also found in Hungary and other eastern European winemaking regions.

Note: Also called Grüner.

HOW WINES ARE NAMED

Most wines are named in one of two ways. Varietal wines are wines named for the main grape variety used to create the wine. Since varietal wines are named after the grape, the wine's main ingredient, you will have a good idea of how the wine will taste. Regional wines are wines named after the place where the grapes used to produce the wine are grown. The grape-growing region can often tell you as much about the characteristics of a wine as the grape variety.

Varietal Wine Names

Common Varietal Wine Names

Red Wine
- Cabernet Sauvignon
- Merlot
- Malbec
- Pinot Noir
- Shiraz
- Zinfandel

White Wine
- Chardonnay
- Gewürztraminer
- Pinot Gris
- Riesling
- Sauvignon Blanc

EST. 1876

STONE CELLARS
by/par
BERINGER.

CALIFORNIA ~ CALIFORNIE
CHARDONNAY
WHITE WINE ~ VIN BLANC
— 2004 —
PRODUCT OF USA ~ PRODUIT DES É.U.

750 ml 13.0% alc./vol.

- Most non-European countries, including the United States, Australia, Chile and South Africa, label their wines using the name of the primary type of grape used to make the wine. Wines named in this way are known as varietal wines.

- Common varietal wine names are shown above.

- Naming a wine using a varietal wine name is very helpful to wine buyers since the type of grape used to make a wine is the main factor in determining how a wine will taste.

- Each country has laws which state the minimum percentage of a grape variety that a wine must contain for the grape variety to appear on a wine's label. For example, to display the grape variety on a wine's label in the U.S., at least 75 percent of the wine must be made from the grape variety.

What else should I know about varietal wine names?

✓ When a wine is named after more than one grape variety, such as Cabernet-Shiraz, the percentages of each grape variety must be stated on the label and add up to 100 percent.

✓ A wine that has a varietal name does not signify that the wine is of higher quality than a wine with a non-varietal name.

✓ Some varietal wines specify that the wine contains 100 percent of a certain grape variety. These wines are ideal for becoming familiar with the characteristics of that particular grape.

TIP **When choosing a varietal wine, should I also look to see where the wine was produced?**

Yes. Quite a few non-European winemaking countries are gaining excellent reputations for producing quality varietal wines. Some of these countries include Argentina, Chile, Australia, New Zealand, South Africa, Canada and the United States. These countries do not have the same winemaking regulations that many European winemakers must follow to ensure quality, but they do produce some great varietal wines and are steadily becoming more regulated.

Regional Wine Names

Region	Primary Grape Varieties	Country
Barolo	Nebbiolo	Italy
Chianti	Sangiovese	
Soave	Garganega	
Valpolicella	Corvina, Molinara, Rondinella	
Bordeaux (red)	Cabernet Sauvignon, Merlot, Cabernet Franc	France
Burgundy (white)	Chardonnay	
Burgundy (red)	Pinot Noir	
Champagne	Chardonnay, Pinot Noir, Pinot Meunier	
Sancerre/ Pouilly-Fumé	Sauvignon Blanc	
Mosel	Riesling	Germany
Rheingau	Riesling	
Rioja (red)	Tempranillo, Grenache	Spain

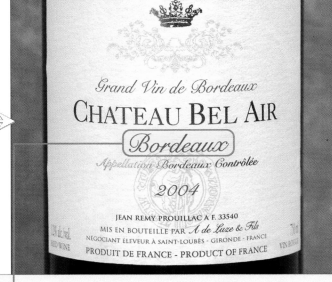

- Most European countries, including France, Italy and Spain, label their wines after the region, or appellation, where the grapes used to make the wine are grown.

- Well-known European winemaking regions are shown in the above chart.

- Each winemaking region has unique characteristics, including the grapes grown, climate and soil, which affect the grapes and ultimately the wine produced from those grapes. Having some knowledge about a region can give you an indication of how a wine will taste.

- In Europe, there are government-registered winemaking regions. Each winemaker must follow the standards and practices defined by the government for their region, which typically include the types of grapes grown and the winemaking and grape-growing methods.

- When a wine name includes a region, the grape variety used to make the wine does not usually appear on the wine label. If you know the region where a wine was made, you can determine the type of grape used to make the wine.

CONTINUED

Aside from varietal and regional names, there are a few other ways that a wine can be named. Generic names are misleading regional names that have been inappropriately given to wines that were not actually produced in the region. Proprietary names are unique names used by specific winemakers for some of their high-quality wines. Brand names are sometimes given to less-expensive wines that do not indicate the grapes used to make the wine or the region in which it was produced.

Generic Wine Names

Generic Wine Name	True Country of Origin
Bordeaux	France
Burgundy	France
Chablis	France
Champagne	France
Chianti	Italy
Port	Portugal
Sauternes	France
Sherry	Spain

- A generic wine is a wine that is named after a famous wine-producing region, but is not actually made using grapes from that region.

- For example, a sparkling wine made in the United States can be named Champagne, even though genuine Champagne is only made in Champagne, France.

- Generic wine names are used to help better market and sell wine, but they often confuse and mislead consumers.

- Wines with generic names tend to be less expensive, inferior wines and do not tell you much about the wine inside the bottle. These wines are typically served as house wines in restaurants and often come in larger-sized bottles.

- Common generic wine names are shown in the above chart.

- Unlike in the United States and some other non-European countries, European countries legally protect the names of famous wine regions and cannot use generic wine names.

TIP *How are wines named on restaurant wine lists?*

Generally, the wines you will see on a restaurant wine list or at a wine shop will be identified by either the grape variety or the region in which the grapes used to make the wine are grown. You may also see the name of the winemaker for each specific wine. For example, Penfolds Shiraz is a wine made from the Shiraz grape by the Penfolds winery. Another example is Conterno Barolo, a wine made in Italy's Barolo region by the winemaker Conterno.

Proprietary Wine Names

Proprietary Wine Name	Producer's Name
Grange	Penfolds
Noble One	De Bortoli
Oculus	Mission Hill
Ornellaia	L. Antinori
Opus One	Mondavi/Rothschild
Sassicaia	I. Rocchetta
Tignanello	P. Antinori
Unico	Vega-Sicilia

- Winemakers all over the world sometimes use a proprietary wine name to label their highest quality wine. Some examples of well-known proprietary wine names are shown in the above chart.

- Wines with proprietary names are often more expensive, higher quality and made in smaller quantities.

- In Europe, wines are often labeled with a proprietary wine name because the wine contains grape varieties that are not permitted by the government regulations. These wines are also often high quality wines.

Brand Names

- Some wine labels provide a brand name, with no indication of the grape variety used to make the wine or the specific region where the wine was made.

- Brand name wines are usually less expensive, lower quality and made in large quantities.

- Brand name wines typically use grapes from many different vineyards within a designated area.

- Although brand name wines tend to be less complex tasting, they can still be very enjoyable to drink.

UNDERSTANDING TERMS ON WINE LABELS

You will be able to make a more informed decision when purchasing wine when you fully understand the terms that appear on wine labels. Most wine bottles have two labels—one on the front and another on the back. The front label is designed to capture your attention and list basic information, while the back label provides more detailed information on the wine. The basic information which must appear on a wine label is typically regulated by the country that produced the wine.

Type of Wine

Table Wine

Sparkling Wine

Dessert Wine

- In the United States, wine is divided into three main categories—table wine, sparkling wine and dessert wine.

- Table wine is the most common type of wine and must have less than 14 percent alcohol.

- In the U.S., the phrase "table wine" is a legal term used to differentiate standard wine from sparkling wine and dessert wine.

- Sparkling wine contains carbon dioxide bubbles.

- Dessert wine, such as Port and Sherry, has more than 14 percent alcohol.

Producer's Name and Country of Origin

Producer's Name
The producer is the name of the company that made the wine. Becoming familiar with the names of good wine producers can help you choose quality wines.

Country of Origin
The country of origin is the country where the wine is produced, not necessarily where all the grapes contained in the wine were grown.

TIP *How reliable are the descriptions found on wine labels?*

Wine labels often include a description of the wine which can help you understand what you are purchasing. Keep in mind, however, that these complimentary descriptions are written by the companies that are selling the wine. A good description of a wine includes objective details about the character of the wine or the winemaking process such as "was aged in new French oak barrels." Subjective details, such as "this wine has a lively personality," do not provide any information on the wine's quality.

TIP *What does the phrase "contains sulfites" mean on a wine label?*

Most U.S. wine labels display the phrase "contains sulfites," which refers to the presence of sulfur dioxide in a wine. Small amounts of sulfur dioxide develop naturally in some wines during the winemaking process. Many winemakers also add sulfur dioxide to their wine to help stabilize and preserve the wine. This phrase is included on most American wine labels as some people, especially those with asthma, can have an adverse reaction to sulfur dioxide.

Grape Variety	Region

- The name of the primary type of grape used to make the wine, such as Chardonnay or Merlot, may appear on a wine label. European wine labels often do not display the grape variety used to make a wine.

- Since grapes are the main ingredient in wine, the grape variety is a good indicator of how a wine will taste.

- In the U.S., to display the grape variety on a wine's label, at least 75 percent of the wine must be made from the named grape variety.

- A wine label may display the region where the grapes used to make the wine were grown.

- In Europe, there are government-registered winemaking regions. Having some knowledge about the various regions can give you an indication of how a wine will taste.

- If a wine is made in a registered winemaking region, a phrase will appear on the wine's label to guarantee that the wine comes from that region.

Note: For a list of regions and guarantees, see page 40.

CONTINUED ▶

Wine labels are packed with useful information. The alcohol content, for instance, will tell you how full-bodied the wine will be. A vintage year can indicate whether the grapes used to make the wine were grown in a year with favorable weather conditions.

The term "Estate-bottled" lets you know that the grapes were grown and made into wine by the same producer. A vineyard name can indicate any unique characteristics in a wine. Most practical of all, volume tells you how much wine you are buying.

Alcohol Content

Vintage

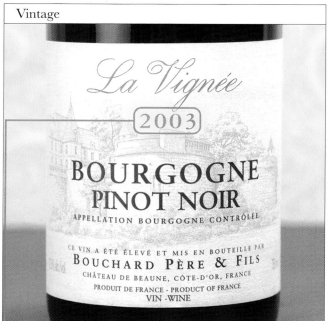

- On a wine's label, the alcohol content of the wine is given as a percentage.

- The alcohol content of a wine can give you an idea of a wine's body. If you taste two different wines, the wine with the higher alcohol content will have a fuller body.

- The vintage is the year the grapes for the wine were picked and the wine was made.

- The vintage of a wine is important when buying medium to high quality wine as the quality of wine can change significantly from year to year due to weather conditions.

- Non-vintage wines, which do not display a year on a wine's label, typically use grapes that were picked in more than one year. Non-vintage wines are not necessarily of lesser quality than vintage wines.

TIP *How does alcohol level correspond to the body of a wine?*

A wine's alcohol content greatly affects the wine's body.

✓ Wine that contains 7 to 10.5 percent alcohol is light bodied.

✓ Wine that contains 10.5 to 12.5 percent alcohol is medium bodied.

✓ Wine that contains more than 12.5 percent alcohol is full bodied.

TIP *What do terms like "reserve" or "special reserve" mean?*

Winemakers sometimes place terms like "reserve" or "special reserve" on a wine label to indicate that the wine is special in some way. For example, the wine may have been made from higher quality grapes or aged longer than usual. The meaning of these terms is regulated in most European countries, such as Italy ("riserva") and Spain ("reserva"). Other countries, such as the United States and France, do not regulate these terms and the terms are often only used to help market and sell a wine.

Estate-bottled

The phrase "Estate-bottled" appears on a wine's label when the company that made and bottled the wine also grew the grapes used to make the wine.

• Since one company was responsible for the entire winemaking process, some people believe that estate-bottled wines are of higher quality.

Vineyard and Volume

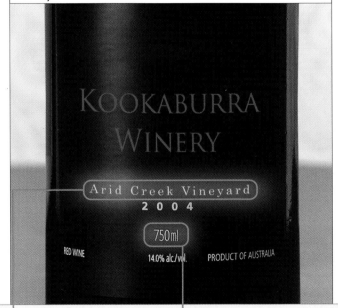

Vineyard
A wine label may display the name of the individual vineyard or vineyards where the grapes were grown. Each vineyard produces unique wine because the wine-growing conditions of each vineyard are different.

Volume
A wine bottle will display the amount of wine in the bottle, which is stated in milliliters (ml) or liters (L). A standard wine bottle is 750ml, but 1L and 1.5L bottles are also available.

HOW EUROPEAN WINE IS CLASSIFIED

Most European winemaking countries have strict laws dictating how wine must be classified. These laws outline various terms that must appear on a wine's label and categorize wine into one of two broad categories—quality wine and table wine. Quality wine has a higher status and usually comes from specific regions where winemakers must follow highly regulated standards for making their wine. Table wine has a lower status and typically comes from regions where winemaking is less regulated.

How European Wine is Classified

Quality wine

Table wine

Quality Wine

Common European Winemaking Regions	Country
Barolo/Barbaresco	Italy
Beaujolais Bordeaux Burgundy Chablis Champagne Châteauneuf-du-Pape	France
Chianti	Italy
Côtes du Rhône	France
Mosel Rheingau/Rheinhessen	Germany
Rioja	Spain
Sancerre/Pouilly-Fumé	France
Soave Valpolicella	Italy

- Most European countries, including France, Italy and Spain, have laws that regulate how wines are labeled.

- Wine produced in most European countries fits into one of two categories—quality wine or table wine.

- Although the status of a European wine can give you an indication of a wine's quality, it does not guarantee the quality of the wine.

- In Europe, wines with the highest status are produced in government-registered winemaking regions, known as appellations of origins.

- In each registered region, winemakers must follow the standards and practices defined by the local government, which typically includes the types of grapes grown and the winemaking and grape-growing methods.

- Some examples of well-known registered winemaking regions are shown in the above chart.

TIP *Does "table wine" have the same meaning in the United States as it does in Europe?*

No. While "table wine" indicates a lower quality wine in Europe, the term has nothing to do with the quality of a wine produced in America. In the United States, table wine is a legal classification for any non-sparkling wine that has up to 14 percent alcohol content.

TIP *Are there registered winemaking regions outside of Europe?*

Yes. The following are examples of winemaking regions you might notice on the labels of wines from outside of Europe.

Country	Winemaking Region
America	American Viticultural Area (AVA)
Australia	Geographic Indication (GI)
Canada	Vintners Quality Alliance (VQA)
South Africa	Wine of Origin (WO)

Country	Highest Status
France	Appellation Contrôlée/ Appellation d'Origine Contrôlée (AC or AOC)
	Vins Délimités de Qualité Supérieure (VDQS)*
Germany	Qualitätswein mit Prädikat (QmP)
	Qualitätswein bestimmter Anbaugebiete (QbA)
Italy	Denominazione di Origine Controllata e Garantita (DOCG)
	Denominazione di Origine Controllata (DOC)
Portugal	Denominação de Origem Controlada (DOC)
	Denominação de Origem (DO)
Spain	Denominación de Origen Calificada (DOC)
	Denominación de Origen (DO)

* These wines are waiting to qualify for AC status.
For each country in the list, the first phrase listed has the highest status.

Table Wine

Country	Higher Status	Lower Status
France	Vin de pays	Vin de table
Germany	Landwein	Deutscher tafelwein
Italy	Indicazione Geografica Tipica (IGT)	Vino da tavola
Portugal	Vinho regional	Vinho de mesa
Spain	Vino de la tierra	Vino de mesa

- If a European wine is made in a registered winemaking region, one of the above phrases will appear on the wine's label to guarantee that the wine comes from that region and the wine is produced according to local regulations.

- Some wine labels may also display **VQPRD** to indicate that a wine is a quality wine from a registered region.

- Although a registered winemaking region cannot guarantee the quality of a wine, it can guarantee most of the elements that go into making the wine.

- In Europe, table wine has a lower status compared to quality wine. You can identify a table wine by looking for one of the phrases listed above on a wine's label.

- Table wines produced in Europe typically come from less regulated regions.

- Some premium wines from registered regions are classified as table wines since the wines are made from grape varieties that are not permitted by the government regulations. In Italy, especially in Tuscany, these wines can be of very high quality.

CHAPTER

2

How Wine
is Made

How Grapes are Grown

How Climate Affects Developing Grapes

How Wine is Made

Making Wine with Oak Barrels

HOW GRAPES ARE GROWN

Since the key ingredient of any wine is grape juice, where and how the grapes are grown is critical to how the wine will turn out. Grapes are grown in vineyards, which is where the grapes develop their unique flavors and qualities. Each vineyard is an environment full of factors that can influence the production of grapes. For example, the type of soil, weather conditions and elevation can have a substantial impact on how the grapes are grown.

Terroir

- Terroir is a French word used to describe the overall growing environment of a vineyard, which influences the taste of a wine. Terroir is pronounced ter-wahr.

- Terroir encompasses factors such as the soil, altitude, climate (sun, wind, rain, humidity) and physical features of the land.

- Every vineyard in the world has its own unique terroir. You will not likely find two vineyards in the world with the exact same terroir.

- If two vineyards grow the same grape, experience the same climate and their grapes are made into wine in the exact same way, the resulting wine from each vineyard can still taste distinctly different.

- A vineyard's unique terroir affects the grapevines that grow in the vineyard, which influences the grapes that grow on the grapevines. As a result, the wine made from the grapes expresses the unique characteristics of the place where the grapes were grown.

Does the region where grapes are grown affect how wines are named?

Yes. European wines are often named after the region where the grapes were grown. This occurs because the location of the vineyards can have such an enormous impact on the taste of a wine. For example, a wine produced in the Burgundy region of France is called a "Burgundy." Non-European wines, on the other hand, are typically named after the type of grape used to make the wine, such as Merlot or Chardonnay.

TIP *What is the difference between viticulture and viniculture?*

Viticulture and viniculture are the two steps involved in producing wine. Viticulture refers to the actual grape-growing process in the vineyard whereas viniculture refers to the process of making the wine from the grapes. These two steps can be performed by either a single winemaking company or by different companies. For example, a grape grower may choose to only grow the grapes (viticulture) and sell the grapes to a winemaker who then makes the wine (viniculture).

Type of Grape

Soil

- Each type of grape responds differently to different environmental factors, including heat, hours of sunshine, water, wind, humidity, soil and the length of the growing season.
- Each type of grape grows best in a certain environment.

- A grape variety might grow superbly in one environment, but struggle to survive in another environment. Some grape varieties are more flexible and can grow well in several environments.

- Grapes can grow in many different types of soil, including clay, granite, gravel, limestone and slate.
- Each grape variety grows best in a certain type of soil. For example, Merlot grapes grow best in clay soil.

- The soil used to grow grapes influences the flavor of the wine. For example, grapes grown in limestone have a chalky flavor.
- Grape growers often say "the worse the soil, the better the wine." Less fertile soil is better for growing grapevines, since "stressing" the grapevines produces better grapes.

CONTINUED

The way grapevines and grapes are handled in the vineyard can make the difference between great wine and mediocre wine. As grapevines mature, they are often cut back, or pruned, and attached to trellises to create optimal grape-growing conditions. Bunches of grapes can also be picked off each vine so the grapes that are left on the vines will develop more concentrated flavors. Harvesting, or picking, the grapes when they are perfectly ripe is essential when producing quality wine. High-quality vineyards often harvest grapes by hand to ensure that the best grapes are chosen.

Canopy Management

Yields

- Canopy refers to the leaves and shoots, or new stems, of a grapevine.
- Canopy management refers to the techniques used to manipulate a grapevine's canopy, including pruning, leaf removal and attaching the grapevine to a trellis, which is a structure that supports the grapevine.

- Canopy management exposes the grapes to more sunlight, makes the grapes easier to reach and reduces moisture within the canopy, preventing mildew from forming.
- Canopy management optimizes the quality of the grapes, resulting in a higher-quality wine.

- The yield refers to the amount of grapes a grapevine or vineyard produces.
- In general, lower yields produce more flavorful grapes since a grapevine's nutrients are shared by a smaller number of grapes, resulting in a higher-quality wine.

- Less expensive, lower-quality, less flavorful wines are generally made from higher yields.
- Most of the best wines in the world are made from low-yielding grapevines and vineyards.

What else should I know about yields?

The size of a yield affects the quality of some grape varieties more than others. For example, the quality of Cabernet Sauvignon and Chardonnay grapes is often not as badly affected by the size of a yield as other grape varieties. Cabernet Sauvignon and Chardonnay grapes can create good wines even when yields are rather high. Other grape varieties, however, lose their best qualities if they are grown to produce high yields. For example, Pinot Noir grapes produce bland wines if the grapevines are allowed to produce high yields.

TIP *How are grapes transported to the winery?*

Great care must be taken not to crush grapes before they arrive at the winery. If the grapes are crushed in the vineyard, the grapes will begin to ferment because of exposure to the air. This will cause the grape juice to lose its fruit flavors and may create wines with unpleasant nutty or cooked aromas. High quality wine-producers take extra precautions to ensure that their grapes are carefully transported to the winery, such as transporting the grapes in small batches.

Harvest

- The harvest is the act of picking ripened grapes.

- As the grapes in a vineyard ripen, the sugar content in the grapes rises while the acidity level falls. The grapes must be picked when these two attributes are well balanced.

- The weather conditions during the harvest are very important. For example, if a large rainfall occurs before the harvest, the rain will swell the grapes with water, diluting the grapes' flavors, resulting in a less flavorful wine.

- The grapes on a vine can be harvested by hand or by a machine.

- Mechanical harvesting is faster, more cost-efficient and can operate 24 hours a day.

- Harvesting by hand allows the grapes to be picked more carefully, reducing the number of unripe grapes and plant material that are picked and the number of grape skins that are unintentionally crushed.

- Most producers of top-quality wines pride themselves in hand-harvesting the grapes used to make their wine.

HOW CLIMATE AFFECTS DEVELOPING GRAPES

The climate in a grape-growing area has a significant effect on grapes developing on the grapevines. The climate can affect the sweetness and flavor of every grape, which in turn affects the wines made from those grapes. Every winemaking region in the world has a unique climate which determines the quality and amount of wine produced.

ABOUT CLIMATE

To grow flavorful grapes for making wine, a vineyard must have just the right combination of climatic factors, such as temperature, sunshine and rainfall. The best grapes are found in areas where the grapevines have to struggle somewhat to produce the grapes. When the grapevines have to struggle with less than adequate sun or water, they produce a limited number of grapes, but those grapes usually have more concentrated flavor and character than grapes grown under perfect conditions.

ABOUT MICROCLIMATES

The unique climate of a small area is called a microclimate. A microclimate may be very small, such as surrounding a single row of grapevines, or may be larger, such as the size of several vineyards. Microclimates are influenced by several factors, including hills, valleys and proximity to bodies of water. For example, one side of a hill may receive more sunlight and wind than the other side of the hill, creating two unique microclimates. The microclimate in which grapes grow affects the wine produced from those grapes.

TEMPERATURE

In cooler climates, grapes have less time to mature. Cooler climates produce grapes that create lighter-bodied wines with good acidity and freshness that are lower in alcohol. In warmer climates, the grapes have more time to fully mature. Warmer climates produce grapes that create full-bodied, fruity wines that are higher in alcohol.

SUNSHINE

The number of days of sunshine and the number of hours of sunshine each day affect how grapevines and grapes grow. If the grapes do not receive enough sunshine, they will not ripen, but too much sunshine can lower the acidity level in the grapes, resulting in an unbalanced tasting wine. Too much sunshine can also cause the grapes to burn and start to shrivel into raisins.

RAINFALL

The number of days of rain and the amount of rain affect how grapevines and grapes grow. Too much rain can cause grapevines to produce a limited number of quality grapes, while severe rain can break open grapes and tear off bunches of grapes from the grapevines. On the other hand, too little rain can cause the grapevines and grapes to stop growing. Additionally, if a large rainfall occurs just before the grapes are picked, the rain will swell the grapes with water and dilute the grapes' flavors, resulting in a less flavorful wine.

WIND

Gentle breezes are beneficial since they circulate air through the grapevines and grapes, which helps protect against mildew, or rot. Gentle breezes also help keep insects off the grapevines and grapes. Severe winds, however, can damage grapevines and tear away grapes from the grapevines.

ALTITUDE

In hot climates, grapes grown at higher altitudes, such as on a mountainside, have an advantage since the temperature is cooler, preventing the grapes from over-ripening. In cold climates, grapes grown at lower altitudes have an advantage since the temperature is warmer, giving the grapes a better chance to fully ripen.

GROWING SEASON

Generally, longer grape-growing seasons produce more flavorful grapes since the various components in the grapes have a longer time to develop. The length of the growing season depends on the region and can vary from year to year.

HUMIDITY

High humidity can result in mildew, or rot, forming on grapevines and grapes, which can damage or destroy the grapevines and grapes. Grape-growers can use windmills or fans to help circulate the air in the vineyards to reduce the humidity level.

TEMPERATURE VARIATIONS

Temperatures can vary from day to night. In very hot wine regions, large temperature variations can be beneficial since the cooler nights slow down the grape development, producing more flavorful grapes.

FROST

Frost is a significant threat to grapevines and grapes. A spring frost can destroy the potential for a crop of grapes, while an early fall frost can stop grapes from fully ripening and destroy the grapevines.

HOW WINE IS MADE

Quality grapes may be the raw ingredient of a great wine, but it is the methods employed by a skillful winemaker that ultimately create a good-quality wine. Wine is made through a process called vinification. This process encompasses all of the steps performed in winemaking and is used to make both red and white wines. The first part of vinification usually involves crushing the grapes, converting the sugars in the grape juice to alcohol and separating the juice from the grape skins.

Step 1—Crushing and Destemming Grapes

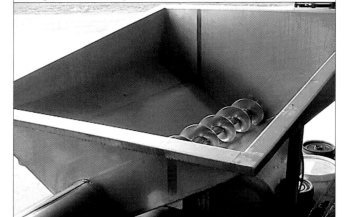

Step 2—Fermentation

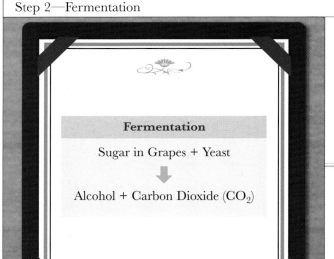

Fermentation

Sugar in Grapes + Yeast

⬇

Alcohol + Carbon Dioxide (CO_2)

- After the grapes are picked, they are put into a crusher-destemmer machine. This machine mechanically "crushes" the grapes to release their sugar-rich juice and "destems" the grapes to remove the stems from the juice.

- The juice of freshly-crushed grapes that will become wine is known as "must."

- When making white wine, the juice is then pressed to separate the grape skins from the juice. When making red wine, the juice is pressed after the fermentation process.

- Fermentation is the natural process that turns grape juice into wine.

- During fermentation, microscopic organisms, known as yeast, consume the sugar in the grape juice and slowly convert the sugar into alcohol as well as carbon dioxide gas which evaporates into the air.

- Although yeast lives naturally on the grapes and in the winery itself, winemakers usually add cultured yeast (yeast produced in a laboratory) to the grapes for better control over the fermentation process.

What is maceration?

Maceration refers to the process of soaking grape skins, seeds and pulp in the wine for a period of time. This is done to add the color, tannin, aroma and flavor from the grape skins to the wine. Maceration naturally occurs during fermentation of red wines since the grape juice is fermented with the grape skins.

TIP *What is malolactic fermentation?*

Malolactic fermentation is a natural process used by winemakers to soften and improve the flavor of wine. This process, which usually occurs during or after fermentation, allows naturally-occurring bacteria to convert the sharp malic acid in a wine to lactic acid, which is softer and less tart. Malolactic fermentation also tends to give wine added complexity and character. This process is typically used in the production of red wines and full-bodied white wines, such as Chardonnay.

Step 3—Pressing

- Red wine is typically fermented in stainless-steel tanks for a few days to a week. The grape juice is fermented with the grape skins to extract color and tannin from the skins.

  Note: Tannin forms the structure of red wine and acts as a natural preservative.

- White wine is typically fermented in stainless-steel tanks or oak barrels for a few days to a couple of weeks. The grape juice is fermented without the grape skins.

- When making red wine, after the fermentation process is complete, the wine is allowed to flow freely into another container in order to separate the wine from the grape skins. This wine is known as free-run wine.

- The solid mixture that remains is then pressed, producing a thick, dark wine, called press wine. Winemakers may later add the press wine to the free-run wine to add more flavor, color and tannin to the final wine.

CONTINUED

The second part of the winemaking process improves the flavor and appearance of the wine and prepares it for sale. Once a wine has fermented, it can be aged in oak barrels for a more complex and richer taste. Most wines are then fined and filtered, which involves removing sediment, cloudiness or undesirable microorganisms from the wine. Next, the winemaker may blend several wines together to create the final wine. After blending, wines are bottled for further aging or for sale.

Step 4—Aging

Step 5—Fining and Filtering

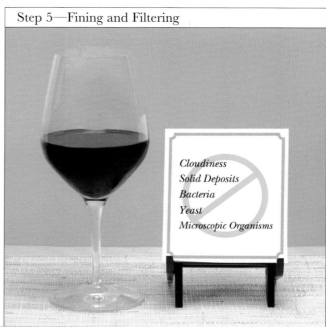

Cloudiness
Solid Deposits
Bacteria
Yeast
Microscopic Organisms

- Aging, or maturation, refers to aging wine in oak barrels for a few months to several years. Some premium white wines and most premium red wines are aged in oak barrels.

- Aging wine in oak barrels makes wine more complex, fuller, sweeter and richer tasting and gives wine an oaky and toasted aroma.

- After the aging process is complete, winemakers fine and filter most wines.

- Fining and filtering removes any cloudiness and solid deposits from the wine, making the wine more clear.

- Filtering also removes any bacteria, yeast or other microscopic organisms that might spoil the wine.

TIP *What is carbonic maceration?*

Carbonic maceration is a method of fermentation in which whole, uncrushed grapes are allowed to ferment in a closed tank where the air has been replaced by carbon dioxide. Once the juice inside the grapes has fermented, the grapes are pressed to release the fermented juice from the grapes. Carbonic maceration creates fruity, light red wines such as the renowned wines from France's Beaujolais region.

TIP *What is lees?*

Lees is sediment that forms in wine after the fermentation process. This sediment is normally filtered out of a wine, but a winemaker may choose to keep the lees in the wine for a period of time. Leaving the wine in contact with the lees gives the wine a somewhat richer texture, a slight nutty flavor and often more complexity.

Step 6—Blending

Step 7—Bottling

- Winemakers may blend together wines made from different grape varieties, different vineyards or both, to make a final wine.

- For high-quality wines, the wines of each grape variety and vineyard are fermented separately and then blended together to make the final wine.

Note: Winemakers may also blend together wines that were fermented or aged in oak barrels with wines that were not fermented or aged in oak barrels.

- For inexpensive, lower-quality wines, all the grapes are fermented together, which results in a simpler-tasting wine.

- Before wine is released for sale, the wine is poured into bottles, corked and labeled.

- After a wine is bottled, the wine may be released to the public right away or may be aged in a wine producer's cellar for a few months to several years.

- Aging wine in bottles enhances aromas and flavors, softens tannins and increases the complexity of the final wine.

MAKING WINE WITH OAK BARRELS

When you read wine reviews, it won't be long before you come across a wine described as "oaky." This term describes aromas and flavors of oak which often come from the oak barrels in which a wine is fermented or aged. Most wine barrels are made from oak. Aside from flavor, oak barrels also add to the price of the wine because these barrels are costly to buy and maintain. The oak for wine barrels is typically grown in France, Slovenia and the United States.

How Oak Barrels Affect Wine

- Placing wine in oak barrels gives wine an oaky aroma and flavor. Other terms used to describe wine placed in oak barrels include toasty, smoky, sweet, spicy, nutty and vanilla flavored.

- Placing wine in oak barrels also makes wine more complex, fuller, sweeter and richer tasting and adds tannin to wine.

- Placing white wine in oak barrels makes the color of the wine darker. Oak barrels do not noticeably affect the color of red wines.

Barrel-Fermented Wine

☑ *Barrel-Fermented Wine*

- When a wine is barrel-fermented, the grape juice for the wine is fermented in oak barrels.

- After the fermentation process is complete, wines that are barrel-fermented often remain in the barrels for a period of time to be aged.

- Some premium white wines are barrel-fermented. Red wines are not usually barrel-fermented.

- When a wine is not barrel-fermented, the wine is typically fermented in a large tank or vat.

TIP *What else should I know about oak barrels?*

✓ The length of time a wine spends in an oak barrel will affect the amount of oak flavor in the wine. The longer a wine spends in a barrel, the stronger the oak flavor will be.

✓ The size of a barrel also has an effect on the oak flavor in a wine. In smaller barrels, the oak flavor becomes stronger.

✓ The age of a barrel affects the oak flavor of a wine. New barrels provide more flavor than older barrels.

TIP *Are there other methods winemakers use to give oak flavor to wine?*

New oak barrels are very costly, so they are normally used for only high quality wines. Many winemakers, however, want to give their less-expensive wines the benefits of oak aging. To achieve an oak flavor, they may place inexpensive oak chips or boards in the wine when it is being aged inside stainless-steel tanks. The resulting oak flavors and aromas are generally not quite as good as those achieved through aging wine in oak barrels. Unless oak barrels are mentioned on a wine's label, an "oaked" wine has often been made using an alternate technique.

Barrel-Aged Wine

Toasted Barrels

- When a wine is barrel-aged, or oak-aged, the wine is stored for a period of time, known as aged, in oak barrels. Wine is typically barrel-aged for a few months to several years.

- Some premium white wines and most premium red wines are barrel-aged.

- When an oak barrel used to store wine is made, the barrel maker toasts, or chars, the inside of the barrel using a flame. A barrel can have a light, medium or dark toast.

- Toasting a barrel acts as seasoning for the winemaker. A winemaker can add different flavors to a wine depending on the amount of toast created on the barrels.

- Lighter toasts give wine a nutty, buttery flavor, while darker toasts give wine a smoky, more intense flavor.

Tasting Wine

Look at a Wine's Appearance

Smelling Wine

Tasting Wine

Writing Tasting Notes

Wine Tasting Tips

LOOK AT A WINE'S APPEARANCE

Wine is a complex beverage that can be experienced just as much through sight as it can through taste. Before a drop of wine touches your tongue, you can tell a lot about the wine by simply observing it in a glass.

While shades of color vary greatly from wine to wine, a wine's color can still provide information on its quality and maturity. Even the way a wine moves in a glass will reveal its thickness and offer some hints about its sugar and alcohol content.

Fill a Wine Glass

Look at the Wine's Color

1 Fill a wine glass about one-third full of wine.

- Make sure you do not fill the glass with too much wine, since this will make it difficult to later swirl the wine in the glass to bring out its aroma.

2 Hold the glass by the stem, not by the bowl of the glass.

- Holding a glass by the stem allows you to clearly see the wine, avoid adding fingerprints to the glass and prevent your hand from warming the wine.

1 Look at the color of the wine in the glass. To clearly determine the color of a wine, tilt the glass of wine away from you in front of a white background, such as a piece of paper, napkin or tablecloth.

- The color of a wine is determined by the grape variety used to create the wine, the age of the wine, the origin of the wine and whether the wine spent time in wood barrels.

TIP

What are the particles at the bottom of my wine glass?

Every once in a while, you may notice small particles floating at the bottom of your wine glass. What you are seeing is sediment. This grainy-looking substance can indicate a good quality wine, since it has not been overly filtered, or a wine that has been aged. While the taste may be on the bitter side and not look very attractive, sediment is completely harmless. You can prevent sediment from appearing in your glass by decanting your wine before drinking. For more information about decanting, see page 96.

TIP

What type of glass should I use for tasting wine?

When you want to truly experience a wine, it is best to use a glass with a narrow top to help direct the aromas toward your nose. The wine glass should be thin, clear and have no decorations so you can easily view the wine's true color. Your glass should also have a stem that you can hold to avoid warming the wine with your hand. For more information on wine glasses, see page 92.

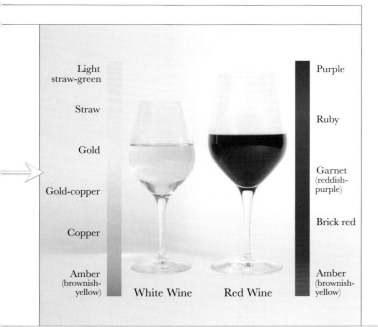

Look at the Wine's Thickness

- As a white wine ages, the wine gets darker in color. As a red wine ages, the wine gets lighter in color.

- If a white or red wine looks brown, it may be past its prime or spoiled.

1 To determine the thickness of the wine, swirl the wine around in your glass and notice how the drops of wine run down the inside of the glass. These drops of wine are known as legs or tears.

- If the wine runs quickly down the glass, the wine has a lighter style and may have a lower alcohol content.

- If the wine runs more slowly down the glass, the wine has a thicker style and may have a higher alcohol content, sugar content, or both.

SMELLING WINE

When it comes to smelling wine, the nose knows. Your nose is extremely sensitive and can detect a wine's subtleties more accurately than your mouth can. Smelling a wine also prepares you for its taste in the same way that smelling a delicious meal stimulates your appetite.

Everyone's sense of smell is different, so there is no right or wrong way to identify the aromas you smell in a wine. With practice, you will quickly become more confident when identifying aromas in wine.

About Smelling Wine

- Smelling wine is the most important part of wine tasting.
- Wine tasters use the word "nose" when referring to the smell of a wine. The terms aroma and bouquet are also used.

- When smelling wine, known as nosing wine, avoid cigarette smoke and wearing perfume, which can distract from the smell of the wine. Also, make sure food with strong aromas is not nearby.

How to Smell Wine

- To evaluate the smell of a wine, you first need to swirl the wine in the glass to mix oxygen into the wine and bring out the aroma of the wine. This is known as "aerating" wine.

1 To best swirl wine in a glass, place the glass on a table and hold the stem of the glass. With the glass remaining on the table, quickly move the glass in small circles.

TIP *How can I improve my ability to identify the aromas in wine?*

You can enhance your ability to identify the aromas in wine by taking the time to familiarize yourself with smells in your daily life. For example, you can smell different fruits, vegetables, spices, herbs and other ingredients when you are cooking. With time, you should have a catalog of smells in your memory that you can refer to when identifying aromas in wine.

TIP *What aromas are commonly found in popular wines?*

White Wines

- Chardonnay
  green apple, lemon, butter
- Riesling
  mineral, lime blossom, honey
- Sauvignon Blanc
  herbaceous, lime zest, asparagus

Red Wines

- Cabernet Sauvignon
  blackcurrant, cocoa, cedar
- Pinot Noir
  cherry, raspberry, spice, cigar
- Sangiovese
  red cherry, dried orange zest

You should learn to identify the aromas that are unique to each wine. Learning to distinguish between the smells of different wines will help you to determine your own wine preferences.

Type of Aroma	Examples
Fruit	peach, cherry, plum, pineapple, mango, blackcurrant
Vegetable (Vegetal)	asparagus, sweet pepper, cabbage, olive, celery
Herb	sage, marjoram, lavender, thyme, tea leaves
Spice	black pepper, clove, licorice, nutmeg, cinnamon
Floral	lime or orange blossom, rose, elderflower, violet, clover
Toasted	nuts, caramel, butter, vanilla, coffee, cocoa, smoky, chocolate
Animal	leather, cat urine, damp fur, barnyard

2 After you swirl wine in a glass, immediately place your nose close to the opening of the glass.

3 Gently sniff the wine and note your first impressions of the wine, which are usually the most accurate. Your sense of smell tires quickly, so you should assess the smell of the wine right away.

4 Determine what substances you smell in the wine, such as fruits, vegetables, herbs and spices. There are hundreds of different aromas that you can identify in wine.

5 Wait a moment and then swirl and sniff again. Smell the wine at least three times. You may smell different aromas each time.

- Higher-quality wines will express more aromas than inexpensive, poorly made wines. If you cannot smell many unique aromas in an inexpensive wine, the wine may not express many aromas.

TASTING WINE

Once you have assessed a wine's appearance and aromas, you can finally taste the wine. Take your time and focus on savoring your first impressions of the wine and enjoy yourself.

When tasting wine, remember there is no right or wrong way to experience a wine's flavors. Everyone has a different sense of taste, so your perception of a wine's taste will be unique. After you have finished tasting the wine, take some time to appreciate the wine's unique flavor.

How to Taste Wine

- Tasting wine allows you to confirm the flavors you sensed when you smelled the wine and also reveals additional characteristics, such as a wine's texture.

1 Take a medium-sized sip of the wine—enough to cover the inside of your mouth.

2 Move the wine around in your mouth for about three to five seconds, making sure it touches your gums, teeth, sides of your mouth and all areas of your tongue.

3 To enhance the flavors in the wine, purse your lips (make an "o" with your lips) and inhale some air over the wine in your mouth. Adding oxygen to the wine will help bring out the wine's flavors.

4 When tasting a lot of wines, you can swallow or spit out the wine after you finish tasting it and reset your palate by eating a plain cracker or piece of bread.

5 Take a moment to evaluate the wine.

TIP *I sometimes have trouble determining whether a fruity wine is sweet or dry. What can I do?*

Fruity aromas are often associated with sweetness. Due to this association, the aromas of an extremely fruity, dry wine can mislead a taster into thinking that the wine is sweet. To determine whether a fruity wine is actually sweet or dry, try tasting the wine while pinching your nose. If the wine continues to taste sweet, it is a sweet, fruity wine. If the wine does not taste sweet any longer, it is a dry, fruity wine.

TIP *What else should I know about sweetness and acidity in wine?*

Sweetness

Only your tongue can detect the sweetness in wine. If most of the sugar in the grapes converts into alcohol when making wine, a wine will taste dry. If only some of the sugar changes to alcohol when making wine, the wine will taste sweeter.

Acidity

Your entire mouth can detect acidity in wine. The higher the acidity of a wine, the more your mouth will salivate after swallowing. Acid is a natural preservative, so wines with low acidity spoil more easily.

Sweetness

Acidity

| Notice the sweetness of the wine, which you can detect mostly on the tip of your tongue. As soon as you sip a glass of wine, you should notice the sweetness of the wine right away.

• The sweetness of a wine is determined by the amount of sugar left in the wine after the fermentation process is complete.

• Some terms used to describe the sweetness of a wine include very dry, dry, off-dry, sweet and very sweet.

| Notice the acidity of the wine, which you can detect on the sides of your tongue and cheek area.

• White wines and some lighter-style red wines typically have a higher level of acidity.

• The acid in a wine provides a crisp and lively taste. Too little acidity creates a flat and lifeless tasting wine, whereas too much acidity creates a sour tasting wine.

• Some terms used to describe the acidity of a wine include flat, flabby, lively, vibrant, crisp and tart.

CONTINUED

When you sample wine, your tongue will respond to its flavors and alcohol content. Your tongue can detect four different types of tastes—sweet, sour, bitter and salty, although the taste of salt is rarely found in wine.

Your tongue and the back of your throat can detect the amount of alcohol in a wine. Alcohol is an important part of wine as it affects the sensation wine produces in your mouth as well as its taste and body.

Tannin

Tannin
- ☐ Soft
- ☐ Firm
- ☐ Tannic
- ☐ Bitter
- ☐ Harsh
- ☐ Astringent

Alcohol

Alcohol
- ☐ Light
- ☐ Medium-Bodied
- ☐ Full-Bodied
- ☐ Hot
- ☐ Alcoholic

1 Notice the level of tannin in the wine, which you can detect all over your mouth. Tannin is found mainly in the skins and pips (seeds) of grapes as well as in oak barrels used to store wine.

- When a wine has a high level of tannin, the wine gives you a drying, mouth-puckering sensation and can taste bitter.

- Red wines usually have more tannin than white wines.

- Some terms used to describe the amount of tannin in a wine include soft, firm, tannic, bitter, harsh and astringent.

1 Notice the amount of alcohol in the wine, which you can detect on the back of your tongue and throat.

- Wines with higher levels of alcohol are rounder (smoother), feel heavier and produce a warm or hot sensation at the back of your throat.

- A wine with too much alcohol will have a hot and harsh taste.

- Some words used to describe a wine's alcohol level include light, medium-bodied, full-bodied, hot and alcoholic.

TIP *Did you know?*

- Red wine generally has more tannin than white wine because the grape skins and seeds, which contain large amounts of tannin, are more often fermented with the juice when making red wine.

- Tannin is found in items other than wine, such as walnuts and tea.

- Tannin improves the aging of wine because it acts as a natural preservative.

- White wines aged in oak barrels often have increased levels of tannin.

TIP *How can tasting wine help me purchase wine at a store?*

Since you will usually purchase wine without tasting it first, you should learn how to communicate what you are looking for in a bottle of wine. You should be able to describe what characteristics you like in a wine so a wine shop employee can help you find something to suit your tastes. Once you understand the terms of wine tasting, such as sweetness, acidity and tannin, you can ask a wine shop employee to recommend a bottle of wine based on your preferences. For example, you could say "I would like a dry, red wine with soft tannins."

Body

Body

- ☐ Thin
- ☐ Light
- ☐ Medium
- ☐ Full
- ☐ Rich

Flavors

Flavor	Examples
Fruit	peach, cherry, plum, pineapple, mango, blackcurrant
Vegetable	asparagus, sweet pepper, cabbage, olive, celery
Herb	sage, marjoram, lavender, thyme, tea leaves
Spice	black pepper, clove, licorice, nutmeg, cinnamon
Floral	lime or orange blossom, rose, elderflower, violet, clover
Toasted	nuts, caramel, butter, vanilla, coffee, cocoa, smoky, chocolate
Animal	leather, cat urine, damp fur, barnyard

1 Notice the weight of the wine on your tongue to determine the body of the wine. Does the wine feel full and heavy, as if you could chew the wine, or thin like water?

- A wine's body is primarily determined by the amount of alcohol and extract (minerals, sugars and other trace elements) in the wine.

- Some terms used to describe the body of a wine include thin, light, medium, full and rich.

1 Notice the individual flavors in the wine, such as fruits, vegetables, herbs and spices. There are hundreds of different flavors that you can identify in wine.

- Most of the flavor in a wine comes from the wine's aroma that evaporates in your mouth and is inhaled through a nasal passageway at the back of your mouth.

- The terms used to describe a wine's flavor are the same terms used to describe a wine's aroma.

CONTINUED

Complex wines contain many distinctive flavors and aromas. Various factors can contribute to a wine's character, such as aging the wine in oak barrels and the variety of grapes used to make the wine.

It can take time to appreciate the multifaceted nature of a complex wine. Simple wines often express all of their personality in the first sip, while complex wines will open up and evolve over the entire course of consumption. Whether a wine is simple or complex, its flavors will linger in your mouth once you have finished drinking the wine.

Complexity

Balance

1 Determine if the wine is complex. All great wines and many good wines are complex.

• Complex wines have many different aromas and flavors and continue to reveal new characteristics over time. Simple wines express all of their personality in the first few sips.

• Stating that a wine is complex is the best compliment you can give a wine.

1 Determine if the wine is balanced. Good wines are well-balanced wines.

• A wine is balanced when you can notice each component in the wine, but one component does not overpower the other components.

• A wine has many different components, including sweetness, acidity, tannin and alcohol.

Can the same wine taste balanced to one person and unbalanced to another?

Since everyone's sense of taste is different, it's entirely possible that you and a friend may not agree on whether a wine is balanced or unbalanced. For most people, nearly all the wines they taste will seem balanced. If you have very strong feelings about specific tastes, such as an extreme dislike of sweets, you might find that some wines taste unbalanced to you.

How can I learn to judge the typicity of a wine?

The typicity of a wine is the extent to which a wine displays the traits that characterize other wines made in the same region. To judge the typicity of a wine, you must be familiar with the qualities of wines from the classic wine regions of the world and the most important grape varieties. Typicity is another thing to consider when tasting wine, but always remember that even an excellent wine can lack typicity.

Finish

Finish
- Short
- Long
- Delicate
- Intense
- Warm
- Bitter
- Crisp

1 After you swallow or spit out the wine, notice the flavors and sensations that linger in your mouth. These flavors and sensations are known as the finish, or aftertaste, of a wine.

2 Notice how long the flavors and sensations last and note whether they are pleasant.

3 Smell your empty glass to determine if any aromas are still present.

- Good wines generally have a long, rich and pleasant aftertaste. The finish of a high quality wine may last for one to several minutes.

- Some words used to describe a wine's finish include short, long, delicate, intense, warm, bitter and crisp.

WRITING TASTING NOTES

You may want to consider writing your own tasting notes as you become increasingly interested in tasting different wines. Although it can be challenging to describe the complex flavors and aromas of a wine, it is well worth the effort to make notes on your wine tasting experiences.

You can photocopy the tasting notes sheet provided on the opposite page to write your own wine tasting notes. You may eventually want to create your own customized tasting sheet based on your own preferences for assessing wines.

Writing Tasting Notes

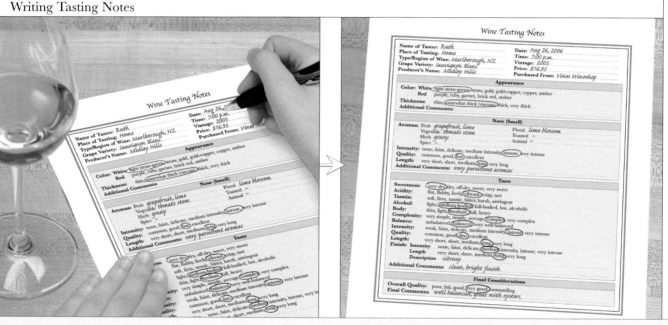

- Writing a description of a wine, known as a tasting note, allows you to express your opinion of a wine that you taste.

- Writing tasting notes allows you to recall the taste of a wine months or years later and helps you to communicate your opinion of a wine to other people. The act of writing a tasting note also helps you better appreciate a wine that you drink.

- When tasting wine, you will describe the many sensations that you experience, including the nose (smell) and taste of the wine.

- When you first start writing tasting notes, your notes may be brief, such as "gold in color, fruity and dry." With experience, your tasting notes will become longer and more descriptive.

- Wine tasting is a personal experience. Your tasting notes can be very different from another person's tasting notes.

Wine Tasting Notes

Name of Taster: _____ **Date:** _____
Place of Tasting: _____ **Time:** _____
Type/Region of Wine: _____ **Vintage:** _____
Grape Variety: _____ **Price:** _____
Producer's Name: _____ **Purchased From:** _____

Appearance

Color: White light straw-green, straw, gold, gold-copper, copper, amber
Red purple, ruby, garnet, brick red, amber
Thickness: thin, somewhat thick (viscous), thick, very thick
Additional Comments: _____

Nose (Smell)

Aromas: Fruit _____ Floral _____
Vegetable _____ Toasted _____
Herb _____ Animal _____
Spice _____
Intensity: none, faint, delicate, medium intensity, intense, very intense
Quality: common, good, fine, excellent
Length: very short, short, medium, long, very long
Additional Comments: _____

Taste

Sweetness: very dry, dry, off-dry, sweet, very sweet
Acidity: flat, flabby, lively, vibrant, crisp, tart
Tannin: soft, firm, tannic, bitter, harsh, astringent
Alcohol: light, medium-bodied, full-bodied, hot, alcoholic
Body: thin, light, medium, full, rich
Complexity: very simple, simple, average, complex, very complex
Balance: unbalanced, balanced, very well-balanced
Intensity: weak, faint, delicate, medium intensity, intense, very intense
Quality: common, good, fine, excellent
Length: very short, short, medium, long, very long
Finish: Intensity none, faint, delicate, medium intensity, intense, very intense
Length very short, short, medium, long, very long
Description _____
Additional Comments: _____

Final Considerations

Overall Quality: poor, fair, good, very good, outstanding
Final Comments: _____

WINE TASTING TIPS

When a group of trained wine experts declares that a wine is good, their decision is generally considered authoritative. However, a person's preference for wine is as individual as their taste in food. You will always be the best judge of whether a wine tastes good to you.

Although it's currently rare to encounter a bad, or flawed, bottle of wine, it is possible to experience problems with an individual bottle. If you purchase a flawed bottle of wine, you may be able to return the wine.

What is a Good Wine?

What is a Bad Wine?

- A good wine is a wine that you enjoy drinking. You are the only person who can decide which wines you like to drink and which wines you do not like to drink. Do not allow others to influence your decision on which wines are good wines.

- Wine experts, who are trained to rate the quality of wine, may give a high rating to a wine that you do not like. Don't worry. Just because many experts like a particular wine does not mean that you should also like it.

- You may occasionally taste a wine with an unpleasant aroma or flavor, which indicates that the wine is flawed. Flawed wines are known as faulty, off or tainted wines.

- When a wine is flawed, you will usually notice that the wine has an unpleasant aroma right away.

- Most winemakers produce good wines. If you encounter a faulty bottle of wine, it is usually just a bad bottle and does not mean that all wine with the same label is faulty.

TIP *How can I become a more knowledgeable wine taster?*

The best way to improve your wine tasting skills is with practice. The more wines you taste, the more your skills will develop. If you are serious about developing your wine tasting skills, consider taking a wine tasting course where an expert will give you information about wines and possibly lead you through an actual wine tasting. Wine tasting courses can range from a simple one-hour class to more extensive courses offering certification with your local Sommelier Guild.

TIP *What is a good wine tasting exercise?*

A simple tasting exercise can help you distinguish between the different grape varieties. Taste several types of red wine, such as wines made from different grape varieties like Cabernet Sauvignon and Pinot Noir. Take tasting notes (see page 68) and try to distinguish between the unique characteristics of each wine. Next, do the same for several different types of white wine, such as wines made from Chardonnay and Sauvignon Blanc grapes. You could also pick one grape variety, such as Merlot, and compare the wines that were produced in several different regions using those grapes.

Examples of Unpleasant Aromas and Flavors in Wine

Aroma or Flavor	Reason
Cork or musty	Defective cork.
Sherry/nutty	Overexposure to oxygen due to age or improper storage.
Sulfur or burnt matches	Too much sulfur dioxide, which is added to wine as a preservative.
Vinegar	Too much acetic acid in the wine, which naturally occurs during the winemaking process.

Wine Tasting Order

Wine Tasting Order

1. Sparkling wine
2. Light white wine
3. Full-bodied white wine
4. Rosé wine
5. Light red wine
6. Full-bodied red wine
7. Sweet wine

- Wine with a defective cork, known as a corked wine, is the most common type of flawed wine. A corked wine has a corky or musty aroma and taste.

- Do not confuse corked wine with a glass of wine containing pieces of floating cork, which is caused by a cork that was incorrectly removed from a wine bottle. Wine with pieces of floating cork is still fine to drink, but you may want to remove the cork pieces with a spoon or other object before drinking the wine.

- When tasting many different wines, the order in which you taste the wines is important. Trying wines in the right order will help your senses maintain their sensitivity so you can better judge each wine that you taste.

- You should taste wine in the order shown in the above chart. Generally, you should start with sparkling wines before moving on to light white wines, heavier red wines and finally, sweet wines.

CHAPTER

4

GERMANY

Buying Wine

Where to Buy Wine

Choosing a Wine Shop

Strategies for Buying Wine

About Wine Ratings

WHERE TO BUY WINE

In some areas, the purchase of wine is regulated by the government. These regulations may affect where you can buy wine. Depending on where you live, you may be able to purchase wine from supermarkets, large discount retailers, specialty wine shops and wine catalogs. Each of these retailers will offer different prices, selection and levels of customer service.

Specialty wine shops are likely to have knowledgeable staff members who can recommend wines that suit your tastes. For information on finding a specialty wine shop, see page 75.

Supermarkets

Large Discount Retailers

- In some areas, wine can be purchased in supermarkets, just like any other beverage.

- Buying wine at the supermarket with the rest of your groceries is very convenient and the prices are usually reasonable.

- At supermarkets, you may be limited to a selection of only popular wines that appeal to a broad range of tastes.

- Supermarkets may not have staff that can recommend wines that will suit your tastes.

- In many areas, large discount retailers, such as Costco, now sell wine. In general, the prices are quite good.

- You will often find a selection of good, popular wines at large discount retailers. Some also sell higher-priced, fine wines.

- The availability of certain wines can vary from week to week at discount retailers. If you see a wine that you like, you should buy the wine immediately.

- Like supermarkets, large discount retailers may not have a knowledgeable wine staff.

What are shelf-talkers?

A shelf-talker is a small sign that accompanies a particular wine to promote the wine to customers. These signs tend to use flattering terms to describe the wine's qualities. Although it may be tempting to buy a bottle of wine after reading the shelf-talker, you should also consult a well-informed staff member. Shelf-talkers are frequently created by the company that is selling the wine, so they are designed to sell the wine, not to provide an unbiased description of its characteristics.

 Is it acceptable to purchase wine at a gas station or convenience store?

Gas stations and convenience stores are not the ideal places to purchase a bottle of wine. They are, however, convenient and will usually have inexpensive to moderately priced wines for sale. If you must purchase wine from a gas station or convenience store, make sure the bottle is in good condition. The plastic covering the cork should be intact and the bottle should not be dusty or sitting in direct sunlight.

Specialty Wine Shops

- Specialty wine shops are stores that focus on selling wine and wine-related products.
- These specialty wine shops tend to offer the widest selection of wines from around the world in a broad range of prices.
- Specialty wine shops usually have a very knowledgeable staff that can assist you in finding wines to suit your tastes.
- Specialty wine shops sometimes have wine tastings, so you can try a wine before purchasing.

Wine Catalogs

- Wine catalogs, offered by many wine shops, allow you to shop from home for a large selection of wines.
- Purchasing from a catalog may allow you to buy wine at a better price than you can find in your area.
- A wine catalog may also give you access to wines that are not available in your area.
- While catalog shopping is convenient, you may not have the benefit of a staff that can recommend wines suited to your tastes.

75

You can purchase unique or hard-to-find wines from wineries, auctions, wine clubs or Internet vendors.

At auctions, you can purchase wines that may not have been sold in stores for many years. Before you buy a wine at an auction, you should try to find out about the wine's condition and how it has been stored. Wine clubs provide an easy way to try new wines. If you join a wine club, a selection of wines based on your preferences is sent to your home on a regular basis.

Wineries

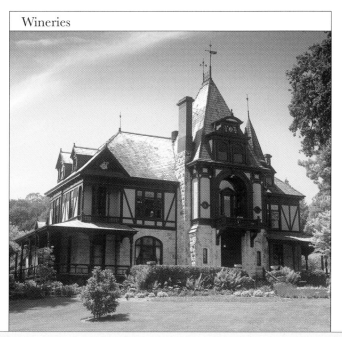

Auctions

You're invited to attend the
15th Annual Smithson Wine Auction

6:30 to 8:30 p.m.
Friday, April 14th, 2006
2890 Maplewood Avenue
New York

Reservations required. Call 212-555-2867

- Most wineries sell the wines they make directly to the public.
- You can usually purchase wine from a winery by visiting the winery in person or by ordering over the phone or the Internet.

- When buying directly from a winery, you may be able to buy older wines or unique styles of wine that are not available anywhere else.
- The prices at a winery are typically the same as you would find in local specialty wine shops.

- Buying wine at an auction allows you to purchase mature and hard-to-find wines that may not be available in stores.
- Auction prices depend on the interest of the bidders and can range from reasonable to expensive.

- At an auction, you must often pay the auction house an additional fee of 10 to 15 percent on the wine you purchase.
- One drawback to buying wine at an auction is that you do not always know the conditions in which the wine was stored.

How is wine sold at auctions?

At an auction, wine is usually sold by the lot. A lot is a grouping of three, six or twelve bottles of wine. It's a good idea to purchase wine by the lot if you already know that you enjoy that type of wine. Wine is also sold at auctions in mixed lots. A mixed lot usually consists of three, six or twelve different bottles of wine. Purchasing a mixed lot is a great way to sample different types of wine.

 What should I know before having wine shipped to me?

Before you arrange to have wine shipped to your address, you should find out whether there are any laws prohibiting the shipment of wine to your area. You should always ask the company selling the wine to determine whether they can legally ship wine to you before you make a purchase. You must also ensure that a person of legal drinking age will be available to receive the delivery.

Wine Clubs

- Wine clubs are organizations that send their members a selection of wines each month.

- Wine clubs are convenient because they save you the time of having to shop for and select wines. Wine club prices tend to be reasonable.

- Since wine clubs often choose the wines you will receive, it is important to choose a wine club that offers the types of wines that you enjoy.

Buying on the Internet

- Shopping for wine on the Internet can be an excellent way to purchase wines that are difficult to find locally.

- You can buy wine from Web sites that have been set up by online-only retailers, real-world stores, wineries and auction houses.

- Wine that you purchase on the Internet may be priced reasonably, but the shipping can be expensive.

CHOOSING A WINE SHOP

A good wine shop can make the experience of shopping for wine more enjoyable. You should choose a wine shop that has an extensive selection of wines, good prices and knowledgeable staff members. Although wine ratings (see page 82) can help you choose a wine, staff members of a good wine shop should be able to tell you more about a wine than just its rating. A truly knowledgeable staff member will describe a wine's characteristics to help you find a wine to suit your tastes.

Choosing a Wine Shop

- When you are searching for a good wine shop, look for a store with a good selection of wine, proper storage conditions and knowledgeable staff.

- A good wine shop should be a place where you can find wines that suit both your tastes and your budget.

- While price is important, you should not automatically select a wine shop that offers wine at the lowest prices.

Good Selection of Wines

- You should look for a wine shop that stocks a wide variety of wines from around the world.

- A wine shop that stocks products from smaller wine producers and lesser-known regions will provide a lot of interesting options for your wine purchases.

- A good wine shop will be thoughtfully organized. Look for wine shops that arrange their wines by region and feature a good selection of hard-to-find wines.

TIP *What questions should I ask before purchasing wine at a wine shop?*

Here are some questions you can ask before purchasing wine:

✓ How would you describe this wine?

✓ What makes this wine interesting?

✓ Are you familiar with the producer of this wine?

A good staff member will answer any questions you have. If a staff member answers your questions with general statements, rather than specific information about the wine you are asking about, you may want to speak with someone more knowledgeable before purchasing the wine.

TIP *What other useful services are provided by good wine shops?*

Many good wine shops provide customers with a monthly or quarterly newsletter. Newsletters often contain detailed descriptions of selected wines and may notify customers about upcoming special events. Some wine shops may also have a Web site that provides customers with information about their selection of wines, along with serving and storage instructions. You can look at the Web sites of many different wine shops to compare the prices of your favorite wines.

Storage Conditions

Knowledgeable Staff

- Wine can spoil when it is exposed to light and extreme temperatures, so it should be stored away from direct sunlight, heat sources and cold temperatures.

- Good wine shops store bottles on their sides so the corks stay moist and tight in the bottles.

- Inspect the wine bottles in the shop. The bottles should be in good condition overall and not covered in dust.

- When visiting a wine shop, ask if you can see where the wine is stored.

- A reputable wine shop will have staff who have a good understanding of the wines they sell and experience tasting the wines.

- After a staff member determines your preferences, he should be able to recommend several wines in a variety of price ranges.

- Over time, if you like the wines a staff member has recommended, you can begin to trust him to recommend more unfamiliar but interesting wines you might not have previously considered.

STRATEGIES FOR BUYING WINE

If the only wines you are purchasing are old favorites, it may be time to try something new. You can start by purchasing wines that you have enjoyed at restaurants or you could ask a staff member of a wine shop to recommend something you have never tasted.

Before you start shopping, research some different types of wine and decide how much money you would like to spend. Subscribing to wine newsletters offered by different wine shops can help you learn about new wines and where they can be purchased.

Buying Wines You Have Tried

Buying New Wines

- When you encounter a wine you enjoy at a friend's house or restaurant, take a moment to write down information about the wine, such as the producer's name, grapes used to make the wine, vintage (year) and region where the wine was produced.

- Information about a wine you like will help you find the wine the next time you go shopping for wine.

- If your local wine shop does not carry the wine you liked, a knowledgeable wine store employee should be able to use the information to suggest another similar wine.

Before You Go Shopping

- You can gather ideas for new wines to try from many sources, including friends, magazines and store newsletters.

- Keep an open mind about the wines you are willing to buy and be prepared to experiment.

- Before shopping, decide how much money you plan to spend on a bottle of wine.

- Wines vary from a few dollars to hundreds of dollars in price. Fortunately, there are good wines available in every price range.

Why is it difficult to find some recently released wines?

Many stores receive limited quantities of some recently released wines, so they tend to sell out quickly. In addition, when a new wine is given a high rating by wine critics, the wine may quickly sell out in local stores. If you want to purchase a highly-rated new wine, you should find out when your wine shop will be receiving the wine so you can be one of the first in line to purchase the wine. For information on how wines are rated, see page 82.

Why can't I find older wines at my wine shop?

Wine stores usually purchase wine just after the wine is bottled and is still relatively new and young. If a wine store would like to sell wine that is closer to its ideal consumption age, the wine must be aged in a cellar in the store. For some wines, like Barolo, this would mean aging the new wine in a cellar for 5 to 20 years. Many wine stores do not sell older wines because they cannot afford to keep wine for such a long period of time before selling the wine.

Questions to Ask When Buying Wine

- If you are unsure of what wine to buy, let a staff member of a wine store help you.

- Tell the staff member how much money you would like to spend and describe the characteristics you like in a wine, such as "fruity" or "dry."

- You can also tell the staff member the type of food you plan to serve with the wine.

- After the staff member has made a few suggestions, ask if any of the wines are available for sampling.

After You Choose a Wine

- Once you find a wine that you enjoy, consider buying several bottles or even a case of the wine to enjoy in the future.

- Remember, even if you buy a bottle of wine that you do not like, you will at least gain a better understanding of your wine preferences and will know what to avoid the next time you shop for wine. Every new bottle you taste is a learning experience.

ABOUT WINE RATINGS

A wine rating is the opinion of a wine critic about a wine's quality. Most wine critics rate wines using a 100-point scale. Many people will purchase a wine based on its rating. If critics give high scores to a new wine, the wine's sales will likely increase. Keep in mind that although wine ratings can be a helpful guide for buying wine, the ratings are subjective. Even though a wine is highly rated, it may not suit your tastes.

About Wine Ratings

86 Grace's Gate 2004 Chardonnay, California, $18 Crisp, lively and well-balanced. Ripe peach and apricot flavors with a hint of grapefruit and hazelnut. Long, fresh finish.

88 Spencer Creek 2005 Cabernet Sauvignon, South Australia, $28 Appealing black currant, mint and smooth chocolate flavors with intriguing undertones of eucalyptus. Rich and full with a lively finish. Well-balanced.

The 100-Point Scale

Score	Wine Quality
95-100	Exceptional
90-94	Outstanding
85-89	Very good
80-84	Good
70-79	Average
60-69	Below average
50-59	Poor

- A wine rating is an evaluation of a wine's quality by a wine critic.

- Wine critics judge a wine's quality based on its appearance, smell, taste and aftertaste. Smell and taste are the most important considerations.

- The cost of a wine is not generally taken into consideration when judging its quality.

- Most wine ratings include a description of the wine's characteristics and a numerical score that indicates the wine's quality, based on a 100-point scale.

- The above chart is an example of the 100-point scale that many wine critics use to score wines.

- In most cases, the lowest possible score a wine could earn is 50 points.

- When a wine's score is shown as a range of points, such as 87-89, it indicates a wine that has not yet been bottled and released to the public. The score is an estimate of the wine's final quality.

Where can I find reliable wine ratings?

You can find reliable wine ratings in magazines such as *Wine Spectator* (www.winespectator.com), *Decanter* (www.decanter.com), *Wine Advocate* (www.wineadvocate.com) and *Food and Wine* (www.foodandwine.com). If you live close to a wine region, you can also consult local wine magazines.

 Can I create my own wine ratings?

Yes. Your own rating of a wine can help you accurately remember the wine's unique qualities in the future. You can create your own wine ratings by using the 100-point scale to assign a score to every different bottle of wine you taste. You can also write wine tasting notes. For more information on how to write wine tasting notes, see page 68.

Using Wine Ratings

- Wine ratings can help you decide whether or not a new or unfamiliar wine is a good choice.

- Try wines suggested by several wine critics until you find a critic who has preferences similar to your own.

- Once you find a critic who has preferences similar to your own, you can use his reviews to help pick new wines.

- To help ensure you purchase a wine you will enjoy, read the whole review rather than relying on just the numerical score for the wine.

- When reading a wine rating, keep in mind that the wine score can tell you about the quality of the wine, but will not indicate if you will enjoy the wine.

- Do not let the opinions of wine critics keep you from trying new styles that might suit your tastes.

- Relying on the ratings of critics alone may prevent you from developing your own preferences for wine.

CHAPTER

5

Serving Wine

Tools for Removing a Cork

Removing a Cork

Serving Wine at the Right Temperature

Types of Wine Glasses

Aerating Wine

Decanting Wine

Storing Leftover Wine

Entertaining with Wine

TOOLS FOR REMOVING A CORK

With practice and the right tools, removing the cork from a bottle of wine is a simple process. The waiter's corkscrew, also called the waiter's friend, is frequently used in restaurants. The twist-style corkscrew, which is easy to use, is gaining in popularity.

Despite its strange name, the ah-so cork remover is well-known for its ability to extract the cork from a bottle of wine without damaging the cork. The wing-type cork remover is also popular, although it tends to damage corks during removal.

Waiter's Corkscrew

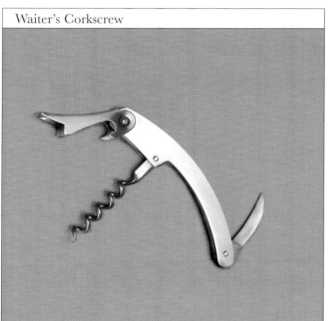

Twist-Style Corkscrew

- The waiter's corkscrew, or waiter's friend, features a handle with a corkscrew, lever and small knife folded into it.

- You twist the corkscrew of this device into the cork and then use the lever to pull the cork from the bottle.

- The waiter's corkscrew is an easy-to-use, inexpensive and reliable cork remover. It is suitable for almost any type of bottle or cork.

  Note: For more information on using a waiter's corkscrew, see page 88.

- The twist-style corkscrew features a long corkscrew attached to either a twisting handle or lever.

- This type of cork remover sits on top of the bottle. You twist the handle or use the lever to insert the corkscrew into the cork and remove the cork from the bottle.

- The twist-style corkscrew is fast and easy to use, though it sometimes does not work well on synthetic corks or bottles with a wide lip at the top of the neck.

TIP *What is a foil cutter?*

A foil cutter is a small device that can quickly and easily cut through the top of the foil or plastic capsule on a bottle of wine. To use a foil cutter, place the device on top of a bottle, twist it around once or twice and remove the top of the foil or plastic capsule. Keep in mind that a foil cutter will not work on the foil or plastic capsule on a bottle of champagne or on a flanged bottle, which has a wide lip at the top of its neck.

The Ah-So

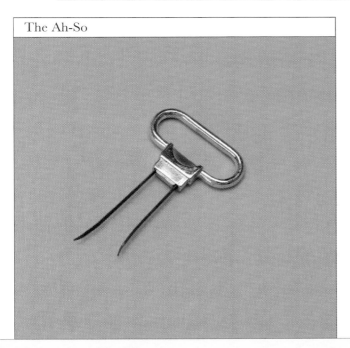

Wing-Type

- The ah-so, or butler's friend, is a cork removal device that features two flat metal rods attached to a T-shaped handle.

- Using a rocking motion, you insert the flat metal rods between the cork and the bottle. Once the handle is touching the cork, you twist and gently pull the ah-so until the cork comes out of the bottle.

- The ah-so is good for removing fragile and tight-fitting corks, but is not well-suited to loose-fitting corks.

- The wing-type cork remover features a corkscrew and two arms that open out to the sides, like wings, as the corkscrew is twisted into the cork.

- Wing-type cork removers are a poor choice for cork removal.

- This style of cork remover tends to break up corks, making them difficult to remove, and often causes cork fragments to fall into the wine.

REMOVING A CORK

Before removing the cork from a bottle of wine, you must cut off the capsule, which is a foil or plastic cover protecting the cork, with a small knife or foil cutter (see page 87). Once you have removed the capsule, check the top of the cork for mold. A moldy cork is a good sign as it indicates that the wine was properly stored. Simply wipe the cork clean and then remove the cork.

Removing the Cork

Step 3

Step 4

- The following steps illustrate how to remove a cork using a waiter's corkscrew.

  Note: For information on waiter's corkscrews, see page 86.

  1 Cut the foil or plastic on the top of a wine bottle with the knife in your waiter's corkscrew.

- If the bottle has a plastic plug instead of a foil or plastic covering, pry off the plug with the tip of the knife in your waiter's corkscrew.

  2 Wipe the rim of the bottle with a clean, damp cloth to remove any debris.

3 Insert the sharp point of your waiter's corkscrew into the center of the cork.

4 Holding the neck of the bottle with one hand, slowly twist the corkscrew clockwise with the other hand until only one ring of the corkscrew is visible above the cork.

- Stopping when one ring of the corkscrew is visible above the cork helps ensure the corkscrew does not go through the bottom of the cork, dropping pieces of the cork into the wine.

TIP *Should I smell the cork once it is removed from the bottle?*

Although there is no need to smell the cork, you should examine the bottom of the cork for moisture. A moist cork indicates that the wine has been stored properly on its side. You should be cautious if the cork appears dry and shrunken as the wine has most likely been stored upright. If you store a bottle of wine upright, rather than on its side, air can penetrate the bottle and ruin the wine.

TIP *What should I do if I end up with a piece of cork in the wine?*

You can use a cork retriever to easily remove floating pieces of cork from a bottle of wine. This device is made up of three thin metal skewers, about 10 inches long, with hooked ends. Alternatively, you can pour the wine through a clean coffee filter into a decanter, which will separate the small bits of cork from the wine. You can also use a spoon to remove the cork from your wine once you have poured the wine into a glass.

Lever — Neck of the bottle

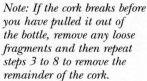

5 Place the lever of your corkscrew against the rim of the wine bottle and hold the neck of the bottle securely with your hand.

6 With your other hand, lift the end of the corkscrew handle that is opposite the lever upward to begin removing the cork.

7 When the cork is almost out of the bottle, release the corkscrew and grasp the cork.

8 Gently wiggle the cork back and forth until it comes out of the neck of the bottle.

- Removing the cork by hand prevents a loud popping sound.

Note: If the cork breaks before you have pulled it out of the bottle, remove any loose fragments and then repeat steps 3 to 8 to remove the remainder of the cork.

SERVING WINE AT THE RIGHT TEMPERATURE

The temperature at which wine is served can greatly affect its flavor. You may love a particular wine at one temperature, and dislike it at another. Unfortunately, wine is commonly served at the wrong temperature. Red wine is often served at room temperature, 70°F or 21°C, which is too warm. When red wine is served at room temperature it can taste flat and the taste of the alcohol can be exaggerated, causing an unpleasant, warm sensation in your mouth. Conversely, white wine is often too cold when served.

About Serving Wine at the Right Temperature

- Temperature plays an important role in your enjoyment of the aromas and flavors of wine.

- When wine is served at the correct temperature, the wine displays all of its best characteristics in perfect balance.

- When a wine is served at the wrong temperature, the wine can taste bland and unbalanced. You can miss out on many of the wine's best characteristics.

- Red wines are generally best served just below room temperature.

- When a red wine is served too cool, the wine can taste acidic, watery and metallic. If red wine is served too warm, the taste of alcohol can be overpowering.

- White wines are typically chilled to make them taste lively and fresh.

- When a white wine is served too cool, the wine's aromas and flavors fade. If white wine is served too warm, the taste of alcohol can be overpowering and the wine's crispness disappears.

TIP *What is the fastest way to chill a bottle of wine?*

If you have forgotten to place your wine in the fridge before serving, the fastest way to chill a bottle of wine is to submerge the bottle, up to its neck, in an ice bucket filled with equal parts of ice and water. This method chills a bottle of wine in approximately half the time of a bucket filled only with ice. You should chill fruity red wines, such as Beaujolais, for approximately 15 minutes in an ice bucket. White wine should be chilled for a bit longer, from 15 to 25 minutes.

Wine Thermometers

Wine Serving Temperatures

Type of Wine	°F	°C
Dry, light, fruity white wines	43°–46°F	6°–8°C
Rosé wines	43°–50°F	6°–10°C
Dry, medium-bodied white wines	50°F	10°C
Light, fruity red wines	50°–53°F	10°–12°C
Full-bodied, complex, oaked white wines	53°–61°F	12°–16°C
Medium-bodied, medium tannin red wines	53°–57°F	12°–14°C
Tannic, full-bodied red wines	59°–64°F	15°–18°C

- Wine thermometers are instruments you can purchase at wine shops and kitchen supply stores that allow you to accurately determine the temperature of a wine.
- Cuff-style wine thermometers fit around the outside of a wine bottle and display a digital reading of the wine's temperature.

- Long, probe-style wine thermometers are placed in the neck of an open bottle of wine and display the wine's temperature.

- The above chart indicates the best temperatures for serving most types of wine.
- When your wine has reached the right temperature, touch the bottle with your hand to determine how cold the bottle feels.

- You should also note how a wine tastes when it has reached the ideal temperature.
- With practice, you should eventually be able to tell if a wine is at the right temperature simply by touching the bottle and tasting the wine.

TYPES OF WINE GLASSES

Well-made wine glasses can help good wine taste even better. Look for wine glasses with a long stem and a generous bowl that narrows toward the rim. A long stem encourages you to hold a glass by the stem, instead of the bowl, to avoid raising the wine's temperature.

A bowl that narrows toward the rim helps to direct the wine's aromas toward your nose. You can purchase wine glasses in a variety of shapes, which are all designed to help you enjoy different types of wines, such as sparkling or sweet wines.

About Wine Glasses

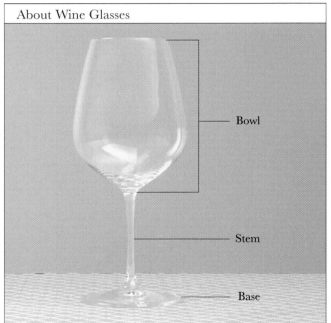

Bowl

Stem

Base

- Wine glasses are generally made up of a bowl, base and stem. The top of the bowl is called the rim.
- Drinking wine out of a high-quality glass or crystal wine glass allows you to fully appreciate the wine's appearance, aromas and flavors.

- The shape, size and thickness of the glass or crystal affect the way you experience wine.

Shape

Red wine

White wine

- While wine glasses come in a wide variety of shapes, red wine glasses are generally balloon shaped and white wine glasses are more tulip shaped.

- The wide bowl of a red wine glass provides the wine with a large surface area that allows oxygen to interact with the wine and improve its aromas and flavors.
- The narrower bowl of a white wine glass concentrates the wine's delicate aromas and helps keep the wine cool.

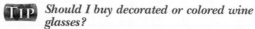

TIP *Can I purchase one type of glass for both red and white wine?*

It's perfectly acceptable to purchase one set of wine glasses to use for both red and white wines. In fact, many people do not have enough space in their homes to store two different sets of wine glasses. Balloon-shaped or tulip-shaped wine glasses that are between 12 and 14 ounces are suitable for both red and white wines.

TIP *Should I buy decorated or colored wine glasses?*

Although decorated wine glasses may look beautiful, they can interfere with your ability to fully appreciate wine. Colored wine glasses or glasses that are covered with a pattern may obscure or alter the true color of your wine. A good-quality wine glass will be clear so that it does not alter the wine's color or divert your attention away from the wine.

Size

Widest section of the bowl

12 oz

10 oz

Thickness

Thinner rim

Thicker rim

- To give you enough space to fully enjoy the wine, red wine glasses should hold at least 12 ounces and white wine glasses should hold at least 10 ounces.

- When pouring wine, you should fill the glass only to the widest section of the bowl—usually between one-third and halfway full.

- Only partially filling the glass leaves room to swirl the wine and space for the wine's aromas to collect.

- The bowls of high-quality wine glasses are made from very thin crystal or glass.

- A thin rim allows you to take a sip of wine into your mouth while inhaling the wine's aromas through your nose.

- A thicker rim causes you to suck wine out of the glass, drawing your breath through your mouth and preventing you from smelling the wine's aromas.

- A thinner bowl is usually more transparent and allows you to better view the wine's appearance.

AERATING WINE

Aeration is a process that exposes wine to oxygen, which can enhance the wine's aromas and flavors. This process is used mainly on red wines and is especially beneficial for young, tannic red wines such as Bordeaux and Cabernet Sauvignon. The aeration process makes the tannins in these wines soften, so the wine tastes less harsh.

The more tannic a wine is, the more aeration it requires. Darker-colored red wines, which tend to be younger, require more aeration than lighter-colored red wines, which are usually more mature and require less aeration.

About Aeration

- Aeration is the process of exposing wine to oxygen, which can enhance the wine's aromas and flavors. This is sometimes referred to as letting wine breathe.

- You normally aerate wine by pouring the wine into a wine glass or container and allowing it to sit in the wine glass or container before serving the wine.

- Aeration can help enhance young, tannic red wines as well as full-bodied red wines.

- As a wine is aerating, you should occasionally taste small samples to determine when the wine's aromas and flavors reach their peak.

- Approximately one hour of aeration will soften the tannins in a young, tannic red wine, making the wine less harsh. The same amount of aeration will enhance a full-bodied red wine's aromas and flavors.

TIP *Do white wines need to be aerated?*

Although white wine is not aerated as often as red wine, some varieties of white wine can benefit from the aeration process. Dry white wines, such as those from Burgundy, Bordeaux and Alsace, do not always give off many noticeable aromas or flavors until they are exposed to oxygen. If you allow these types of white wines to aerate for approximately 15 minutes, the aromas and flavors of the wine will often improve.

 TIP *What is the best way to aerate wine that is served at a restaurant?*

At some restaurants, the waiter will offer to remove the cork from a bottle to let the wine breathe. However, the neck of a wine bottle is far too narrow to allow the wine to breathe, or aerate, sufficiently. It is much more effective to pour the wine into a glass and allow the wine to sit in the glass and breathe for a few minutes before drinking.

Aerating with a Decanter

Decanter

Aerating with Wine Glasses

- Before serving wine, you can aerate the wine by pouring it into a decanter, which can be a crystal or glass container. Pouring wine into a decanter is known as decanting.

  Note: For information on decanting, see page 96.

- The container that you pour the wine into should be wide so the wine has a large surface area to interact with the oxygen in the air.

- Allow the wine to sit in the container for approximately one hour or until the wine is sufficiently aerated. Then serve the wine.

- If you do not have a decanter, you can pour the wine into wine glasses to aerate the wine before serving.

  Note: For information on wine glasses, see page 92.

- The bowl of wine glasses that you use should be relatively wide to create a large surface area for the wine to interact with the oxygen in the air.

- Allow the wine to sit in the wine glasses for approximately half an hour or until the wine is sufficiently aerated. Then serve the wine.

DECANTING WINE

Decanting is a simple process in which you remove the sediment from wine. The term sediment refers to the grainy deposits at the bottom of a wine bottle. When you are about to decant a bottle of wine, you should handle the bottle gently to avoid disrupting its sediment.

Many white wines and lighter-bodied red wines do not require decanting. Wines that are more than 25 years old may be too fragile to decant and should be consumed directly after opening.

About Decanting

- Decanting is the process of pouring a bottle of wine into a glass or crystal container before serving the wine.

- Many full-bodied red wines should be decanted to remove the unpleasant sediment that has accumulated at the bottom of a bottle as the wine has aged.

- Most decanted wine should be served soon after being decanted. If the wine is exposed to oxygen for too long, the wine's aromas and flavors will eventually spoil.

How to Decant Wine

Decanter

- Before decanting a bottle of wine, the bottle should be left standing upright for a day or two. This allows the sediment to settle to the bottom of the bottle.

1 Place the decanter, a tall candle and the bottle of wine on a table.

2 Remove the cork from the bottle (see page 88).

96

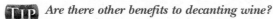

TIP *Are there other benefits to decanting wine?*

Decanting wine also allows you to quickly aerate the wine. Aeration involves exposing wine to oxygen, which can enhance the wine's aromas and flavors. You can improve tannic red wines and some dry white wines, such as wines from Burgundy and Bordeaux, by decanting the wines to expose them to oxygen before serving. For information on aerating wine, see page 94.

TIP *Why should I use a candle when decanting wine?*

A lit candle can help you to see the wine in the neck of a bottle as you pour the wine into a decanter. While pouring, make sure to hold the neck of the bottle several inches above the candle's flame to avoid heating up the wine. You should use a tall, taper-style candle for decanting wine rather than a short, votive-style candle.

3 Light the candle so you can use it as a light source to make it easier to see the wine in the neck of the bottle when pouring the wine into the decanter.

4 With your hand grasping the widest part of the wine bottle, hold the neck of the bottle several inches above the candle's flame.

5 Begin to slowly and smoothly pour the wine from the bottle into the decanter.

6 As you pour the wine into the decanter, watch the wine as it flows through the neck of the bottle.

7 When you notice the grainy sediment approaching the neck of the bottle, stop pouring.

8 Discard the small amount of wine that remains in the bottle.

• You can now serve the wine in the decanter.

STORING LEFTOVER WINE

To keep leftover wine fresh, you need to limit its exposure to oxygen by sealing the bottle with its original cork, or a novelty stopper that fits snugly into the bottle's neck. You can store any leftover wine, even red wine, in the refrigerator to keep the wine fresh. When you remove red wine from the fridge and pour it into a glass, the wine will quickly warm to proper serving temperature. For information on serving wine at the proper temperature, see page 90.

Storing Leftover Wine

- After you open a bottle of wine, the wine is exposed to oxygen, which will gradually begin to spoil the wine's subtle flavors and aromas.

1 After serving the wine, insert the cork back into the wine bottle to help prevent the oxygen from affecting the wine.

- To reduce the amount of oxygen that will be trapped inside the bottle with the wine, you can pour any leftover wine into a smaller, clean wine bottle before inserting the cork.

2 After inserting the cork into the wine bottle, store the wine in your refrigerator to slow down the effects of the oxygen on the wine.

- Red wine that has been recorked and refrigerated will stay fresh for about three days.

- White or rosé wine that has been recorked and refrigerated will stay fresh for about two days.

When should I recork a bottle of wine after it has been opened?

Once you have opened a bottle of red wine, you can leave it uncorked for up to two hours before replacing the cork in the bottle and refrigerating the wine. If you have opened a bottle of white or rosé wine, you should recork the bottle and refrigerate it right away. However, if you have opened an oaky, full-bodied white wine, such as Chardonnay, you can leave it uncorked for up to two hours before replacing the cork and refrigerating the bottle.

 What are some signs that a wine is no longer fresh?

If a bottle of wine has been open for too long, the wine loses its fresh aromas and flavors. Examining the wine's aromas and flavors will quickly tell you whether the wine is still fresh. When a wine is past its prime condition, the wine's aromas will fade and most of its fruit flavors will disappear. You may also notice a nutty smell in a spoiled bottle of wine. This is the result of the wine being exposed to oxygen for too long.

Air Pumps

- An air pump is a device that allows you to pump and seal most of the oxygen out of a wine bottle. Air pumps usually come with a supply of caps used to seal the bottles.

- Red wine that has been sealed and refrigerated will stay fresh for three days.
- White or rosé wine that has been sealed and refrigerated will stay fresh for two days.

Gas Preservatives

- A gas preservative is a product you can spray into a wine bottle immediately before inserting the cork. This product replaces most of the oxygen in the bottle with a gas that will not affect the wine.

- Red wine that has been treated with a gas preservative and refrigerated will stay fresh for four days.
- White or rosé wine that has been treated with a gas preservative and refrigerated will stay fresh for three days.

ENTERTAINING WITH WINE

Are you planning to serve wine at a dinner party or celebration? There are several guidelines you can follow to ensure that serving wine at your next event will be a success.

When entertaining, you may choose to serve two types of wine with a meal. White wines are usually served with the first course while red wines are often served with the second course. When you serve wine with a meal, it's important to make sure the wine complements your food. For information on matching wine with food, see page 128.

About Entertaining with Wine

Wine Serving Guidelines

Guidelines

- Serve white wines before red wines.
- Serve light-bodied wines before heavy-bodied wines.
- Serve simple wines before complex wines.
- Serve lower-quality wines before higher-quality wines.
- Serve dry wines before sweet wines.

- When entertaining with wine, such as at a dinner party or on a special occasion, you should consider the types of wines you want to serve and when you want to serve the wines.

- At dinner parties, it is common for more than one wine to be served during the meal. Sometimes a different wine is served with each course.

- You may also want to serve wine as your guests arrive at the event and with a cheese course after the meal.

- In order for wines to taste their best, you should consider the order in which you serve the wines.

- The above chart provides some general guidelines for serving wine when entertaining.

- You do not have to follow all of these guidelines when entertaining. Consider the wines you intend to serve at your event and try to follow the guidelines that apply.

TIP *How many glasses should I use when serving wine with a meal?*

You should provide each guest with a different glass for each type of wine you serve. If the event is casual, you can place the glasses on the table as you serve each type of wine. For a more formal event, you should set the glasses on the table ahead of time. When a guest is sitting at the table, the white wine glasses should be placed to the left of the red wine glasses. You should also provide guests with a water glass.

TIP *How often should I refill my guests' wine glasses?*

You should refill a guest's wine glass when it contains enough wine for approximately two more sips. If you refill your guests' glasses too frequently, they will not be able to appreciate the different flavors and aromas that develop in a wine while it is in the glass. You should also avoid frequent refilling if you are serving chilled white wine or Champagne. If you refill a glass that contains wine that has warmed somewhat, the chilled wine or Champagne you add to the glass will warm up past the proper serving temperature.

Buying Enough Wine

Buying Enough Champagne

- For dinner parties, you should buy one 750-ml bottle of wine per person. This will likely be a little more than you will need, but having too much wine is better than running out of wine before your event is over.

- If you are planning a longer meal or event, you may need to buy more than one bottle per person.

- For celebratory events, remember to purchase extra wine for making toasts.

- The amount of Champagne you will need depends on how you will be serving the Champagne.

- When Champagne is served before a meal, a 750-ml bottle of Champagne will typically serve three or four people.

- When Champagne is served with a meal, expect a bottle to serve two or three people.

- If Champagne is only going to be used for making toasts, less Champagne is usually required. A bottle should serve six to ten people.

Grand Vin de Bordeaux

CHATEAU BEL AIR

Bordeaux

Appellation Bordeaux Contrôlée

2004

JEAN REMY PROUILLAC À F. 33540
MIS EN BOUTEILLE PAR A de Luze & Fils
NÉGOCIANT ÉLEVEUR À SAINT-LOUBÈS · GIRONDE · FRANCE
PRODUIT DE FRANCE · PRODUCT OF FRANCE

Storing and Collecting Wine

How to Properly Store Wine

Where to Store Wine

How Long to Store and Age Wine

About Collecting Wine

Wine Collecting Strategies

HOW TO PROPERLY STORE WINE

Wine is a very sensitive product that needs to be stored properly. Factors like extreme temperatures, low humidity, bright light and vibrations can all have a negative effect on a bottle of wine. If your wine is not stored properly, it may gradually lessen in quality rather than improve. If you don't store your wine properly, any aging potential your wine has may be lost and you will most likely be disappointed when you open the bottle.

How to Properly Store Wine

Temperature

60°F
53°F

Humidity

75
95

Temperature

- Wine should be stored at a cool, but not cold, temperature. Warmer temperatures speed up the aging process and spoil wine more quickly.

- Large fluctuations in temperature are also harmful to wine. For example, wine will quickly spoil in a poorly insulated room which heats up during the day and cools down at night.

- The best temperature for storing wine is 55°F (13°C), but a constant temperature between 53°F and 60°F (12°C and 16°C) is acceptable.

Humidity

- Wine should be stored in a room with between 75 percent and 95 percent humidity, although 75 percent humidity is ideal.

- If the humidity level is too low, the corks in the wine bottles will dry out. A dry cork can allow wine to leak out or evaporate and allow oxygen to enter a wine bottle, which will quickly spoil the wine.

- To determine the humidity level in a room, you can purchase a hygrometer, which is a device that measures the humidity level.

Can I store a bottle of wine in the refrigerator?

While the refrigerator is a fine place to chill your wines, it should not be used to store them over a long period of time. The cold temperatures can dull the flavors of the wine over time. In addition, the vibrations created by the refrigerator's motor can also damage the wine. You should only keep bottles of wine in the refrigerator for a few days at the most.

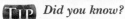 *Did you know?*

✓ After you have chilled a bottle of wine, you should drink the wine immediately. Do not transfer wine from storage to the fridge more than once as several temperature fluctuations will damage the wine.

✓ You should not store your wine in extremely cold conditions. If the wine freezes, the cork can be pushed out and the wine will spoil.

✓ If you store your wine in a location with too much humidity, the labels may develop mildew or come off the bottles.

Orientation
- Wine bottles are best stored lying on their sides. Storing a wine bottle on its side allows the wine to be in constant contact with the cork, preventing the cork from drying out.

Darkness
- Wine should be stored in a dark room, away from any source of light, especially direct sunlight. The ultraviolet rays of the sun are especially damaging to wine.
- Make sure you avoid storing wine in a room with windows.

Smells
- Avoid storing wine near chemical odors and strong smells, such as paint and gasoline. Strong smells can affect the flavor of wine.

Vibrations and Movement
- Excessive vibration and movement can damage wine, so you should not store wine next to refrigerators, washing machines, dryers or near heavy traffic. You should also avoid unnecessary transportation of your wine.

WHERE TO STORE WINE

If you plan to assemble a collection of wine, you need to ensure the bottles are stored properly. Wine needs a stable environment to maintain and develop its best qualities. There are a number of different storage options for wine, from a cool basement in your home to a rented storage space. How you choose to store your wine will usually depend on the amount of money you are willing to spend and the size of your wine collection.

Wine Cellars

- If you have a large wine collection and enough space in your home, you can set up a wine cellar, which is a room for storing wine.

- A wine cellar needs to be cool, damp, dark, vibration free, insulated and well ventilated.

- A wine cellar usually needs a temperature and humidity control unit to keep the wine stored at the right temperature and humidity level.

- You can have a custom-built wine cellar professionally installed or install a wine cellar yourself using a do-it-yourself kit.

Wine Racks

- Most wine cellars have racks to store the wine.

- Wine racks can be made of various materials, ranging from less-expensive plastic or metal to more-expensive redwood.

- Diamond-shaped wine racks allow you to store several bottles in each section and make efficient use of storage space.

- Wine racks that have a separate space for each wine bottle are typically more expensive. Before purchasing these wine racks, make sure your oversized bottles will fit in the racks.

TIP *I only have a few bottles of wine. Where should I store them?*

Even if you consume your wine shortly after purchase, you should put some thought into how you store the bottles. You don't need a cellar, but you should store the bottles on their sides and keep them away from heat sources or direct sunlight. Do not store your wine on the kitchen counter as it may be too warm or bright. An ideal location to store a few bottles of wine is a cool space under a bed or at the bottom of a closet.

TIP *Can I store my wine in wooden crates?*

The wooden crates in which some wines are sold are good places to store your bottles. Closed wooden crates block out the light and temperatures tend to change slowly because of the number of bottles stored so closely together. One drawback of storing your wine in crates is that bottles on the bottom row inside the crate can be inconvenient to remove. If your wine did not come in a wooden crate, you can usually find wooden crates at a wine shop.

Wine Storage Units

Rented Storage Space

- You can buy a wine storage unit, also called a wine refrigerator or wine cabinet, to store your wine. Make sure the storage unit allows you to control the temperature and the humidity level.

- Wine storage units range in size. Small units can store 24 bottles, while large units can store several hundred bottles.

- You can purchase stainless-steel wine storage units and units that look like pieces of furniture. Some units have glass doors, some units have interior lighting and most units can be locked.

- If your home or apartment does not have the room for a wine cellar or wine storage unit or your wine collection has grown too large, you can rent storage space in a temperature and humidity-controlled wine storage facility.

- Renting storage space can be inconvenient, since you need to determine which wines you want to drink in advance so you have enough time to pick up the wines.

- Renting storage space is ideal for wines that you do not plan to drink for several years.

HOW LONG TO STORE AND AGE WINE

Many people think that all wine improves with age. This isn't actually true. While there are a number of wines that will improve over time, the majority of wines available in your local wine shop are best when consumed right away. If you plan on creating a space in your home to age wines, you should know which wines will age well and which ones should be enjoyed with tonight's dinner.

About Storing and Aging Wine

- For most wine, you should drink the wine young, while the wine's aromas and flavors are still fresh and vibrant.

- Most red wines should be consumed within two to five years of the vintage, or year, shown on the label.

- Most white wines should be consumed within one to three years of the vintage, or year, shown on the label.

  Note: If a vintage is not shown on a wine's label, drink red wine within two years and white wine within one year after you purchase the wine.

- Less than one percent of all wines should be aged for more than five years.

- For wines that are meant to be aged, the wine's aromas and flavors change over time from fresh and fruity to more complex aromas and flavors. A wine's tannins also soften over time, resulting in a smoother wine.

- Red wine becomes lighter in color as it ages. White wine becomes darker in color as it ages.

TIP *What factors help a wine to age well?*

- **High tannin:** Red wine can generally age much longer than white wine since red wine contains significantly more tannin, which is a natural preservative. Some red grape varieties, such as Cabernet Sauvignon, have more tannin than other grape varieties.

- **High acid:** Some white wines, like German Rieslings, are quite high in acid and can be aged for a long time since acid is a natural preservative.

- **High sugar:** Sweet wines, such as Port and ice wine, can age for longer periods since sugar is a natural preservative.

- **Production method:** The way a wine is made can affect how well it ages. For example, if a wine is fermented or aged in oak barrels, the wine's aging potential will most likely be greater.

- **Region:** Some regions of the world produce more age-worthy wines, such as French Bordeaux and Italian Barolo.

- **Vintage:** Wines that are produced in years with more ideal weather conditions are more likely to age well.

Age-Worthy Red Wines

Country	Wine	Years
Argentina	Malbec	3–15+ years
Australia	Cabernet Sauvignon	5–15+ years
	Shiraz	5–15+ years
France	Bordeaux	5–30+ years
	Burgundy	3–15+ years
	Hermitage	5–25+ years
	Vintage Champagne	5–25+ years
Italy	Barolo and Barbaresco	5–25+ years
	Brunello di Montalcino	3–15+ years
	Chianti Classico Riserva	3–10+ years
	Super-Tuscans	3–25+ years
Portugal	Vintage Ports	10–40+ years
Spain	Rioja Gran Reserva	5–20+ years
United States (California)	Cabernet Sauvignon	5–15+ years
	Merlot	2–10+ years
	Pinot Noir	2–10+ years
	Zinfandel	5–15+ years

Age-Worthy White Wines

Country	Wine	Years
France	Alsace Gewürztraminer	2–10+ years
	Alsace Riesling	3–30+ years
	Bordeaux	3–15+ years
	Burgundy	2–20+ years
Germany	Riesling	3–30+ years
United States	California Chardonnay	3–15+ years

- The above list shows some of the red wines that are suitable for aging. When you plan to age a red wine, make sure you buy the wine from a high-quality producer of red wine.

- Red wines that age the best have high amounts of tannin and acid. Both tannin and acid act as a natural preservative.

- The above list shows some of the white wines that are suitable for aging. When you plan to age a white wine, make sure you buy the wine from a high-quality producer of white wine.

- White wines that age the best have high amounts of acid. Acid acts as a natural preservative.

ABOUT COLLECTING WINE

As you learn to appreciate wine, you may develop the urge to buy several bottles each time you go shopping. This may be a sign that you should consider starting a wine collection. Whether you start a collection of 20 or 200 bottles, you can build the collection to suit your preferences. Your collection will also give you an opportunity to buy a range of wines from all over the world. With a wine collection, both old favorites and new tasting experiences will be as close as your cellar.

Reasons for Collecting Wine

- When you collect wine, you have a variety of wines to choose from, which allows you to select wine based on your current mood or the food you plan to serve at your next meal.

- Collecting wine also gives you great wines to choose from for special occasions, such as dinner parties, birthdays, holidays and graduations. You will also have good wines to offer at unplanned events, such as last-minute dinner parties or after the arrival of unexpected guests.

Types of Wine to Collect

Everyday wines

Age-worthy wines

- A wine collection should maintain a balance between wines that can be consumed right away and wines that require aging.

- You can enjoy less expensive, ready-to-drink, everyday wines during family dinners and on casual occasions and more expensive, fine wines on special occasions.

- The percentage of everyday wines versus wines that require aging depends on your personal preferences and your budget. You may want to start with 75 percent everyday wines and 25 percent age-worthy wines in your collection.

TIP *What else should I consider when collecting wine?*

You should make sure that your wine collection is diverse. Aside from everyday favorites, think about including wines from different regions. You can also purchase a variety of wines from a specific region that you enjoy, such as Bordeaux. Be sure to include some wines that go well with food and others that you would enjoy on their own. You can also include sparkling wines, fortified wines and sweet wines in your wine collection.

TIP *What is the best bottle size for aging?*

If you plan to age a bottle of wine, you might want to consider buying the wine in a 1.5-liter Magnum bottle. Wine tends to mature more slowly and last longer in these bottles, which are twice the size of standard wine bottles.

Everyday Wines

- The majority of wine collections consist mostly of everyday, ready-to-drink wines.

- You should select a variety of everyday wines for your collection so you can enjoy trying different types of wines.

- You should also choose everyday wines to go well with a variety of meals.

- If there is a particular wine that you really enjoy, you may want to purchase a case of the wine.

Note: For information on buying a case of wine, see page 115.

Age-Worthy Wines

- A wine collection should include some wines that require aging. Many fine wines need to age for at least five years.

- You can buy age-worthy wines when they are young and the prices are more affordable. Some age-worthy wines are difficult to find and expensive to purchase when the wines are ready to drink.

- When you collect wine, you can buy several bottles of an age-worthy wine and try the wine every year or two to taste the wine at different stages of its development.

WINE COLLECTING STRATEGIES

Collecting wine is an activity you should approach with a strategy. Having a plan for building your wine collection will save you from buying too much of the same type of wine and wines that mature too quickly.

To get your wine collection started, consider buying an initial selection of 20 to 100 bottles. You should then continue to purchase wine at a rate that keeps pace with your wine consumption. This should always give you a good selection of wine in your collection.

Determine How Much Wine You Drink

Determine Size of Wine Collection

- Before becoming a wine collector, determine how many bottles of wine you drink in a month, including the number of bottles consumed when you entertain.

- For example, if you enjoy a glass of wine with dinner each night, you will need about 2 bottles of wine a week, assuming a regular-sized bottle serves about 5 glasses. If you entertain twice a month, you will need about $1/2$ to 1 bottle of wine per person on each occasion.

- Determine how many months you want your supply of wine to last. For example, do you want a one-month, six-month, one-year or five-year supply of wine in your collection?

- Make sure you do not buy more wine than you can drink. You do not want the wine in your collection to spoil before you have an opportunity to drink the wine.

Note: For information on how long you can store wine, see page 108.

TIP *When should I drink the older wines in my collection?*

It can be difficult to know when a wine has hit its peak because wines mature at different rates. There are, however, a couple of ways you can estimate when a wine is at its best to drink. First, read any reviews written by wine critics and note their estimates of when they think the wine will reach its peak. You can also contact the winery and ask the winemakers when they think the wine will be at its best to drink.

TIP *How do I know if a wine in my collection is too old to drink?*

The only way to tell if a wine is too old to enjoy is to sample the wine. If the wine has passed its prime, the wine may smell of wood or dried fruit, or it may have no aromas at all. Another way to determine if a wine has passed its prime is to examine the wine's color. Both red and white wines become a brownish-yellow when they are too old to drink.

Consider Your Storage Space

Set Financial Limits

Monthly Wine Budget

$200
7 to 10 wine bottles

- Before starting a wine collection, consider how much space you have to store your wine.

- You should also make sure the area where you plan to store your wine has the proper conditions for storing wine. This is especially important for wines that you plan to age for many years.

Note: For information on how to properly store wine and where to store wine, see pages 104 to 106.

- Determine how much money you want to spend on your wine collection and the number of bottles you want to purchase with the money.

- Set a budget for your wine purchases and stick to the budget, otherwise you may spend too much money on your wine collection. For example, you may want to set a weekly or monthly budget to limit your spending.

- When buying wine, look for sales and specials at wine stores to help you save money.

CONTINUED ▶

When you have a wine collection, you should keep an accurate inventory of your wine. Your inventory will keep you aware of which wines you have, which wines you should purchase and when your wines should be consumed. An accurate inventory also makes it easy to compare notes with your wine-loving friends.

As you build your collection, buying 12-bottle cases of the wines you drink most often can be a good option that will sometimes earn you a discount.

Keeping a Wine Inventory

Wine Inventory	
Producer	Little Berries Estate Winery
Wine Name/ Vineyard	Hillside Vineyard
Region	Napa
Country	U.S.
Grape Variety	Merlot
Vintage	2000
Type of Wine	Red
Number of Bottles	6
Price Paid/Bottle	$30.00
Bottle Size	750 ml
Date Purchased	June 2, 2004
Purchased From	Bacchus Wine Shop

- You should record information about each wine in your wine collection and keep track of the total number of bottles in your entire collection.

- Some information you may want to record for each wine in your collection is shown above.

- You can record your wine inventory on paper or you may want to use a spreadsheet or database program on your computer for your wine inventory.

- Make sure you update your wine inventory on a regular basis.

- Creating and maintaining an inventory of your wine collection allows you to quickly find a particular bottle that you want to drink.

- Keeping a wine inventory also stops you from unintentionally buying too many bottles of the same wine.

- Maintaining a wine inventory also prevents you from forgetting about a wine that you own, only to later discover that the wine is past its prime.

Can I manage my wine collection on my computer?

Yes. There are a number of software programs that allow you to keep track of your wine collection on your computer. These software packages are designed to help you easily and efficiently manage the wine in your collection. Some of these software packages allow you to create your own rating system and generate lists that classify and sort your wines. Critics' ratings and notes about the winery and winemaker are also included with some software packages.

 What else do I need to know about buying wine by the case?

- Instead of buying an entire case of wine, you can inquire about purchasing a half-case, which typically contains six bottles of the same wine.
- You can also purchase mixed cases, which contain a variety of different wines at various prices.
- There are several places that you can purchase a case of wine. You can buy cases from a wine shop, an Internet retailer, at an auction or directly from a winery.

Buying a Case of Wine

- When you find a wine that you really enjoy, consider buying a case of the wine, which typically contains 12 bottles. Some stores may offer a discount when you purchase a case of wine.

- When you buy a case of wine, you will always have your favorite wine available to enjoy and you will also have extra bottles to use as gifts. When you buy a case of wine that can be aged, you can try the wine every year or two to taste the wine at different stages of development.

- Before buying a case of wine, make sure you really enjoy drinking the wine. Do not buy a case of wine just because your friends or critics give the wine a high rating. Buy a case of wine based on your own personal taste.

- Before buying a case of wine, consider that the wine may age faster than you expect, leaving you with several bottles of wine that are past their prime. You may also get bored of the wine or your tastes may change over time.

CHAPTER

7

Selecting Wine in Restaurants

How Wine is Sold in Restaurants

How Wine Lists are Organized

Wine Service in Restaurants

HOW WINE LISTS ARE ORGANIZED

Wine lists, also known as "cartes des vins" in French, can be organized in a number of different ways. For example, some display just the names and prices of the wines, while others may include descriptions of the wines, interesting tidbits of information or even maps of the wine regions. You can often tell how serious a restaurant is about serving quality wines by the amount of information on the list and how often it is updated.

About Restaurant Wine Lists

Traditional Style Wine Lists

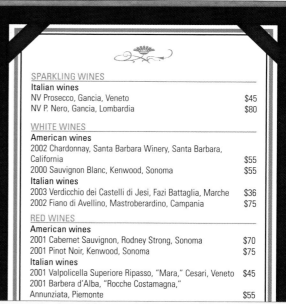

SPARKLING WINES
Italian wines
NV Prosecco, Gancia, Veneto $45
NV P. Nero, Gancia, Lombardia $80

WHITE WINES
American wines
2002 Chardonnay, Santa Barbara Winery, Santa Barbara, California $55
2000 Sauvignon Blanc, Kenwood, Sonoma $55
Italian wines
2003 Verdicchio dei Castelli di Jesi, Fazi Battaglia, Marche $36
2002 Fiano di Avellino, Mastroberardino, Campania $75

RED WINES
American wines
2001 Cabernet Sauvignon, Rodney Strong, Sonoma $70
2001 Pinot Noir, Kenwood, Sonoma $75
Italian wines
2001 Valpolicella Superiore Ripasso, "Mara," Cesari, Veneto $45
2001 Barbera d'Alba, "Rocche Costamagna," Annunziata, Piemonte $55

- Most restaurants use one of three styles of wine lists to present their wine selections to the customer.

- Understanding how wine lists are organized and how to read them will allow you to more confidently order wine with your meal.

- No matter how a wine list is organized, every wine list should provide the essential information about each wine—the wine's name, producer, vintage, or year, and price.

- Depending on the length of the wine list, you may also find a short description of each wine.

- A traditional style wine list organizes wines by category, such as sparkling wines, white wines and red wines.

- Each category of wine is then organized by region. For example, under the White Wines category, the wines may be listed as American wines, Italian wines and Australian wines.

- If you are not very familiar with wines from regions around the world, a traditional style wine list may make it difficult for you to determine which wine you want to order.

What is the purpose of the numbers listed beside the wines on some wine lists?

You may have noticed that some wine lists feature numbers beside each wine. Sometimes referred to as bin numbers, these numbers correspond to a specific location in the restaurant's wine cellar or storage room. This system helps the restaurant to more efficiently manage its wine inventory and also allows the server to quickly locate a wine in the wine cellar or storage room.

TIP *Can I view a restaurant's wine list ahead of time?*

Many restaurants publish online versions of their wine lists on their Web sites. If you would like to know what wines they serve before you arrive, you can simply review the wine list on the Internet before you go to the restaurant. You can narrow the list down to a few options and then make your final decision at the table.

Progressive Style Wine Lists

SAUVIGNON BLANC

Oyster Bay, Sauvignon Blanc - New Zealand	$48
Geyser Peak, Sauvignon Blanc - California	$45

CHARDONNAY

Affinité, Chardonnay - France	$31
Lindemans 'Bin 65,' Chardonnay - Australia	$29

PINOT NOIR

Henry of Pelham 'Unfiltered,' Pinot Noir - Canada	$45
Louis Jadot, Bourgogne, Pinot Noir - France	$53

CABERNET SAUVIGNON & CABERNET FRANC

Caliterra, Cabernet Sauvignon - Chile	$28
Penfolds 'Koonunga Hill,' Shiraz/Cab Sauv - Australia	$42

MERLOT

Leaping Horse, Merlot - California	$40
Affinité, Merlot - France	$30

SYRAH or SHIRAZ

Laurent Miguel, Syrah - France	$48
Wolf Blass 'Eaglehawk,' Shiraz - Australia	$29

- A progressive style wine list organizes wines according to the main grape variety used in the wine. For example, white wines may be divided into categories of Sauvignon Blanc and Chardonnay, while red wines may be divided into categories of Pinot Noir and Cabernet Sauvignon.

- Within each grape variety category, the wines are normally listed by style, from lightest- to fullest-bodied.

- Progressive style wine lists can help you determine which wine you want to order by giving you a clear indication of the wine's style.

New Trend in Wine Lists

WHITE WINES
JUICY AND REFRESHING
These delicious white wines deliver mouth-watering and lively flavors.

Verdicchio, Fazi Battaglia, Italy	$27
Sauvignon Blanc, Landskroon, South Africa	$37

FULL-FIGURED AND VOLUPTUOUS

Pinot Gris, Malivoire, Canada	$46
Chardonnay 'Gold Label,' Coppola, California	$78

RED WINES
FRUITY AND LIGHT-BODIED
These easy-drinking reds are packed with fresh fruit flavors.

Merlot, Mezzacorona, Italy	$32
Beaujolais, George Duboeuf, France	$40

FULL-BODIED

Merlot, Woodbridge, California	$35
Cabernet Sauvignon, Concha Y Toro, Chile	$38

- Some newer wine lists organize wines according to the taste of the wine. For example, white wines may be divided into categories of "juicy and refreshing" and "full-figured and voluptuous" while red wines may be divided into categories of "fruity and light-bodied" and "full-bodied."

- Within each taste category, the wines are normally listed from least expensive to most expensive.

- This new trend in wine list organization is excellent for people who do not have a lot of wine expertise, as it describes the flavor of the wine.

WINE SERVICE IN RESTAURANTS

Before serving you a bottle of wine at a restaurant, your waiter will usually go through a short ritual of presenting the wine for your inspection. Although the process may seem a bit pretentious and fussy, it is designed to ensure that you receive the wine you wanted and that the wine is not flawed. Some people find the wine presentation ritual intimidating, but if you understand the reasoning behind each step you will feel more comfortable with the process.

Wine Service in Restaurants

- When you order a bottle of wine at a good restaurant, your waiter or the restaurant's sommelier will usually go through a short ritual of presenting the wine for your inspection.

  Note: A sommelier is a person who specializes in restaurant wine service.

- The wine presentation ritual allows you to examine the wine and determine whether you want to accept the bottle or reject the bottle if the wine is flawed.

- When the server arrives with the bottle of wine, the server will show the bottle to you.

1 Check the wine's label to ensure that the wine is the same wine and vintage, or year, that you ordered from the wine list.

2 If the server has brought you the correct bottle, tell the server that you approve.

- If the server has brought the wrong bottle, point out the mistake and the server will bring you the correct bottle.

TIP *Should I smell the cork?*

There is no need to smell the cork when the waiter presents it to you. You may have seen this done on television or in a movie, but a cork's scent will not tell you very much about the condition of the wine or its quality. When the waiter presents you with the cork, all you need to do is look at the cork to make sure that it is in good condition. You should look for a cork that is moist and not shriveled as this indicates a bottle of wine that was properly stored on its side.

- After you have inspected and approved the bottle label, the server will remove the cork from the bottle and present the cork to you for inspection.

3 Look at the cork to determine if it is in good condition.

4 If the cork is in good condition, tell the server you approve.

- If the cork is crumbly, looks moldy or is saturated with wine, there may be something wrong with the wine. You should still taste the wine before rejecting the bottle.

- After you have inspected and approved the cork, the server will pour a small sample of wine into your glass for you to examine.

Note: If the wine requires decanting to remove sediment from the wine, the server may decant the wine before pouring you a sample of the wine. For information on decanting, see page 96.

CONTINUED ▶

Most of the time, the short ritual of presenting wine will be a mere formality before you enjoy a pleasant glass of wine. On rare occasions, however, you may come across a bottle that is flawed. If this happens, you should explain the problem to the server and ask for a replacement. Do not allow the server to make you feel uncomfortable or guilty if you suggest that the bottle of wine is flawed. Upon recognizing the problem, the server should bring you another bottle.

Wine Service in Restaurants (continued)

5 Sniff the sample of wine to determine if the wine has any unpleasant aromas that may indicate that the wine is flawed.

- Damp or moldy aromas are an indication that a wine is "corked."

- When a wine is corked it means that it was inadvertently sealed with a defective cork that has ruined the flavor of the wine.

- An aroma of vinegar or rotten eggs is also an indication that the wine is flawed.

6 Take a small sip of the sample of wine to check for any unpleasant flavors.

- The absence of fruit flavors may indicate that a wine is flawed.

- Do not feel rushed when tasting the sample. You may want to take a second sip to confirm any faint impressions you got from the first sip.

Can I send the bottle back if I don't like the wine?

While it's perfectly acceptable to send back a flawed bottle of wine, it is not appropriate to return a bottle of wine just because it doesn't suit your tastes. If the wine that has been opened for you is in good condition, you are generally expected to accept the bottle. There is one exception to this rule of etiquette. If you don't like a wine that your waiter has strongly recommended, you may send back the bottle.

 What should I do if my sample of wine doesn't taste right?

If you are unsure about the condition of a wine, ask your waiter to give you five minutes. Allowing the wine to have a few minutes of exposure to the air should bring out any flaws in the wine. After five minutes, you should taste the sample again to see if any flaws in the wine are more noticeable. If the wine seems flawed after tasting the sample again, you should explain the problem to your server.

- When you sip the wine, also pay attention to the temperature of the wine. Red wine should usually be slightly below room temperature, while white wine should usually be cool.

  Note: For information on serving temperatures for wine, see page 90.

- You do not need to reject a bottle of wine based on its temperature. A bottle of wine that is too warm can be placed in an ice bucket and a wine that is too cool will warm up after being poured.

7 After sampling the wine, you can give your approval to the server or reject the bottle if there is something wrong with the wine.

- If you approve of the wine, the server will pour the wine for your guests and then for you.

- If there is something wrong with the wine, describe to the server what you find objectionable.

- When you reject a bottle of wine, the server should bring you another bottle of the same wine or allow you to select another wine.

Matching Wine and Food

Combining Wine with Food

Suggested Wine-and-Food Pairings

COMBINING WINE WITH FOOD

Wine and food are a dynamic combination. Each time you pair wine and food together, the taste sensations in the wine react with the flavors present in the food.

Understanding a few basic principles of combining wine and food will make your next dining experience a delight for your taste buds.

HOW WINE AND FOOD INTERACT

When paired correctly, wine and food pleasantly complement one another. However, if they are paired incorrectly, you may bring out any unfavorable qualities in the wine or the food.

When you understand how certain types of wine affect certain types of food, you can make good wine and food matches.

Similar Characteristics

As a general guideline, when you consume wine and food that have a similar aroma, flavor, texture or weight, the combination generally makes both the wine and the food taste better. For example, rich, flavorful wines, such as a Cabernet Sauvignon, pair well with rich, flavorful foods, such as a rib-eye steak.

Dissimilar Characteristics

When you consume food and wine that have dissimilar characteristics, the characteristics of one will sometimes clash with or overwhelm the other. For example, the delicate flavors of a filet of sole will be overwhelmed by a rich, flavorful red wine. Certain foods and wines can even create an unpleasant taste when they are consumed together. For example, creamed spinach has a metallic taste when it is consumed with red wine.

TIPS FOR SELECTING WINES TO COMBINE WITH FOOD

When you create a complementary combination of wine and food, the flavorful experience is far better than tasting the wine and food separately. For example, a good, tannic red wine may be delicious on its own, but when paired with a rib-eye steak, the wine and food both taste sensational. The following are some tips that may help you to select the perfect wine to accompany your food.

Ask For Help

When you first start trying to match wine with food, finding the right wine at a wine shop can be an intimidating experience. Fortunately, a knowledgeable wine shop employee will have extensive knowledge of the wine he sells and should be able to suggest several wines that will complement your meal.

Consider the Food's Dominant Flavor

Selecting a wine to serve with a dish that has a complex range of flavors may seem challenging at first. You should focus on trying to determine the most dominant flavor present in the dish and choose a wine to enhance the dish's main flavor.

Red Wine

Garlic

Consider a Wine's Flavors

Wine can add interesting new flavors to a dish it is served with. For example, if you serve a fillet of salmon in butter sauce with a Sauvignon Blanc wine, you will be able to taste citrus and herb flavors from the wine in the food. When choosing a wine for your meal, consider the flavors of the wine and whether those flavors will complement the flavors of the food.

Know Your Own Preferences

Remember that taste is a personal preference, so feel free to experiment and discover your own unique wine and food combinations. As you experiment and learn, you will develop your own instincts when choosing wine to accompany a meal.

CONTINUED

When choosing wine to pair with food, you should consider the characteristics of the wine, such as if the wine is high in alcohol, acid or tannin. You should also consider if the wine is off-dry or sweet or an aged wine.

HIGH-ALCOHOL WINES

Wines that are high in alcohol include Italian Barolo and Barbaresco wines, some Californian wines and many wines from Australia. High-alcohol wines are a good match with very flavorful and substantial dishes, such as roasted or grilled lamb. High-alcohol wines also pair well with foods that are slightly sweet, such as meats with a barbecue sauce.

⚠ Be careful when pairing high-alcohol wines with subtly-flavored, light dishes, as the wine can overpower the food's flavors.

HIGH-ACID WINES

Wines that have a lot of acid include dry Sauvignon Blancs, Pinot Noirs and Chiantis. Salty foods, such as smoked salmon, work well with high-acid wines, making the wine taste somewhat softer and less acidic. High-acid wines are also a great accompaniment for rich foods, such as dishes with cream sauces, since the wines can help rinse your taste buds between bites.

⚠ Be careful when pairing acidic wines with foods that are also acidic, as the acidity in the food can make the wine taste too acidic.

HIGH-TANNIN WINES

Red wines with a lot of tannin include Cabernet Sauvignons and Italian Barolos. When consumed with more fatty foods, such as steak, wines that are high in tannin can help dry the oiliness in your mouth and enhance the flavor of the food. High-tannin wines also tend to taste less bitter when paired with high-protein foods, such as roast beef, and salty foods, such as Parmesan cheese.

⚠ Wines high in tannin are not the best match for spicy or sweet foods.

OFF-DRY WINES

Off-dry wines, which are slightly sweet, include many German wines that are not labeled as dry and medium-dry French Vouvray wines. Off-dry wines are a good match for savory and spicy foods, such as spicy Thai noodles.

⚠ Be careful not to match an off-dry wine with food that is rich or creamy, as these foods can make the wine taste overly sweet and heavy.

SWEET WINES

Sweet wines include Port, ice wines and late harvest wines. Sweet wines are a good match with salty foods, such as blue cheese, because salty foods make sweet wines taste fruitier and slightly less sweet. Sweet wines also pair well with foods that are slightly sweet, such as light pastries.

⚠ Be careful not to pair a sweet wine with food that is very sweet, as the food may overpower the sweetness of the wine and make it taste acidic.

FINE, AGED WINES

When you plan to serve a fine, aged wine with a meal, you need to find a dish that will not compete with or overpower the intriguing and often delicate flavors that have developed in the wine. For example, when serving an aged Bordeaux, a delicious simple main course of prime rib would be a perfect dinner companion. Remember this rule of thumb: the more complex the wine is, the more neutral the meal should be.

SUGGESTED WINE-AND-FOOD PAIRINGS

When you have found a perfect combination of wine and food, the flavors in every mouthful simply taste better. The following suggested wine-and-food pairings will help you put together a number of delicious combinations with ease. Remember, however, that these pairings are just suggestions. Sauces, food-preparation methods and even the region where the wine was made can change how certain wines and foods will taste together. Don't be afraid to experiment. If you find a combination that tastes great, it's a good match!

RED MEAT

As a general rule, red meats match well with full-bodied wines. Both beef and lamb are delicious when paired with red wines that are high in tannin.

Dish	Suggested Wines
Beef stew	Grenache or Pinot Noir
Beef ribs	Syrah or Cabernet Sauvignon
Chili	Zinfandel or Italian Nero d'Avola
Game meat, such as venison	Syrah
Grilled steak	Cabernet Sauvignon
Hamburgers	Zinfandel or Merlot
Rack of lamb	Pinot Noir or Cabernet Franc
Roasted beef	Cabernet Sauvignon
Shepherd's pie	Grenache or Italian Barbera
Steak with barbecue sauce	Zinfandel or Merlot

WHITE MEAT

A common misconception when pairing food and wine is that white meat should only be served with white wine. There are, however, a number of light- to medium-bodied red wines that pair well with white meats.

Dish	Suggested Wines
Roasted chicken	Viognier, oaked Chardonnay* or a Sémillon-Sauvignon Blanc blend
Chicken parmesan	Italian Pinot Grigio or Italian Barbera
Fried chicken	Grüner Veltliner or Italian Verdicchio
Glazed ham	Riesling, Viognier or Merlot
Grilled herbed chicken	Sauvignon Blanc or Portuguese Vinho Verde
Grilled pork chops	Pinot Noir, Cabernet Franc or oaked Chardonnay*
Pork sausages	Sangiovese, Italian Barbera or Italian Dolcetto
Pork tenderloin with cream sauce	Sémillon or oaked Chardonnay*
Pork ribs	Merlot, Zinfandel, Syrah or Italian Nero d'Avola
Thanksgiving turkey	Chenin Blanc, Pinot Noir or Grenache

* Note: An oaked Chardonnay is a Chardonnay that was aged in oak barrels.

SEAFOOD

Seafood dishes often have very delicate flavors, so it is important that an accompanying wine does not overpower the flavors of the seafood.

Dish	Suggested Wines
Shrimp in garlic butter sauce	Italian Inzolia or Italian Greco di Tufo
Battered fish	French Muscadet or unoaked Chardonnay*
Grilled salmon	Pinot Grigio or Pinot Noir
Lobster	Champagne, a Sémillon-Sauvignon Blanc blend or oaked Chardonnay*
Mussels in white wine sauce	Sauvignon Blanc or French Muscadet
Oysters	Champagne or French Muscadet
Rainbow trout with butter sauce	Sauvignon Blanc or Riesling
Seafood chowder	Chardonnay or a Sémillon-Sauvignon Blanc blend
Seared tuna	Gamay or Viognier
Smoked salmon	Champagne, unoaked Chardonnay* or Sauvignon Blanc

* Note: An unoaked Chardonnay is a Chardonnay that was not aged in oak barrels. An oaked Chardonnay is a Chardonnay that was aged in oak barrels.

DISHES WITH COMPLEX FLAVORS

Dishes that have many different flavor elements are best paired with a wine that complements the dominant flavor of the dish. If you are serving a spicy dish, you can rely on aromatic, full-bodied wines to complement the meal.

Dish	Suggested Wines
Stir-fries	Muscat Ottonel or Riesling (off-dry versions)
Cured meats, like salami	Sangiovese or Pinot Gris
Curry dishes	Gewürztraminer or Sauvignon Blanc
Fajitas	Zinfandel
Mushroom risotto	Primitivo, Grenache or Italian Barbera
Pasta in cream sauce	Italian Verdicchio or oaked Chardonnay*
Pasta in tomato sauce	Sangiovese or Merlot
Pizza	Sangiovese or Shiraz
Sushi	Sauvignon Blanc or unoaked Chardonnay*
Indian Tandoori dishes	Viognier

* Note: An oaked Chardonnay is a Chardonnay that was aged in oak barrels. An unoaked Chardonnay is a Chardonnay that was not aged in oak barrels.

CHEESES

While wine and cheese is a well-known combination, you need to consider the texture and flavors of a cheese to choose the appropriate wine to serve.

Dish	Suggested Wines
Brie or Camembert	Pinot Noir or oaked Chardonnay*
Cheddar	Cabernet Sauvignon or Merlot
Gouda	Chardonnay or Riesling
Fontina	Pinot Blanc or Grenache
Gorgonzola	Madeira or French Banyuls
Gruyere	Grüner Veltliner or Champagne
Munster	Gewürztraminer or Riesling
Roquefort	Sauternes, Pinot Gris (off-dry) or Zinfandel

* Note: An oaked Chardonnay is a Chardonnay that was aged in oak barrels.

DESSERTS

There's a simple rule that must be remembered when serving wine with dessert—the dessert should always be less sweet than the wine. A very sweet dessert will overpower the wine.

Dish	Suggested Wines
Pear tart	Sweet Chenin Blanc
Apple pie	Sweet Chenin Blanc
Baked peaches	Sparkling Muscat
Crème brûlée	Canadian Vidal ice wine
Crepes with orange butter	Hungarian Tokaji
Dark chocolate tart	Port or French Banyuls
Lemon tart	Late Harvest Riesling
Pastry cream puffs	Champagne
Strawberries and cream	Rosé Champagne
Tiramisu	Madeira

FOODS THAT DO NOT PAIR WELL WITH WINE

There are certain foods that simply do not pair well with any type of wine. Foods that are extremely acidic or tannic tend to overpower and negatively affect the flavor of wine.

Uncooked tomatoes

Asparagus

Bitter greens, such as arugula and radicchio

Extremely spicy foods

Artichokes

Very sweet desserts and chocolates

Vinaigrette salad dressings

CHAPTER

9

French Wines

About French Wine

Bordeaux

Burgundy

Rhône

Loire

Alsace

Provence

Languedoc-Roussillon

ABOUT FRENCH WINE

Not only is France one of the world's largest producers of wine, it also has one of the world's highest levels of wine consumption per person. With these statistics, it's not surprising that France grows many of the world's most distinguished grape varieties, such as Chardonnay, Pinot Noir and Cabernet Sauvignon. French winemakers produce a wide variety of red, rosé and white wines. France also produces the famous sparkling wine, Champagne. See page 218 for information on Champagne.

About French Wines

Wine Name	Primary Grape Varieties
Beaujolais	Gamay
Burgundy (red) (white)	Pinot Noir Chardonnay
Châteauneuf-du-Pape	Grenache, Mourvèdre, Syrah and others
Côtes-du-Roussillon	Carignan, Mourvèdre, Syrah and Grenache
Entre-Deux-Mers	Sauvignon Blanc, Sémillon and Muscadelle
Haut Médoc	Cabernet Sauvignon
Hermitage	Syrah
Pomerol	Merlot
Pouilly-Fumé	Sauvignon Blanc
Vouvray	Chenin Blanc

- In France, there are hundreds of government registered winemaking regions, called appellations.
- Most French wines are named after the appellation where the grapes are grown.

- Some common French wines are shown in the above chart.
- The grape variety used to make the wine, such as Chardonnay or Merlot, does not usually appear on the wine label.

- Each winemaker must follow the standards and practices defined by the government for their region, which typically includes the types of grapes that can be used and the methods of grape-growing and winemaking.

- Each winemaking region has unique characteristics, including the type of grapes grown, climate and soil. Having some knowledge about a winemaking region can indicate how a wine will taste.

TIP *Does the term "appellation" only refer to a winemaking region?*

Although the word "appellation" usually refers to a winemaking region, it can also refer to a district, village or even a specific vineyard that is registered with the French government. Wines that are named after a smaller location, or a more specific place, like a vineyard, are usually of higher quality and may be more expensive.

 TIP *What does "Vieilles Vignes" mean on a French wine label?*

"Vieilles Vignes" means "old vines" in French. This phrase may appear on a French wine label to indicate that the grapes used to produce the wine were grown on older vines. These grapes are valued because the wine they produce is considered stronger and more flavorful than grapes grown on younger vines. The government, however, does not regulate the use of this phrase, so any winemaker can list this term on their wine labels.

Classifying French Wines

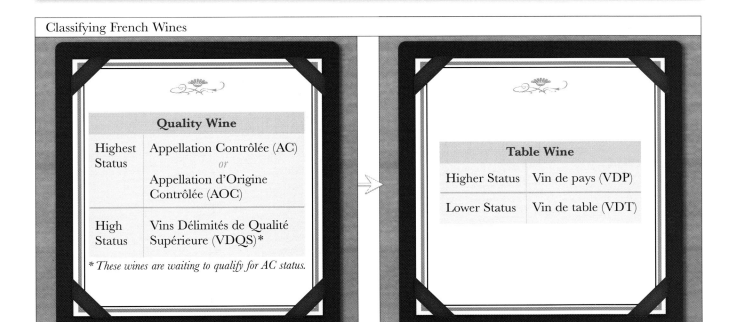

Quality Wine	
Highest Status	Appellation Contrôlée (AC) *or* Appellation d'Origine Contrôlée (AOC)
High Status	Vins Délimités de Qualité Supérieure (VDQS)*

* These wines are waiting to qualify for AC status.

Table Wine	
Higher Status	Vin de pays (VDP)
Lower Status	Vin de table (VDT)

Quality Wine

- If a French wine is made in a registered winemaking region, one of the above phrases will appear on the wine's label.

- These phrases guarantee that the wine comes from that region and that the wine is produced according to local regulations.

- Although a registered winemaking region cannot guarantee the quality of a wine, it can guarantee most of the elements that go into making the wine.

Table Wine

- In France, table wine has a lower status than quality wine. One of the above phrases will appear on the label of a table wine.

- Table wines produced in France typically come from less-regulated regions.

- The name of the region where a wine was made always follows "vin de pays" or "VDP" on a wine label.

- By law, the label of a French vin de table wine cannot display the area of France where the wine was made or the grape variety used.

BORDEAUX

The Bordeaux region is one of France's major winemaking areas, producing ten percent of the country's wine. A bottle of Bordeaux wine may cost anywhere from ten dollars to one thousand dollars, depending on the wine's quality.

Bordeaux wines are commonly purchased when they are young and then aged in an individual's home until the wine is at its best to drink. When Bordeaux wine is still young, the wine is often very dry, with dark cranberry colors and flavors of blackcurrants and spice.

Bordeaux Region

- The Bordeaux region in western France surrounds the city of Bordeaux and stretches to the Atlantic Ocean.

- In the Bordeaux region, there are approximately 57 government-registered winemaking regions, known as appellations. For information on appellations, see page 138.

- Bordeaux has a reputation as one of the largest and best wine regions in the world.

- The Bordeaux region's warm summers, mild winters and ample rainfall create excellent conditions for making the dry red wines for which the region is famous.

- The soil in the Bordeaux region varies from area to area and may contain limestone or gravel.

TIP *I would like to try a variety of wines from Bordeaux. Where should I start?*

The best way to experience Bordeaux wines is to sample the less expensive and easier-drinking wines before you try any of the more expensive or finer wines from this region. For example, you could try wines like Calvet St-Emilion and Moueix before moving on to higher quality Bordeaux wines like Château Calon-Ségur and Château d'Issan. Becoming familiar with less expensive Bordeaux wines will help you to better appreciate the subtleties of finer Bordeaux wines.

TIP *Why is the blending of different grapes so important for Bordeaux wines?*

The blending of different grape varieties helps improve a wine's taste. Each grape variety has different characteristics, such as varying levels of tannin and acid. A winemaker can blend different grape varieties to make a wine that brings out the best qualities in each grape variety, which creates a wine that is well-balanced and complex. Using different grape varieties also provides winemakers with more flexibility. Different varieties of grapes ripen at different times, so harvesting grapes can be completed in stages instead of all at once.

Red Bordeaux

- Most red Bordeaux wines are made from a blend of up to 5 different grapes, including Cabernet Sauvignon, Merlot, Cabernet Franc, Malbec and Petit Verdot.
- The type of grapes and the percentage of each type that go into a wine is determined by the winemaker.
- Red Bordeaux wines become more complex as they age. The best red Bordeaux wines can take from 20 to 100 years to reach their prime.
- Red Bordeaux wines set the standard for every other Cabernet Sauvignon and Merlot wine made in the world.

White Bordeaux

- Most white Bordeaux wines are made from a blend of different types of grapes, including Sauvignon Blanc, Sémillon and Muscadelle.
- White Bordeaux wines are usually aged in oak barrels.
- Most white Bordeaux wines are crisp within the first few years after bottling, but need to age at least 5 to 10 years to develop a rich, honeyed and complex flavor.

CONTINUED

BORDEAUX CONTINUED

Over 80 percent of the wine produced in the Bordeaux region is red wine. In fact, this region is famous for producing red wines which require decades to mature. However, most of the red wine produced in Bordeaux is suitable for everyday drinking and can be consumed three to five years after bottling.

The label on a bottle of Bordeaux wine usually indicates which winemaking estate, called a château, has produced the wine. The label should also specify the town or district where the winemaking estate is located.

Important Subregions of Bordeaux

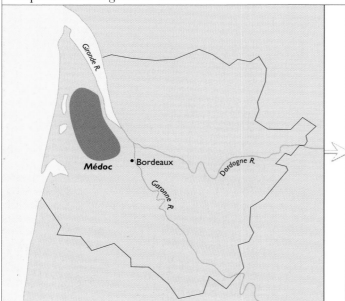

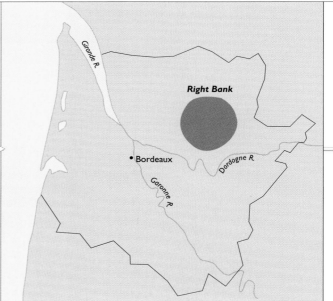

Médoc

- The Médoc area begins at the city of Bordeaux and runs north along the Gironde River.

- This area includes the appellations of Médoc and Haut Médoc, as well as several popular winemaking communes.

- The red wines produced in this area are usually made from the Cabernet Sauvignon grape.

- These red wines tend to be tannic with a blackcurrant flavor. The best examples of this wine should be consumed 10 or more years after bottling.

Right Bank

- The Right Bank area lies to the east and north of the Dordogne River.

- This area includes several appellations, such as St-Emilion and Pomerol.

- The red wines produced in this area are usually made from the Merlot grape.

- These red wines are often less tannic than other Bordeaux wines and should be consumed five or more years after bottling.

What does "cru classé" or "grand cru classé" mean on a Bordeaux wine label?

The term "cru classé" means "classed growth" and the term "grand cru classé" means "great classed growth." Winemakers in Bordeaux may use these terms to indicate that their wine is of a higher quality. The term "cru classé" was introduced in 1855, when the first system for classifying Bordeaux wines was created.

 Do prestigious châteaus offer more reasonably priced wines?

Yes. Many châteaus sell less-expensive wine, called "second label" wine. Although second label wine is not of the same quality as their more expensive wines, this type of wine allows you to taste the style of wine that a top level château produces at a more affordable price. If you want to purchase a second label wine, you need to know the name under which it is sold, since the words "second label" will not appear on the wine's label. For example, Château Margaux sells second label wine called Pavillon Rouge de Château Margaux.

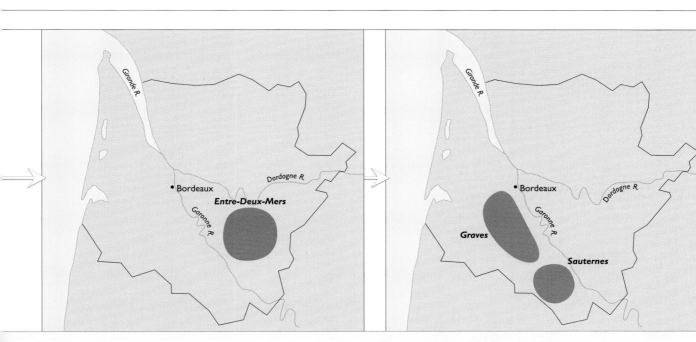

Entre-Deux-Mers

- The Entre-Deux-Mers area is found between the Garonne and Dordogne Rivers.

- Several appellations are found in this area, including Entre-Deux-Mers and Premières Côtes de Bordeaux.

- This area is known for dry white wines which are crisp and fruity.

- This area also produces large quantities of good, generic red Bordeaux wine. This wine is sold without any reference to a specific vineyard or chateau.

Graves and Sauternes

- The Graves area, south of the city of Bordeaux, includes the Pessac-Léognan appellation.

- This area produces red wines made from the Merlot and Cabernet grapes. The area also produces a dry white wine with a citrus flavor.

- The Sauternes area is southeast of the Graves area.

- This area produces sweet white wines made mostly from the Sémillon grape blended with a small amount of Sauvignon Blanc grapes.

BURGUNDY

The Burgundy region is fairly small in terms of annual wine production. The high quality of Burgundy wines, however, has made it one of France's top winemaking regions.

If you enjoy Pinot Noir, you may want to try a Burgundy Pinot Noir, as the region is thought to produce the best Pinot Noir grapes in the world. If you enjoy red wines, you may want to try drinking a red Burgundy wine with your next meal. Red wines from Burgundy are extremely versatile and will complement a pork, fish, poultry or more substantial seafood dish.

Burgundy Region

Distinctions in Burgundy

Distinction	Quality-Level	Wine Produced in Region
Grand cru	World class. The best quality and most expensive.	1% of Burgundy wine
Premier cru, or 1er cru	First-class quality.	11% of Burgundy wine
Commune, or village	Above-average quality.	25% of Burgundy wine
Region and district names	Average quality. Most affordable.	63% of Burgundy wine

- The Burgundy, or Bourgogne, wine region is located in the eastern part of France, from Dijon to Lyon.

- The Burgundy region has warm summers and cold winters.

- In the Burgundy region, there are approximately 100 government-registered winemaking regions, known as appellations. For information on appellations, see page 138.

- The soil in this region is mostly limestone and clay, but it can vary from one vineyard to another or within a single vineyard.

- A Burgundy wine label usually displays the wine's distinction, indicating the quality of the wine.

- Grand cru is the top distinction. It is given to a small number of very prestigious vineyards.

- Premier cru indicates a vineyard which produces great wines at a lower price than grand cru.

- The commune, or village, distinction indicates a typical Burgundy wine. There are 54 official Burgundy communes.

- Everyday Burgundy wines are identified simply by the region and district names.

What does the term "négociant" mean on a wine label from Burgundy?

The term négociant means merchant or wine shipper. A négociant is a company that purchases grapes to create wine and then bottles the wine under its own name. In addition to grapes, négociants also purchase, blend and age wine and then bottle it for sale under their own name. Two prominent négociants are Louis Jadot and Georges Duboeuf. Négociants are an important part of the Burgundian wine trade, as they sell 65 percent of all wines produced in Burgundy.

 What is Aligoté?

Aligoté is the name of a grape variety and a type of wine. Aligoté is a variety of white grape which is grown in Burgundy, mainly in the Mâconnais district. These grapes are used to produce Aligoté wine, which is an affordable, light and neutral-tasting white wine. Keep in mind that some winemakers may add a small percentage of Chardonnay grapes to their Aligoté wine for added complexity. If you purchase Aligoté wine, you should drink the wine while it is young, as the wine does not age well.

Red Burgundies

White Burgundies

- Red wines made in the Burgundy region are typically made from either the Pinot Noir or Gamay grape.
- Red Burgundy wines are often full-bodied and low in tannin, with flavors of berries.

- Many red Burgundy wines become richer and rounder as they age, but most can be consumed just a few years after bottling.

- White wines made in the Burgundy region are usually made from the Chardonnay grape or from a blend of Chardonnay and Aligoté grapes.
- White Burgundy wines often have flavors of apples, citrus, peaches, flowers or honey and various amounts of oak.

- White Burgundy wines become more complex as they age, but many can be consumed just a few years after bottling.

CONTINUED ▶

The Burgundy region contains five different winemaking areas, called districts. Each of these districts is known for producing unique wines such as Pouilly-Fuissé and Beaujolais. Pouilly-Fuissé wines commonly have the flavors of fresh fruit and nuts and are frequently aged in oak barrels, as are most of the wines produced in the Burgundy region.

Beaujolais is a fruity red wine with low levels of tannin. For those who prefer white or rosé wines, Beaujolais can provide a great introduction to red wines.

Districts of Burgundy

Côte Chalonnaise

- The Côte Chalonnaise area is located south of Dijon.

- This area produces both red and white wines of good to above-average quality.

Côte d'Or

- The Côte d'Or area lies just north of the Côte Chalonnaise area and includes the appellations of Côte de Nuits and Côte de Beaune.

- The most famous red and white Burgundy wines are produced in this area.

Chablis

- The Chablis area is northwest of the main part of the Burgundy region, surrounding the city of Chablis.

- This area is known for its white wines made from the Chardonnay grape, which are usually aged and fermented in stainless steel.

- The cooler climate of the Chablis area produces lighter-bodied, very dry wines.

- A simple Chablis wine is best consumed a few years after bottling, while a Grand Cru Chablis is best consumed up to 15 years after bottling.

What is Beaujolais Nouveau?

Every year, on the third Thursday in November, a new vintage of six-week-old Beaujolais Nouveau is released worldwide. This specialized release date has helped to create a strong winemaking industry in the Beaujolais district. Beaujolais Nouveau is a young, fruity wine that has strong grape flavors and almost no tannins. This wine is easy to drink and will be at its best if consumed during the first year after the wine is bottled.

 What makes Burgundy wines so distinctive and expensive?

Wines from the Burgundy region are special and costly because they are produced in small quantities on small vineyards. When grapes are grown on a small plot of land and used to make a small amount of wine, the grapes can affect the flavor and character of the wine more easily than grapes that were grown over a large area and blended with other grapes. The smaller scale of production makes the wine produced in Burgundy more unique and expensive.

Mâconnais

- The Mâconnais area lies south of the Côte Chalonnaise area.

- This area is known for its affordable white wines made from Chardonnay grapes.

- Mâconnais wines are usually medium-bodied, crisp and are typically best consumed within three years of bottling.

- Pouilly-Fuissé is one of the best-known Mâconnais white wines.

Beaujolais

- The Beaujolais area is just north of Lyon and produces approximately 75 percent of the wine made in Burgundy.

- The dry, red wines in this area are made from the Gamay grape.

- Beaujolais wines have lots of fruit flavor and are usually best consumed right after bottling.

- Beaujolais Cru is a top-level wine produced by only 10 villages and is best consumed up to 15 years after bottling.

RHÔNE

The Rhône region contains over 50 government-registered winemaking areas. Winemakers in the southern part of the Rhône region often produce wines using a combination of different grapes, including Syrah, Grenache and Carignan. In the northern part of the Rhône region, winemakers primarily use Syrah grapes to make red wine. All of the wine produced in this region, regardless of location, is aged in oak barrels.

You can usually find great, inexpensive red wines produced in the Rhône region. In general, the red wines made in this region are intense, full-bodied and high in alcohol.

Rhône Region

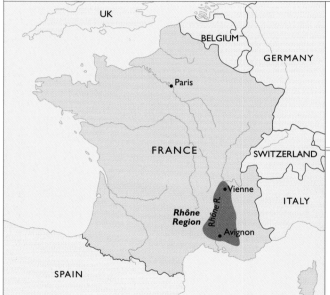

- The Rhône wine region in southeastern France runs along the path of the Rhône River, from the city of Vienne to the city of Avignon.

- The southern and northern areas of this region are quite different and produce different types of wines.

- The south has mild winters and hot summers. The soil is composed mostly of limestone.

- The north has cold winters and warm summers. The soil is composed mostly of granite.

Southern Rhône Region

- The southern Rhône region produces 90 percent of Rhône wines.

- Southern Rhône red wines may be made from a combination of grapes, including Grenache, Syrah and Carignan. These wines are usually inexpensive and easy-to-drink.

- Châteauneuf-du-Pape is the best-known red wine of this area.

- A small amount of white wine is also produced here, from a combination of grapes, including Clairette, Marsanne and Roussanne.

TIP   *What is a Côtes du Rhône wine?*

Eighty percent of the wines produced in the Rhône region are called Côtes du Rhône. This term can be applied to wine made anywhere in the entire Rhône region. A red wine labeled Côtes du Rhône is usually a medium- to high-quality, full-bodied red wine. You can enjoy a red Côtes du Rhône wine soon after the wine is bottled or after it has been aged for a few years.

A Côtes du Rhône wine may also be a white or rosé wine. The white wines from the Rhône region tend to be dry with intense aromas. The rosé wines from this region tend to be fruity with intense flavors.

Northern Rhône Region

- The northern Rhône region produces red wines made from the Syrah grape.

- Côte-Rôtie, Cornas and Hermitage are three popular red wines produced in this area.

- These full-bodied, tannic red wines may have spicy, berry, tar or plum flavors and may be consumed 15 or more years after bottling.

- White Hermitage is a popular white wine made in the northern Rhône region. This full-bodied wine is made from Marsanne and Roussanne grapes and should typically be consumed 5 to 8 years after bottling.

- Condrieu is a popular white wine produced in this area using the Viognier grape. This dry wine has flavors of apricot and peach and is typically best consumed within a few years of bottling.

LOIRE

For a refreshing change from Chardonnay, the white wines from the Loire region make a fine choice. This relatively cool region is best known for its delicate and flavorful white wines. To avoid giving their wines the oaky flavor that is often characteristic of some barrel-aged wines, many wineries in the Loire region use only stainless-steel tanks for fermenting and aging. Producing wines such as Muscadet, Vouvray, Pouilly-Fumé and Sancerre, the Loire region ranks third in AOC wine production, just after the Bordeaux and the Rhône regions. For information on the AOC, see page 138.

Loire Region

- The Loire wine region runs along the path of the Loire River, from the center of France west to the Atlantic Ocean.

- The cool climate found in the Loire region produces mostly grapes well suited to making white, light-bodied wines.

- In the Loire region, there are approximately 70 government-registered winemaking regions, known as appellations. For information on appellations, see page 138.

- The soil in the Loire region varies from area to area and may be composed of limestone, gravel and sand.

Central Loire Valley

- The Central Loire Valley lies about 300 miles inland from the Atlantic Ocean and is slightly south of Paris.

- The wines produced in this area are usually made from the Sauvignon Blanc grape.

- Pouilly-Fumé and Sancerre are the two main wines produced in this area.

- These wines tend to be dry with tangy, spicy, green-grass flavors and are best consumed within four years of bottling.

TIP *Does the Loire region also produce red and rosé wines?*

While it is renowned for its white wines, the Loire region also produces several red and rosé wines. In fact, some of the world's only sparkling red wines are produced in this region. The most notable red wines from the region include Bourgueil, Chinon and St-Nicolas-de-Bourgueil, all from the Touraine area.

TIP *What does the term "sur lie" mean on a wine label?*

"Sur lie" means "on lees." Lees is sediment that is created during the fermentation process. Some winemakers choose to filter the lees out of their wines before aging, while others leave it in the wine for a longer period of time to create more flavor and complexity. When this sediment is left in the wine, it sinks to the bottom of the tank or barrel, leaving the wine "on lees." The sediment is removed before bottling. This winemaking process is popular in the Loire region.

Touraine and Anjou-Saumur

- This part of the Loire region, surrounding the cities of Tours, Angers and Saumur, is the best area in the world for growing the Chenin Blanc grape.

- The main Chenin Blanc wines produced in this area are Savennières, Vouvray and Coteaux du Layon.

- These wines may be dry (sec), medium-dry (demi-sec) or sweet (moelleux) and often have fruity, apple and honey flavors.

Pays Nantais

- Pays Nantais refers to the area where the Loire River meets the Atlantic Ocean and is most known for the Muscadet, or Melon de Bourgogne, grape.

- The wine produced from the Muscadet grape is also called Muscadet. This wine is an inexpensive, light, dry, floral wine with some apple flavors.

- Muscadet wine is typically best consumed within two years of bottling.

ALSACE

Alsace is the only region in France that is permitted to grow the two grape varieties of Riesling and Gewurztraminer. These grapes, along with the Muscat and Pinot Gris varieties, are used to produce the majority of wine in the Alsace region.

Most wines from Alsace are typically aged in stainless-steel or cement tanks rather than oak barrels. This allows the wine to retain more pure grape flavor and prevents the wine from tasting oaky.

Alsace Region

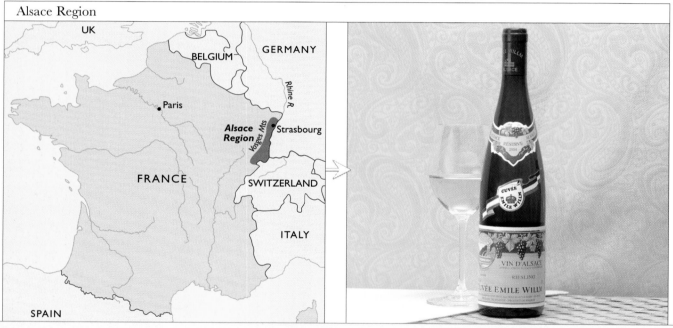

- The Alsace wine region is France's smallest wine region and is found in northeastern France, between the Vosges mountains and the Rhine river.

- The climate in the Alsace region is dry with warm summers and cool winters.

- The soil in the Alsace region varies and may contain granite, limestone, clay or sandstone.

- Most wines made in this region are white and are made using only one grape variety.

- Alsace wines differ from wines in the rest of France in the type of wine bottle used and the way the wines are named.

- All Alsace wines must be bottled in a long-necked bottle, called a flûte.

- In Alsace, there are only two government-registered winemaking regions, known as appellations—Alsace AOC and Alsace Grand Cru AOC. For more information, see page 138.

- Within these two appellations, the wines of Alsace are named according to the main grape variety used.

Are there any other wines that are commonly produced in Alsace?

Yes. Pinot Blanc wines, which account for about 20 percent of the region's wines, are typically light, inexpensive and medium-dry to very dry. The Pinot Blanc wines from Alsace have creamy, baked-apple flavors and are usually best consumed within a couple of years of bottling. Pinot Noir wines, which account for less than 10 percent of the region's wines, are simple, light-tasting red wines which are best consumed soon after bottling.

TIP Does Alsace produce any late harvest wines?

Yes. There are two types of late harvest wines that come from the Alsace region. Wines classified as "vendange tardive" (VT) can be either sweet or dry and are made from grapes that have been allowed to ripen late into the season. Wines classified as "sélection de grains nobles" (SGN) are made from extremely sweet grapes that have been affected by the botrytis, or noble rot, fungus. Both types of wine are rare and expensive.

Main Grape Varieties

Riesling

- Riesling is the most widely-used grape in Alsace. It creates a very dry white wine that often has flavors of peaches and lime.

- Most Alsace Rieslings are best when consumed within a few years of bottling.

Pinot Gris

- The Pinot Gris grape from the Alsace region creates a full-bodied, spicy white wine that often has flavors of ginger, smoke and vanilla.

- Pinot Gris from Alsace is sometimes also called Tokay Pinot Gris.

Gewurztraminer

- The Gewurztraminer grape from the Alsace region creates a unique white wine that often has flavors of rose, lychee, grapefruit, smoke and baking spices.

- Gewurztraminer wines are typically best when consumed within a few years of bottling.

Muscat

- The Muscat grape creates a dry white wine that often has flavors of orange peel and peaches.

- Muscat wines from Alsace often blend two different types of Muscat grapes— Muscat d'Alsace and Muscat Ottonel.

PROVENCE

The Provence region of France is one of the country's largest producers of wine. This region is located in the south of France, which is the oldest winemaking area in the country.

Provence is well-known for producing rosé wines, although its red wines have started to earn critical acclaim. Red wines currently make up only 15 percent of all the wines produced in the Provence region. The production of red wines, however, is continuing to increase in Provence.

Provence Region

- The Provence wine region runs along the coast of the Mediterranean sea, from the Rhône region to the city of Cannes.

- The hot, dry climate is ideal for producing the region's red and rosé wines.

- In the Provence region, there are 8 government-registered winemaking regions, known as appellations. For information on appellations, see page 138.

- The soil in the Provence region varies from area to area, but often contains limestone.

- The main appellations in Provence include Côtes de Provence, Coteaux d'Aix-en-Provence and Bandol.

- These appellations produce rosé and red wines, often using a blend of the Grenache, Cinsault, Mourvèdre, Carignan or Syrah grapes.

- Provence's rosé wines are generally dry, fruity and best when enjoyed soon after bottling.

- Provence's red wines can vary greatly in quality level. Some wines are low-quality, while others are complex and can age well.

LANGUEDOC-ROUSSILLON

The Languedoc-Roussillon region makes 80 percent of all the vin de pays, or table wine, produced in France. Vin de pays wine is a good value because of its low cost and relatively good quality. For more information on vin de pays, see page 139.

Although Languedoc-Roussillon is known primarily for producing red wines, some producers in the region make high-quality sweet wines and fortified wines. Fortified wines are wines that have had an extra dose of alcohol added.

Languedoc-Roussillon Region

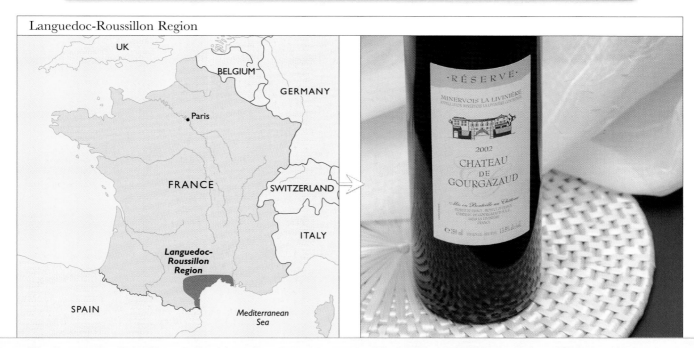

- The Languedoc-Roussillon wine region runs along the Mediterranean sea, from the Rhône region to the border of northern Spain.

- The hot, dry climate is ideal for producing the region's increasingly popular red wines, along with some rosé and white wines.

- In this region, there are approximately 25 government-registered winemaking regions, known as appellations. For information on appellations, see page 138.

- The soil in this region varies from area to area, but often contains chalk, gravel and limestone.

- The main appellations in Languedoc-Roussillon include Minervois, Costières de Nîmes, Corbières, Coteaux du Languedoc, Maury, Côtes du Roussillon and Banyuls.

- These appellations produce red wines, often using a blend of the Grenache, Cinsault, Mourvèdre, Carignan or Syrah grapes.

- The wines from this region are generally fruity and spicy with wild herb flavors, known as garigue.

- Most wines from this region are best when enjoyed soon after bottling, although the wines of high quality become better with age.

BENI DI
BATASIOLO

Barolo

denominazione
di origine controllata
e garantita

2002

The Barolo growing
area lies to the southeast
of the town of Alba.
Barolo is the most
illustrious of all the
great red wines that
since antiquity
connoisseurs have highly
praised as great art.

Carlo Pecrone - Viaggio in Italia

Italian Wines

About Italian Wine

Piedmont

Tuscany

Northeastern Italy

Other Important Italian Regions

ABOUT ITALIAN WINE

Italy is one of the world's largest wine producers and its wines are among the world's best. Many wines produced in Italy are unique because they are made with grape varieties, such as the Nebbiolo, Barbera and Sangiovese grapes, that do not exist anywhere else. Italy has almost two thousand native grape varieties as well as many different soil types, climates and winemaking methods, which allow the country to produce a wide range of wines.

About Italian Wines

Region	Primary Grape Varieties
Piedmont	Nebbiolo, Barbera, Dolcetto, Moscato, Arneis
Veneto	Corvina, Molinara, Rondinella, Garganega
Tuscany	Sangiovese, Brunello, Prugnolo Gentile, Vernaccia, Trebbiano
Friuli-Venezia Giulia	Merlot, Refosco, Tocai Friulano, Ribolla Gialla, Sauvignon Blanc
Umbria	Trebbiano, Sangiovese, Sagrantino, Grechetto, Chardonnay
Campania	Aglianico, Greco di Tufo, Fiano, Primitivo
Sicily	Nero d'Avola, Inzolia, Syrah, Chardonnay

STANDARDS & PRACTICES

- Italy, like most European countries, has laws that regulate how wines are labeled.
- There are hundreds of government-registered winemaking regions where grapes are grown in Italy.

- Some well-known Italian winemaking regions are shown in the above chart.
- Most Italian wines are named after the region where the grapes are grown. Some wine names also include the type of grape used to make the wine.

- In each registered region, winemakers must follow the standards and practices defined by the local government, which typically indicates the types of grapes that can be used and the methods of grape-growing and winemaking.

- Each winemaking region has unique characteristics, including the type of grapes grown and the climate and soil, which affect the grapes and ultimately the wine produced.

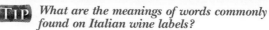

TIP *How important is the DOC or DOCG status in determining a good Italian wine?*

Some winemakers do not have DOC or DOCG status because they think the system has little merit and winemakers are concerned that its regulations could affect the quality of their wine. In fact, some of the best Italian wines have IGT or VdT status. While knowing the DOC or DOCG status of an Italian wine is useful, you should pay more attention to the producer of the wine to determine a wine's true quality.

TIP *What are the meanings of words commonly found on Italian wine labels?*

Italian Term	Definition
Azienda, Fattoria, Tenuta or Podere	A winemaking estate that grows their own grapes
Cantina	Winery
Classico	Wine produced in the region's historical center
Riserva	Wine that has been aged longer than regular wines and contains higher alcohol levels
Vigna or Vigneto	Vineyard

Classifying Italian Wines

Quality Wine	
Highest Status	Denominazione di Origine Controllata e Garantita (DOCG)
High Status	Denominazione di Origine Controllata (DOC)

Table Wine	
Higher Status	Indicazione Geografica Tipica (IGT)
Lower Status	Vino da Tavola (VdT)

Quality Wine

- Wine produced in Italy fits into one of two categories—quality wine or table wine.
- If an Italian wine is made in a registered winemaking region, one of the above phrases will appear on the wine's label.
- These phrases guarantee that the wine comes from that region and is produced according to local regulations.
- Although the status of an Italian wine can give you an indication of a wine's quality, it does not guarantee the quality of the wine.

Table Wine

- In Italy, table wine has a lower status than quality wine. You can identify a table wine by looking for IGT or VdT on a wine's label.
- Vino da Tavola (VdT) wines produced in Italy typically come from less regulated regions.
- Some wines from registered regions are classified as table wines since the wines are made from grape varieties that are not permitted by the government regulations. In some regions, such as Tuscany, these wines can be of very high quality.

PIEDMONT

Some of the world's greatest wines, such as Barolo and Barbaresco, are made in Piedmont. Piemonte, as it's known in Italy, is famous for its red wines, although the region also uses Moscato and Arneis grapes to make dry and sweet white wines. Chardonnay and Sauvignon Blanc wines also have a strong presence in Piedmont. One of Italy's most renowned red grape varieties, Nebbiolo, is used to produce some of Piedmont's most famous wines. Nebbiolo grapes produce wines with strong tannins, high acidity and complex fruit flavors.

Piedmont

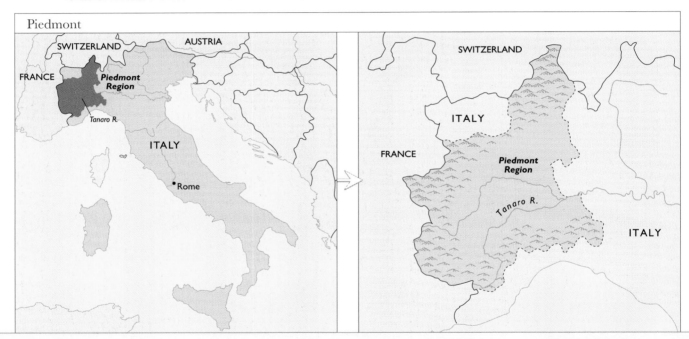

- The Piedmont region is located in Italy's northwest and borders on both Switzerland and France.

- Piedmont contains 7 DOCG areas and 50 DOC areas. For information on DOCG and DOC, see page 158.

- The climate of the Piedmont region varies greatly. In general, the mountains that surround the region protect it from extreme heat and cold. Warm summers, mild winters and lots of fog are common.

- The soil in Piedmont consists mostly of clay, sand, gravel and limestone.

TIP *What is the difference between the traditional and modern styles of winemaking in Piedmont?*

There are two main styles of winemaking in Piedmont—traditional and modern. Wine labels do not indicate which style of winemaking was used to create a wine. However, wine produced using the modern style will frequently have a more contemporary label.

Traditional Style

✓ Wine is aged in traditional, large barrels made of Slovenian oak

✓ Wine is more tannic and needs more time to develop

✓ Wine is frequently less fruity and may have a slightly nutty taste

Modern style

✓ Wine is aged in barrels made of French oak, giving the wine a sweet, oaky flavor

✓ Wine is less tannic as the grapes' skins are handled more delicately

✓ Wine is more fruity and requires less aging

Piedmont Wine Regions

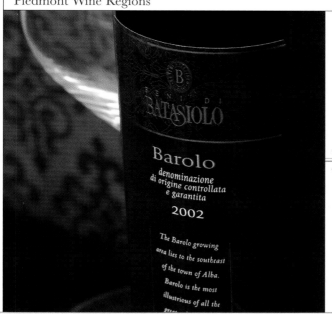

Barolo

- The Barolo region, located on the banks of the Tanaro River, produces the world-renowned red wine called Barolo.

- Barolo wine is made using the Nebbiolo grape.

- This wine is full-bodied, dry and tannic, with flavors of plums, strawberries, licorice, chocolate, dried tea and roses.

- Barolo wines must age for three years before leaving the winery and are typically best consumed up to 20 years after bottling.

Barbaresco

- The Barbaresco region lies north of the Barolo region. This region produces a well-known red wine named for the region—Barbaresco.

- Barbaresco wine is made using the Nebbiolo grape.

- This wine, considered a softer version of Barolo, is a full-bodied, dry wine, with aromas of strawberries, vanilla and roses.

- Barbaresco wines must age for two years before leaving the winery and are typically best consumed up to 15 years after bottling.

CONTINUED ▶

Wines produced in Piedmont can vary significantly depending on the winemaker. In fact, most of the wines from this region are produced on family estates. Winemakers in this region work diligently to create wines that are elegant and unique.

In addition to the Nebbiolo grape, Piedmont is also home to the Barbera and Dolcetto grape varieties. Most of the grapes planted in Piedmont are Barbera grapes, which often make crisp, fruity red wines. Dolcetto grapes often produce a light-bodied red wine.

Piedmont Wine Regions (continued)

Alba and Asti

- The regions of Alba and Asti are found along the Tanaro river in the central part of Piedmont. Asti is just north of Alba.

- The wines of these regions are often named using the grape variety followed by "d'Alba" or "d'Asti."

- In Alba and Asti, red wines made using the Barbera grape are produced in many styles, from fresh and fruity to rich and spicy.

- Red wines made using the Dolcetto grape in these regions are often dry and tannic with flavors of fruit and spice.

- The region of Alba also produces red wines made using the Nebbiolo grape. These wines are typically dry, with flavors of strawberries and licorice.

- The region of Asti is famous for its sweet, sparkling white wine made using Moscato grapes, which has flowery, peachy flavors.

TIP *Are there any other wines from the Piedmont area that I should try?*

There are many other wines produced in Piedmont that are worthy of tasting. For example, Gavi, named after the region in southern Piedmont, is a very dry, crisp white wine made from the Cortese grape. This wine has a subtle aroma and is enjoyable to drink. Roero, named after the region west of Alba, is a dry white wine made from the Arneis grape. This rich, lemony tasting wine is sometimes called white Barolo.

TIP *Are there any white wines made in Piedmont using foreign grape varieties?*

Some Piedmont winemakers produce white wines using French grape varieties, such as Chardonnay and Sauvignon Blanc. The white wines made with foreign grapes are often full bodied and are made using the modern style of winemaking. These white wines are a definite contrast to the red wines made in Piedmont, which are produced mainly from local grape varieties in the traditional winemaking style.

Gattinara

- The region of Gattinara in the north of Piedmont produces red wines which are normally made using the Nebbiolo grape.

- Nebbiolo wines from Gattinara are robust and dry and often have aromas of violets and spices.

- Gattinara's Nebbiolo wines must age for four years before leaving the winery and are typically best consumed up to 10 years after bottling.

Ghemme

- The region of Ghemme is east of the Gattinara region.

- The winemakers of Ghemme produce red wines using the Nebbiolo grape.

- Nebbiolo wines from Ghemme are dry, with aromas of roses and spices. These wines often have a slightly orange color.

- Ghemme's Nebbiolo wines must age for four years before leaving the winery and are typically best consumed up to eight years after bottling.

TUSCANY

Tuscany is located in the central part of Italy, on the west coast. Winemakers in this region produce mainly red wines and Sangiovese grapes are used for all of their classic red wines.

The Chianti region has a variety of climate and soil types, so the characteristics of Chianti wines vary depending on the producer of the wine. During the past two decades, many wineries have upgraded their facilities to improve the production of Chianti and create varieties of Chianti that taste clean and fresh.

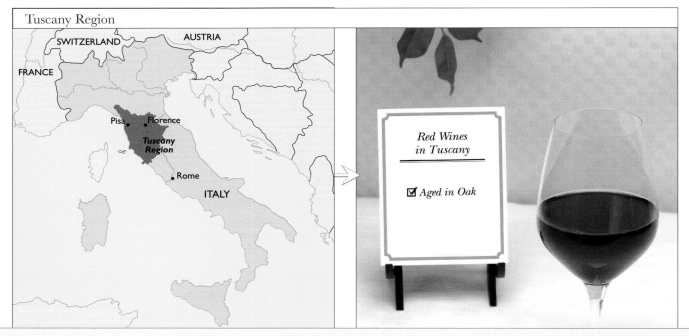

Tuscany Region

Red Wines
in Tuscany

☑ Aged in Oak

- The Tuscany region is found on the western coast of Italy. The cities of Florence and Pisa are both in Tuscany.

- The climate varies throughout Tuscany, but in general the coastal areas are warm and dry while the hillside areas are hot and dry.

- The soil in Tuscany is often sandy and may contain clay, stones and minerals.

- All of the red wines in the Tuscany region must be aged in oak, according to regional winemaking laws.

- The amount of time a wine must be aged in oak depends on the laws of each specific winemaking region.

TIP *Does Tuscany produce any white wines?*

Tuscany produces three white wines of note: Vernaccia di San Gimignano, Chardonnay and Trebbiano.

Vernaccia di San Gimignano is a refreshing wine produced with Vernaccia grapes that grow near San Gimignano, a town southwest of Florence. This wine is produced by almost 500 different winemakers in Tuscany and is Tuscany's only white wine with a DOCG rating. For information on DOCG ratings, see page 158.

Chardonnay has become very popular in Tuscany. Chardonnay grapes are being grown more frequently in Tuscany and the wine they produce is the most expensive white wine in the region.

Trebbiano grapes are widely planted in Tuscany and many white wines in the region are made using these grapes.

Wine Regions of Tuscany

Chianti

- The Chianti wine region is made up of seven smaller districts and lies south of the city of Florence.

- The entire Chianti region has DOCG status, which is the highest status for a government-recognized winemaking region in Italy.

- The red wines produced in this region are made from the Sangiovese grape. These red wines may simply be named Chianti, but also often include the name of the area where the grapes were grown.

- Chianti red wines tend to be light, refreshing and very dry with flavors of tart cherries and violets. The best examples of Chianti should be consumed 3 to 5 years after bottling.

- Chianti Classico wines are produced in the very center of the Chianti region, which is known to be one of the best grape-growing and winemaking areas in the region. Chianti Classico is usually a higher quality wine than other Chiantis.

CONTINUED

The region of Brunello di Montalcino started making wine only three decades ago, but the region is already producing some of the finest red wines in the world. Considering that wines from this region usually have strong tannins, younger versions of this wine should be aerated (see page 94) for several hours before serving. Although Super Tuscan wines are considered a luxury wine, many different wineries have started to make these wines, so their quality has become more varied. The original Super Tuscan wines, which are still among the world's most sought after wines, include Sassicaia, Solaia, Ornellaia, Masseto and Tignanello.

Wine Regions of Tuscany (continued)

Brunello di Montalcino

- The Brunello di Montalcino wine region is located south of the Chianti region.

- This new winemaking area produces one of Italy's greatest red wines and has already earned DOCG status.

- Brunello di Montalcino wine is made using a variation of the Sangiovese grape, called Brunello.

- Wines from this region are full-bodied, tannic and tend to have flavors of black cherry and chocolate. They are typically best consumed at least 5 years after bottling.

Vino Nobile di Montepulciano

- The Vino Nobile di Montepulciano wine region lies to the southeast of the Chianti region.

- The red wines produced in this region are usually made from a variation of the Sangiovese grape, called Prugnolo Gentile.

- These wines tend to be tannic with tart cherry and spicy, earthy flavors.

- Vino Nobile di Montepulciano wines are typically best consumed 5 to 10 years after bottling.

Are there less-expensive alternatives to the red wines made in Tuscany?

There are several different versions of the Brunello di Montalcino, Vino Nobile di Montepulciano and Carmignano red wines. If you are looking for a slightly lighter and less-expensive alternative to these red wines, you may want to try the Rosso versions. For example, you can try Rosso di Montalcino as an alternative to Brunello di Montalcino. Similarly, you can try Rosso di Montepulciano as a substitute for Vino Nobile di Montepulciano.

TIP *What is Vin Santo?*

Vin Santo is a type of dry to sweet wine produced from Trebbiano and Malvasia grapes. The grapes are allowed to dry for a few months before they are crushed, fermented and aged for a few years. This process gives the wine a creamy, roasted, honey flavor. Winemakers only produce small amounts of Vin Santo, so this wine may be more expensive than other wines. For more information on sweet, or dessert, wines, see page 254.

Super Tuscans

Carmignano

- The Carmignano wine region is found northwest of the city of Florence.

- The red wines produced in this region are often made from a blend of Sangiovese and Cabernet Sauvignon grapes.

- Carmignano wines may be medium- to full-bodied and have a good amount of tannin and acidity.

- These wines are typically best consumed 2 to 10 years after bottling.

- Some expensive, high-quality Tuscan wines, referred to as "Super Tuscans," have only Vino da Tavola (VdT) status because the winemakers do not conform to regional regulations.

- Super Tuscan wines are usually made from Sangiovese grapes blended with other grapes, such as Merlot or Cabernet Sauvignon.

- These wines are usually aged in oak barrels and are typically best consumed 5 to 20 years after bottling.

- Super Tuscan wines usually have brand names, such as Tignanello and Sassicaia.

NORTHEASTERN ITALY

There are three winemaking regions in northeastern Italy: Veneto, Trentino-Alto Adige and Friuli-Venezia Giulia. In the past, these regions were a part of the Venetian Empire, so they are sometimes referred to as "The Three Venices." Veneto, Trentino-Alto Adige and Friuli-Venezia Giulia are home to about 50 different grape varieties. Winemakers in northeastern Italy produce wines in many different varieties, from dry white wines and rosé wines to red wines. In fact, the Veneto region produces one of Italy's most famous red wines called Amarone.

Northeastern Italy

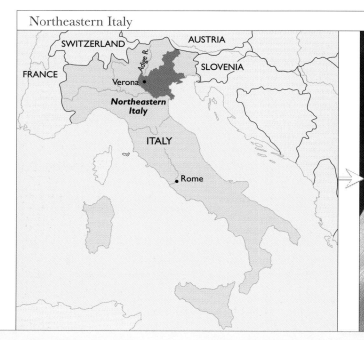

- The northeastern corner of Italy contains three wine regions, called Veneto, Trentino-Alto Adige and Friuli-Venezia Giulia.

- Sheltered by the Alps mountains, these regions generally have hot summers and mild winters, with little frost.

- The soil in northeastern Italy may be volcanic bedrock, limestone or sandy gravel.

Veneto

- The Veneto wine region surrounds the city of Verona and is the most southern of the northeastern Italian regions. Veneto produces several popular wines.

- Italy's popular white wine, Soave, is made with the Garganega grape and features lemon and almond flavors.

- Valpolicella and Bardolino are light, red, cherry-flavored wines made from a blend of Corvina, Molinara and Rondinella grapes.

- Amarone is an intense, dry, red wine made from dried Corvina, Molinara and Rondinella grapes.

Are there any other wines from Veneto that I should try?

Winemakers in Veneto also produce dessert wines called Recioto. Recioto wines are called "passito" wines because the grapes are dried before fermentation to concentrate the grapes' flavors and sugars. Recioto della Valpolicella is the red variety of this wine, made from Corvina, Molinara and Rondinella grapes. This wine is rich, bittersweet and tastes similar to Port. There is also a sweet, white version of Recioto wine, called Recioto di Soave, made from Garganega grapes.

 Do I need to age wine from northeastern Italy?

It is not necessary to age wines from northeastern Italy since most of these wines are meant for early consumption. The flavors and aromas of wines like Soave and Valpolicella will be at their best when the wine is consumed soon after bottling. Amarone wine, however, is an exception to this rule. A bottle of Amarone wine can be aged for 7 to 15 years before drinking.

Trentino-Alto Adige

- Trentino and Alto Adige are two newer wine regions that produce distinctly different wines.
- These regions, which run along the Adige River, are treated as one region for administrative purposes.
- Trentino produces white Chardonnay wines and dark, spicy Teroldego Rotaliano wines.
- Alto Adige is best known for its white wines, including Pinot Grigio, Chardonnay and Pinot Blanc.

Friuli-Venezia Giulia

- The Friuli-Venezia Giulia wine region, on the border of Slovenia, is known for producing a clean, crisp, fruity style of wine in both red and white versions.
- This region grows many grape varieties not found in other regions, such as Ribolla Gialla, Verduzzo, Picolit and Refosco.
- The best winemaking districts within this region are Colli Orientali, Gorizia and Collio.

OTHER IMPORTANT ITALIAN REGIONS

Although the best-known winemaking regions of Italy are Piedmont, Tuscany and regions in northeastern Italy, there are several other important winemaking regions in the country. Sicily, Umbria and Campania are all up-and-coming wine regions where the production of high-quality wines is on the rise. All of these regions use local and imported grape varieties as well as new and traditional winemaking methods. The wines produced in these regions are a great value for consumers because of their high quality and relatively low cost.

Other Important Italian Regions

- In addition to the main winemaking areas of Piedmont, Tuscany and the regions of northeastern Italy, there are several other renowned winemaking regions in Italy.

- Three of the most important winemaking regions include Sicily, Umbria and Campania.

Sicily

- Sicily is a large Italian island in the Mediterranean Sea. This island is quickly becoming one of Italy's most important winemaking regions.

- The sunny, warm climate is ideal for the Nero d'Avola grape, which is used to make full-bodied, spicy red wines.

- Sicily also produces full-bodied white wines made from the Inzolia grape.

- In addition, Sicily produces one of Italy's most famous fortified wines, called Marsala.

TIP *Are there any other important Italian wine regions?*

Some of the other well-known winemaking regions in Italy include:

- Lombardy
- Emilia-Romagna
- Liguria
- Le Marche
- Latium
- Abruzzo
- Basilicata
- Apulia
- Sardinia

Many of these regions are known more for the quantity of wine they produce than for the wine's quality. The quality of wine from these regions may range from mediocre to great, depending on the particular wine and the producer of the wine.

Umbria

- The Umbria region is found in central Italy, to the southeast of Tuscany.

- Many important wineries from other parts of Italy have purchased vineyards and modernized wineries in Umbria, so the quality of the wines produced in this area is quickly increasing.

- The best-known wines from the Umbria region include the white Orvieto, as well as the red Sagrantino di Montefalco and Torgiano.

- Three renowned Umbrian wine producers are Arnaldo Caprai, Cervaro della Sala and Lungarotti.

Campania

- The Campania winemaking region in southern Italy runs along the Amalfi Coast and surrounds the city of Naples.

- Some of the wines produced in this region using local grape varieties are among the most interesting wines in Italy.

- Campania produces Taurasi, which is a dark red wine made from the Aglianico grape, as well as white wines made with the Fiano and Greco grape varieties.

SZEREMLEY

Badacsonyi Muscat Ottonel
Quality dry white wine

Estate bottled

Other European Wines

Spanish Wines

Portuguese Wines

German Wines

Austrian Wines

Hungarian Wines

Greek Wines

SPANISH WINES

Like most European countries, Spain's winemaking regions are defined by its strict grape-growing and winemaking laws. Each region has its own unique characteristics, such as soil conditions and grape varieties grown, which impact the wines of each region.

While Spain is generally dry, hot and mountainous, the country's best wines come from the northern part of the country where the climate is cooler. In these northern regions, the popular Tempranillo grape is widely grown.

Government-Registered Regions

Wine Classifications

Quality Wine	
Highest Status	Denominación de Origen Calificada (DOC or DOCa)
	Denominación de Origen (DO)
High Status	Vino de Calidad con Indicación Geográfica (VCIGS)
Table Wine	
Higher Status	Vino de la Tierra (VdlT)
Lower Status	Vino de Mesa (VdM)

- In Spain, there are hundreds of government-registered winemaking regions where grapes are grown.

- Most Spanish wines are named after the region where the grapes are grown.

- In each registered region, winemakers must follow the standards and practices defined by the local government, which typically dictates the types of grapes that can be used to make wine and the grape-growing and winemaking methods.

- Wine produced in Spain fits into one of two categories—quality wine or table wine. Table wine has a lower status than quality wine.

- You can look for one of the above phrases on a wine's label to determine the quality of the wine.

- If a Spanish wine is made in a registered winemaking region, the wine is considered a quality wine.

- Although the status of a Spanish wine can give you an indication of a wine's quality, it does not guarantee the quality of the wine.

Does Spain produce any sparkling wines?

Yes. Spain produces a well-known sparkling wine called Cava. This sparkling wine is produced in the Penedés region in northeast Spain. Cava is produced using the same traditional method of making Champagne (see page 222). Instead of using the same grapes used to produce Champagne, however, Cava winemakers use the Macabeo, Xarel-lo and Parellada grape varieties.

 Are both modern and traditional winemaking methods used in Spain?

Yes. In a number of Spain's winemaking regions, both modern and traditional winemaking methods are used to create wine, allowing the regions to produce a large variety of styles of wine. For example, Spain produces wine using the traditional method of fermenting wine in large, oak barrels which produce more-tannic, less-fruity tasting wines. More contemporary Spanish winemakers produce wine using more modern methods, such as fermenting wine in stainless steel tanks to produce fruitier-tasting wines.

Rioja

- The Rioja region in the center of northern Spain produces some of the country's best red wines and is important in terms of wine quantity and quality.

- Red wine makes up 75 percent of the wine produced in this region.

- Red wines produced in the Rioja region are normally made from a blend of at least two types of grapes, such as Tempranillo and Garnacha (Grenache).

- Many wine producers in this region age their wines in the bottle, creating fresh-tasting wines.

Navarra

- The Navarra region, northeast of the Rioja region, is best known for its red wines.

- Some French grape varieties, such as Cabernet Sauvignon and Merlot, are used to make wines in the Navarra region.

- Red wines produced in Navarra are also often made from the Garnacha (Grenache) grape and blended with Tempranillo and other grape varieties.

CONTINUED

SPANISH WINES CONTINUED

Spain's vineyards grow more than 600 native grape varieties that supply roughly 10,000 Spanish wineries. With these statistics, it's no wonder that Spain now ranks as the world's third largest producer of wine. However, Spain has not always been a powerhouse in terms of wine production. Despite being the second-oldest country in Western Europe to produce wine, Spain has only recently developed a reputation for producing many exciting and vibrant wines.

Ribera del Duero

Rueda

- The Ribera del Duero region is north of the city of Madrid.

- Ribera del Duero produces Pesquera red wines using the Tinto Fino grape. Pesquera wines are rich and tannic with an abundance of fruit flavors.

- This region also produces Spain's most famous wine, Vega Sicilia's Unico, using Tempranillo and Cabernet Sauvignon grapes.

- Vega Sicilia's Unico is a full-bodied, tannic wine that is typically best consumed at least 10 years after bottling.

- The Rueda region, west of the Ribera del Duero region, produces many affordable, good-quality white wines.

- The Rueda white wines made from a blend of Macabeo and Verdejo grapes are considered one of Spain's best white wines.

- These Rueda white wines are known for their aromas of citrus, herbs and almonds.

- The Rueda region also produces Sauvignon Blanc wines, which are gaining popularity.

TIP *What are some of the most common terms I might see on a Spanish wine label?*

Añejo – wine aged for at least 12 months

Blanco – white

Bodega – winery

Cosecha – harvest or vintage

Coto – estate

Crianza – red wine aged at least 6 months in oak barrels and 18 months in the bottle

Finca/Granja – estate

Gran Reserva – red wine aged 3 years, with at least 24 months in oak barrels and the rest of the time in the bottle

Reserva – red wine aged at least 1 year in oak barrels and 2 years in the bottle

Rosado – rosé

Tinto – red

Viejo – wine aged at least 36 months

Viña/Viñedo – vineyard

Vino – wine

Rías Baixas

Priorat

- The Rías Baixas region in northwest Spain is perfect for growing the white Albariño grapes used to make Albariño wine.

- Albariño wine has flowery aromas and fruit flavors such as peaches and melon.

- Unlike many other white wines, Albariño wine has no contact with oak during the winemaking process.

- Albariño wine is typically best when consumed within 1 to 2 years after bottling.

- The Priorat region in the mountains of northeast Spain is a newly popular red wine region that has become famous for its attention to quality in winemaking.

- Red wines produced in Priorat are made using Garnacha (Grenache) and Carignan grapes.

- The red wines from this region are rich with lots of tannin and a high alcohol content and are typically best consumed within 10 years after bottling.

PORTUGUESE WINES

When it comes to Portuguese wines, many people think of Port (see page 244) or Madeira (see page 250), the country's renowned fortified wines. In recent years, however, Portugal has gained a reputation for producing quality dry wines, including many notable red wines.

Portugal ranks as one of the top ten wine-producing countries in the world. Sixty percent of wines made in Portugal are red, rosé or fortified wines, with the remaining 40 percent being white wine.

Government-Registered Regions

Wine Classifications

Quality Wine	
Highest Status	Denominação de Origem Controlada (DOC)
High Status	Indicação de Proveniencia Regulamentada (IPR)*
Table Wine	
Higher Status	Vinho Regional (VR)
Lower Status	Vinho de Mesa (VdM)

These wines are waiting to qualify for DOC status.

- In Portugal, there are 56 government-registered winemaking regions where grapes are grown.

- Most Portuguese wines are named after the region where the grapes are grown.

- In each registered region, winemakers must follow the standards and practices defined by the local government, which typically dictates the types of grapes that can be used to make wine and the grape-growing and winemaking methods.

- Wine produced in Portugal fits into one of two categories—quality wine or table wine. Table wine has a lower status than quality wine.

- You can look for one of the above phrases on a wine's label to determine the quality of the wine.

- If a Portuguese wine is made in a registered winemaking region, the wine is considered a quality wine.

- Although the status of a Portuguese wine can give you an indication of a wine's quality, it does not guarantee the quality of the wine.

What are some of the terms that often appear on Portuguese wine labels?

Adega—winery

Branco—white

Colheita—vintage (year)

Quinta—wine estate, or vineyard

Reserva—wine of superior quality from one vintage (year)

Rosado—rosé

Seco—dry

Tinto—red

Vinho—wine

Are there any other important wine regions in Portugal?

There are two other noteworthy Portuguese wine regions—the Dão region and the Bairrada region. The Dão region is located south of the Douro region. In the Dão region, 50 different grape varieties are used to create a wide variety of mainly red wines. The Bairrada region is located west of the Dão region. The Baga grape must make up at least 50 percent of every wine produced in the Bairrada region.

Douro

- The Douro region in northern Portugal extends along the banks of the Douro River.
- Some of the Douro region's best red wines are made from several grape varieties, including Touriga Nacional and Tinta Roriz (Tempranillo).
- These red wines are generally dry and full-bodied with flavors of ripe fruit and vanilla and can often age for 20 or more years after bottling.
- One of the best examples of Douro's red wine is called Barca Velha.

Vinho Verde

- The Vinho Verde region in the northwest area of Portugal has cool temperatures that are ideal for growing the grapes used to produce the country's best white wines.
- The best white wines produced in this region are made from Alvariñho, Loureiro or Trajadura grapes.
- White wine produced in the Vinho Verde region is light, spritzy and acidic with mineral flavors and is typically best consumed within a year after bottling.

GERMAN WINES

Germany has the distinction of being the most northern country in Europe to produce wine. Germany's vineyards tend to be damp and cool, which provides an ideal environment for growing white grapes. As a result, 85 percent of wines produced in Germany are white as red grapes do not thrive in the country's cooler climate. Unlike many European countries, the names of German wines usually include the variety of grape, such as Riesling, used to make the wine.

Government-Registered Regions

Quality Wine

Quality Wine	
Highest Status	Qualitätswein mit Prädikat (QmP)
High Status	Qualitätswein bestimmter Anbaugebiete (QbA)

- In Germany, there are 13 large winemaking regions.
- German wines are typically named for the type of grape used to make the wine, although the vineyard name and winemaking region may also appear on the label.

- In each registered winemaking region, winemakers must follow the standards and practices defined by the local government, which typically dictates the types of grapes that can be used to make wine and the grape-growing and winemaking methods.

- If a wine is made in a registered winemaking region, one of the above phrases will appear on the wine's label to indicate that the wine has quality wine status.
- The above phrases guarantee that the wine comes from the registered winemaking region and is produced according to local regulations.

- Although a registered winemaking region cannot guarantee the quality of a wine, it can guarantee most of the elements that go into making the wine.

TIP *What German wine-label terms should I know?*

Einzellage – single vineyard

Grosslage – group of vineyards

Halbtrocken – medium-dry

Rotling – rosé

Rotwein – red wine

Schloss – wine estate, but literally means "castle"

Sekt – sparkling wine

Trocken – dry

Weingut – wine estate

Weisswein – white wine

TIP *What is chaptalization?*

The process of chaptalization allows a winemaker to increase the level of alcohol in wine by adding extra sugar to the grape juice before fermentation. Chaptalization helps to properly balance wines that are made with grapes that do not contain enough natural fruit sugar. Wines with Germany's highest classification, Qualitätswein mit Prädikat (QmP), cannot be chaptalized.

Prädikat	Sugar Concentration in Grapes	Type of Wine
Kabinett	Normal	A light, medium-dry wine.
Spätlese	Slightly higher than normal	A medium-dry wine.
Auslese	Slightly higher than normal	A wine with some sweetness.
Beerenauslese (BA)	High	A moderately sweet wine.
Trockenbeerenauslese (TBA)	Very high	A sweet wine.
Eiswein	Very high	A very sweet wine.

Table Wine

Table Wine	
Higher Status	Tafelwein
Lower Status	Landwein

- German wines with the highest quality status are labeled with a distinction, called a Prädikat, indicating the concentration of sugar in the grapes before they were harvested.

- You will see the distinction on the label of a wine that has the Qualitätswein mit Prädikat (QmP) status.

- The chart above lists the six Prädikat levels, from the lowest concentration of sugar in the grapes to the highest concentration of sugar.

- In Germany, table wine has a lower status than quality wine. One of the above phrases will appear on the label of a table wine to indicate the status of the table wine.

- Table wines produced in Germany typically come from less-regulated regions.

CONTINUED

181

GERMAN WINES CONTINUED

Germany has 13 winemaking regions which are all located in the southwestern part of the country. Many of Germany's vineyards are located along rivers, like the Rhine and Mosel, which have steep slopes that provide grape vines with a good amount of sun exposure.

The Riesling grape is Germany's most-planted grape variety, with other popular grapes being the Silvaner, Müller-Thurgau, Dornfelder and Spätburgunder. German wines are known for being slightly sweet to sweet, fruity and low in alcohol.

Mosel-Saar-Ruwer

Pfalz

- The Mosel-Saar-Ruwer region lies along the banks of the Mosel River.

- This region produces white wines which are most often made from the Riesling grape.

- Riesling wines from the Mosel-Saar-Ruwer region are light, delicate, fruity and fresh-tasting and are typically best consumed within 2 to 10 years after bottling.

- You can identify a bottle of Riesling wine made in this region by its green bottle. Most white wines produced in other areas of Germany have a brown bottle.

- The Pfalz region is the southernmost winemaking region in Germany and produces a wide variety of great wines.

- This region is famous for producing some of the best dry Riesling, Chardonnay and Weissburgunder (Pinot Blanc) white wines in Germany.

- Several good red wines are also produced in this region using Spätburgunder (Pinot Noir) grapes. These medium-bodied wines often have aromas of cherry and spice and are typically best consumed within 4 to 8 years after bottling.

Are there any other notable winemaking regions in Germany?

Yes. The Nahe region, which is west of the Rheinhessen region, has a reputation for producing high-quality wines. Located along the Nahe river, the Nahe region is well-suited to growing Riesling, Silvaner, Scheurebe and Müller-Thurgau grapes. The finest wines produced in the region tend to be made with Riesling grapes and are typically full bodied with intense flavors.

 Do some German winemakers sweeten their wines?

Yes. Some German wines are made using a sweetening process called Süssreserve, which means sweet reserve. Prior to fermentation, a portion of the grape juice is removed and put aside. Once fermentation is complete, the juice that was put aside is added to the wine. This process sweetens the wine with the juice's natural sweetness.

Rheingau

- The Rheingau region lies along the northern bank of the Rhine River.
- This region produces mostly white wines made from Riesling grapes with flavors of violets and honey. These wines are typically best consumed within 1 to 8 years after bottling.
- In addition, this region also produces medium-bodied red wines using the Spätburgunder (Pinot Noir) grape. These wines have flavors of spices and bitter-almond and are typically best consumed within 4 to 10 years after bottling.

Rheinhessen

- The Rheinhessen region, south of the Rheingau region, is Germany's largest winemaking region.
- Liebfraumilch white wines from this region are one of Germany's most famous wines. This wine often has flavors of melon and honey and is best consumed immediately after bottling.
- A small amount of good white Riesling wines are also made in this region. These Riesling wines have flavors of peach and white flowers and are typically best consumed within 5 years after bottling.

AUSTRIAN WINES

Austria may not be among Europe's big wine producers, but the small, central-eastern European nation does produce a number of notable wines. In particular, Austria is known for making excellent dry white wines. More than 30 different grape varieties are grown in Austria, including the local Grüner Veltliner and Blaufränkisch varieties and well-known grapes such as Chardonnay and Riesling. The Grüner Veltliner variety is Austria's most popular grape, producing rich, crisp and full-bodied wines that feature the flavors of grapefruit, white pepper and smoke.

About Austrian Wines

Lower Austria

- In Austria, all wines are produced in the eastern part of the country, where the soil mostly consists of limestone or gravel.

- The mild climate of Austria allows the grapes to ripen longer on the vines than they would in many other European countries.

- The most well-known winemaking regions in Austria are Lower Austria, Burgenland and Vienna.

- For information on Austrian winemaking regulations, see the top of page 185.

- The Lower Austria winemaking region produces more than half of Austria's wines.

- Wachau, in Lower Austria, produces famous lime-scented white wines made from the Riesling grape. These wines are typically best consumed within 5 years after bottling.

- The winemaking district of Kremstal produces white wines with flavors of citrus and white pepper made from the Grüner Veltliner grape. These wines are typically best consumed within 5 years after bottling.

How are Austrian wines regulated and classified?

The standards for winemaking in Austria are typically defined by local governments. These rules generally dictate the grapes that can be used to make wine, as well as grape-growing and winemaking methods. While Austrian winemaking regulations are quite similar to German regulations, the Austrian rules tend to be even more strict. For more information on German regulations, see page 180.

 Does Austria produce any sweet wines?

Yes. Several excellent, full-bodied sweet wines are produced in Austria. These wines are typically produced using grapes that have been affected by the botrytis, or noble rot, fungus (see page 257). The Burgenland region, in particular, is well known for using Furmint grapes and a selection of other grapes to produce sweet wines called Trockenbeerenauslese.

Burgenland

- The Burgenland winemaking region lies along the border of Hungary.
- Red wines made from the Blaufränkisch grape in this region have raspberry and white pepper flavors and are typically best consumed within 8 years after bottling.
- White wines made from the Welschriesling grape in this region have citrus and floral flavors and are typically best consumed within 4 years after bottling.

Vienna

- Vienna is the world's only major city that is designated as a winemaking region.
- White wines made from the Weissburgunder (Pinot Blanc) grape in Vienna have apple and citrus flavors and are typically best consumed within 3 years after bottling.
- Red wines made from the Zweigelt grape in Vienna have cherry flavors and are typically best consumed within 8 years after bottling.

HUNGARIAN WINES

With a centuries-old history of winemaking and an environment that is ideal for grape growing, Hungary is full of wine-producing potential. Hungary is located further north than many other European wine-producing nations, but its land is surrounded by mountains which creates a relatively mild, grape-friendly climate.

The country's varied and often well-draining soils provide an ideal environment for the many native and international grape varieties grown in Hungary. Both red and white wines are produced in Hungary, ranging from dry to slightly sweet.

About Hungarian Wines

Southern Areas

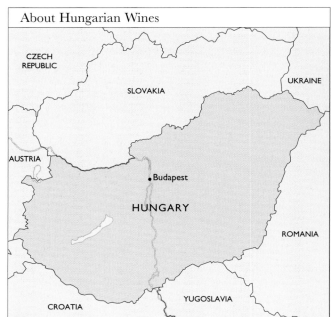

- In Hungary, high-quality wines are produced in government-registered winemaking regions and display "Minőségi Bor" (quality wine) on their labels.

- In registered regions, winemakers must follow the government's winemaking standards, which include the types of grapes grown and the winemaking methods.

- Lower quality wines display "Asztali Bor" (table wine) on their labels and typically come from less-regulated regions.

- Most Hungarian wines are named after the type of grape used to make the wine.

- The majority of Hungary's red wines are produced in the southern area of the country.

- The famous, full-bodied red wine called Bikavér (Bull's Blood) is made in southern Hungary. This wine has flavors of spice and black cherries.

- In southern Hungary, some red wines are also produced using varieties of grapes found in other countries, such as Bordeaux-style red wines that have flavors of plum and cocoa.

TIP *What makes Tokaji Aszú wine so special?*

Tokaji Aszú wine is made using a different process than any other wine in the world. Aszú is the name of a sweet paste which is made of crushed noble rot-affected grapes. The paste is added to the wine to sweeten the wine before fermenting.

The amount of paste added to the wine determines the final sweetness level of a Tokaji Aszú wine. The sweetness level is indicated on the wine's label by a number from three to six, followed by the word "Puttonyos." The higher the number listed on the label, the sweeter the wine.

Western and Northeastern Areas

Tokaji Aszú Wine

- The western and northeastern areas of Hungary produce mostly white wines.
- White wines made from local grape varieties such as Muscat Ottonel and Furmint are generally full-bodied, dry wines with spice flavors.

- The western and northeastern areas of Hungary also produce wines using varieties of grapes found in other countries. These wines tend to be medium bodied and aromatic.

- Hungary's most famous wine is the sweet white wine called Tokaji Aszú (Tokay).
- Tokaji Aszú is made from local white grapes, including Furmint and Hárslevelü, that have been affected by noble rot—a mold that grows on the grapes.

- Tokaji Aszú wines can be found with a variety of flavors and styles from medium sweet to very sweet, depending on the winemaker and the techniques used to make the wine.

GREEK WINES

We have Greece to thank for the creation of wine as ancient Greeks were the first to produce wine more than 6,000 years ago. Today, Greece is the world's thirteenth largest wine producer and makes many exceptional wines.

Greece produces a large selection of wines using more than 300 different grape varieties such as Sauvignon Blanc, Chardonnay, Cabernet Sauvignon and Merlot. Sixty percent of wines produced in Greece are white wines that range from sweet to dry.

About Greek Wines

Macedonia

- Most Greek wines are named after the government-registered winemaking region, or appellation, where the grapes are grown.

- Each Greek winemaker must follow the winemaking standards defined by the government.

- The label of a Greek wine made in a registered winemaking region will display the Appellation of Superior Quality (OPAP) classification.

- Table wine, called vin de pays or topikos oenos, has a lower status than quality wine.

- Macedonia, in northern Greece, produces some of Greece's best wines.

- The cool, high altitudes of the mountains and the soil composed of limestone and volcanic rock create ideal growing conditions for white wine grapes such as Sauvignon Blanc and Assyrtiko.

- One of Greece's best-known red wines, Naoussa, is produced in Macedonia using the Xynomavro grape. Naoussa wines have spicy, fruity flavors and are typically best consumed within 5 years after bottling.

TIP *Does Greece produce any dessert wines?*

Yes. Greece produces several very good dessert wines. The Samos region produces Samos White Muscat wine, which is made from the Muscat Blanc à Petits Grains grape and features flavors of figs, dates and honey. Mavrodaphne of Patras is also a popular dessert wine made from Mavrodaphne grapes in the Patras area of the Peloponnese region. This Port-like wine often has flavors of plums and nuts.

TIP *What is retsina?*

Retsina is a unique type of wine that has been made in Greece for thousands of years. Retsina is usually made with the white Savatiano grape and has a pine flavor. This flavor comes from pine resin that is added to the grape juice as it is fermenting. Retsina, which is best served slightly cool, can be an interesting accompaniment to aromatic Greek foods.

Peloponnese

Crete

- Peloponnese is located in southern Greece.
- Patras and Mantinia are both spicy white wines made in Peloponnese from a blend of grapes, including the pink-skinned Rhoditis grape. These wines are typically best consumed within 3 years after bottling.

- The best red wines in Peloponnese are made in the Nemea region from the Agiorgitiko grape. These wines have a spicy, peppery flavor and are typically best consumed within 6 years after bottling.

- Crete is the Greek island that produces the largest amount of wine.
- Crete has hot summers and mild winters which allow the island to produce several good styles of wine.

- Red wines produced in Crete are often made from the Kotsifali grape. These spicy wines are typically best consumed within 5 years after bottling.
- White wines produced in Crete are often made from the Vilana grape. These fruity wines are typically best consumed within 3 years after bottling.

New World Wines

Australian Wines

New Zealand Wines

South African Wines

Chilean Wines

Argentinean Wines

American Wines

Canadian Wines

AUSTRALIAN WINES

Australia has become a winemaking powerhouse —the country now ranks seventh in terms of wine production in the world. As the industry has grown, Australian wineries have developed a reputation for creating quality wines at reasonable prices. These wines tend to be fruity and are best consumed right after bottling.

Some of the country's best wines are produced in South Australia, a region responsible for just over half of all Australian red wines. Most of the country's largest wineries are based in South Australia.

About Australian Wines

- Australia produces good wines using some of the most technologically advanced methods and equipment available in the world.

- Most of Australia's wines are produced in the southern part of the country, where the climate is warm and dry.

- The soil in Australia's winemaking areas varies, but often consists of sand, limestone or clay.

- Most of Australia's wines are created to be consumed soon after bottling and do not improve with age.

- Although Australia does not have laws regulating grape growing and winemaking methods, the country does have laws dictating how wines are labeled.

- If a grape variety is displayed on a wine's label, at least 85 percent of the wine must be made from the grape variety.

- If a wine is made from a blend of grape varieties, the grape names must appear on the wine's label in order from the highest to the lowest quantities.

- If a winemaking area is named on the label, at least 85 percent of the wine must be produced in that area.

TIP

Do Australian wineries tend to be more traditional or modern in their approach to winemaking?

Generally, the wineries in Australia rely less on traditional methods and more on modern technology to create their wines. Over the years, Australian wineries have enthusiastically embraced many advances in winemaking technology. The country is a world leader in using a modern winemaking approach to produce intensely fruity wines that taste delicious and do not need to be aged after bottling.

 TIP

Some Australian wines have a screw cap instead of a cork. Does this mean the wine is of low quality?

No. Many Australian wine producers, including those who produce premium wines, now use screw caps to seal their bottles. Corks are being replaced with screw caps because corks are only beneficial for wines that are intended to age for a long time in the bottle. Since most Australian wines are produced to be consumed soon after bottling, the majority of Australian wines do not require a cork.

South Australia

- Most of the wine produced in Australia comes from southern Australia.

- The Barossa Valley is famous for red wines made from the Shiraz grape. These wines have a fruity, peppery, oak flavor.

- McLaren Vale is also well-known for its Shiraz red wine, which often has flavors of blackberry and chocolate.

- The Coonawarra area produces Australia's best red wine made from the Cabernet Sauvignon grape, which often has flavors of black currant, chocolate and eucalyptus.

- The Eden Valley is well-known for making great-tasting dry white wines made from the Riesling grape. Eden Valley Rieslings are crisp and have flavors of white flowers and lime.

- The Adelaide Hills area is best-known for white wines made from the Sauvignon Blanc grape. These wines often have flavors of citrus and passion fruit.

CONTINUED

Known for its sophisticated irrigation systems and environmentally-friendly disease management methods, Australia grows a wide range of grape varieties. The Chardonnay grape is the country's most widely grown white grape variety and is used in many of Australia's finest wines. Riesling and Semillon are two other popular white grape varieties grown in Australia. The Shiraz grape is Australia's most widely planted red grape variety. In fact, Australia boasts one of the largest Shiraz plantings in the world.

Victoria

- Victoria is located in the southeastern area of Australia and is the home of many small wineries that produce quality wines. Victoria contains several winemaking areas, including the Pyrenees, Yarra Valley and Goulburn Valley.

- The Pyrenees area is well-known for its red wines made from the Shiraz grape. These red wines often have flavors of mint and spice.

- The Yarra Valley produces several excellent wines, including red wines made from the Pinot Noir grape, white wines made from the Chardonnay grape and sparkling wines made from these two grape varieties.

- The Goulburn Valley is also famous for red wines made from the Shiraz grape. Goulburn Valley Shiraz wines often have flavors of red raspberries and chocolate.

 *Did you know?*

- Australia does not have any native grape varieties. The grapes grown in Australia can be traced back to vines that were imported from Europe and South Africa between the late 1700s and early 1800s.

- Unlike many countries in Europe, Australia does not have to abide by regulations that outline specific regions where only certain types of grapes can be grown. This has given Australian wineries the freedom to experiment with planting different grape varieties throughout the country.

TIP *Why is Australia famous for its wine blends?*

Australia was one of the first countries to start making wine blends with grapes that were not traditionally combined. Shiraz-Cabernet Sauvignon and Semillon-Chardonnay are two wine blends that were invented and popularized by Australian winemakers. The practice of blending wines has now become popular, with other countries also creating their own blends.

New South Wales

- New South Wales is located just north of Victoria on Australia's southeastern coast.

- The Mudgee area is known for producing excellent red wines made from the Cabernet Sauvignon grape. These wines have flavors of chocolate and black currant.

- The Hunter Valley produces wines of exceptional quality, including intensely fruity white wines made from the Semillon grape.

Western Australia

- Western Australia produces a small amount of very good quality wine.

- The Margaret River area in western Australia is known for producing excellent red wines made from the Cabernet Sauvignon grape. These wines often have flavors of black currant, herbs and cocoa.

- The Great Southern area is one of the largest winemaking areas in Australia. Many good wines are produced in this area, but the best wine is a crisp white wine made from the Riesling grape, with flavors of lime blossom and grapefruit.

NEW ZEALAND WINES

New Zealand has a reputation for producing fresh-tasting wines with clean fruit flavors. In fact, the country's lively Sauvignon Blanc wines are world famous. Many popular white grape varieties grown in New Zealand include the widely grown Chardonnay, along with the Müller-Thurgau and Riesling varieties, which thrive in cool conditions. Pinot Noir is the most widely planted red grape variety in the country. Other red grape varieties grown in New Zealand include Cabernet Sauvignon and Merlot.

About New Zealand Wines

- The country of New Zealand consists of two islands located just southeast of Australia.

- New Zealand is a newer winemaking area. This country has been producing a small amount of wines since the 1980s, but the amount of wine produced in the country is increasing every year.

- New Zealand has a cool, damp climate and a long growing season, which allows the grapes to develop slowly, producing flavorful wines.

- Although New Zealand does not have laws regulating grape growing and winemaking methods, the country does have laws dictating how wines are labeled.

- If a grape variety is displayed on a wine's label, at least 75 percent of the wine must be made from the grape variety.

- If a wine is made from a blend of grape varieties, the grape names must appear on the wine's label in order from the highest to the lowest quantities.

Why are wines from New Zealand available in stores sooner than wines from other parts of the world?

New Zealand, which is located in the southern hemisphere, has a grape-growing season that is opposite to countries in the northern hemisphere, such as the United States and France. For example, during the winter months in the northern hemisphere, when grapevines are dormant, the grapevines in New Zealand are flourishing. This head-start on the growing season allows New Zealand winemakers to produce and distribute their wines sooner than winemakers in other parts of the world.

Why do New Zealand's white wines have such crisp flavors?

You will find that the white wines produced in New Zealand, such as Sauvignon Blanc and Chardonnay, tend to have a lot of acidity which gives them refreshingly crisp flavors. To preserve the natural acidity of their wines, New Zealand's winemakers generally avoid using oak barrels for fermenting and aging their wines, as oak tends to soften the character of a wine. Instead, most of New Zealand's winemakers make their white wines in stainless steel tanks which accentuate the wine's acidity.

North Island

South Island

- Approximately 40 percent of New Zealand's vineyards are located on the North Island.
- The best winemaking areas on the North Island include Hawke's Bay and Wairarapa.

- Pinot Noir is the most widely planted red grape in New Zealand. On the North Island, good, red Pinot Noir wines have earthy flavors and are ready to drink soon after bottling.
- Good white wines are also made here using the Riesling and Chardonnay grapes.

- The South Island of New Zealand has a slightly cooler climate than the North Island.
- The best winemaking areas include Marlborough, Nelson, Canterbury and Otago.
- The South Island has many small, independent wineries that produce wines of excellent quality.

- Sauvignon Blanc grapes make the best white wines in New Zealand. White Sauvignon Blanc wines from the South Island have flavors of lime, green vegetables and tropical fruit and are ready to drink soon after bottling.

SOUTH AFRICAN WINES

South Africa is far from being a "new kid on the block" when it comes to winemaking. This country may not have the ancient winemaking history many European countries boast, but South Africa has actually been producing wine since the 17th century.

South Africa grows over 40 different grape varieties in 11 winemaking districts. South African winemakers tend to produce mostly white wines although the production of red wines is increasing steadily.

About South African Wines

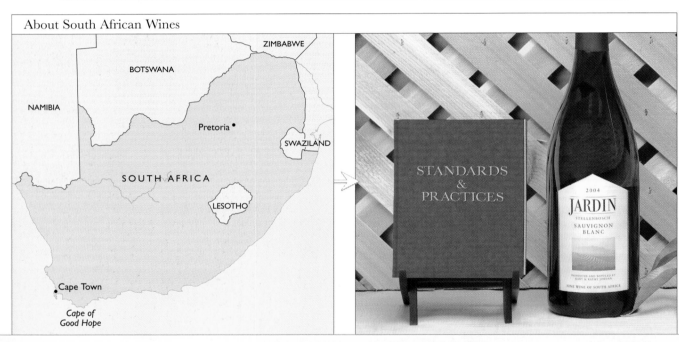

- Most of South Africa's wines are produced in the areas around the Cape of Good Hope.

- The climate in the South African winemaking areas is hot and dry, but is cooled slightly by the wind coming off the ocean.

- The soil in South Africa's winemaking areas varies, but often consists of gravel, sand and rich, red soil called Cape sandstone.

- South Africa has Wine of Origin (WO) regulations, which are based on the wine laws of France.

- Each winemaker must follow the standards defined for their region, which typically includes the types of grapes that can be used and the methods of grape-growing and winemaking.

- If a grape variety is displayed on a wine's label, at least 85 percent of the wine must be made from the grape variety.

- If a winemaking area is named on the label, 100 percent of the wine must be produced in that area.

Why are more South African wines available now than in the 1980s?

During the 1980s, economic sanctions aimed at ending racial segregation in South Africa hurt the country's wine industry. South Africa fell behind as winemakers in other countries evolved and improved. When the sanctions ended, South Africa's wineries were finally able to start catching up with wineries in other parts of the world. Today, the country is the world's eighth largest wine producer and its wineries are delivering high-quality wines.

 Does the southern coast of South Africa produce wine?

The country's southern coast, which is known for its cooler climate, is home to a number of vineyards, or "wine farms" as they are called in South Africa. Two main types of white grape varieties are grown in this region—Chenin Blanc and Colombard. Chenin Blanc grapes produce white wines that have aromas and flavors of white flowers and honey. White wines made with Colombard grapes tend to be inexpensive, neutral tasting and crisp.

Cape Peninsula

Western Coast

- The Cape Peninsula refers to the winemaking areas surrounding the Cape of Good Hope and Cape Town.

- Two of the most important winemaking districts, Stellenbosch and Paarl, are located in the Cape Peninsula.

- This area is known for making white wines using the Sauvignon Blanc grape, which have flavors of herbs, smoke and gooseberries.

- Good-quality red wines are also produced in the Cape Peninsula using Cabernet Sauvignon, Merlot and Shiraz grapes.

- The western coast of South Africa produces red wines using the Pinotage grape, which is a cross of the Pinot Noir and Cinsaut (Cinsault) grape varieties. Pinotage wines often have fresh, plummy, earthy flavors.

- The western coast is also well-known for the white wines produced in this area using the Chenin Blanc grape, called Steen. Steen wines often have flavors of honey and white flowers.

CHILEAN WINES

Wines from Chile are a wonderful balance between the refinement of European wines and the fruitiness of California wines. In fact, several wine producers from France, Spain and the United States operate wineries in Chile. With a growing reputation for quality, Chile is now the world's tenth largest producer of wine.

The Cabernet Sauvignon grape is the most widely grown grape variety in Chile. This grape is often used to create easy-to-drink red wines with flavors of mint, black currants and olives.

About Chilean Wines

- Chile, in South America, has been producing wine for hundreds of years. The first vineyards were started in the 1500s.

- Chile has a long grape-growing season. The wine regions of Chile are generally warm during the day, cool at night and very dry.

- The soil in Chile varies but is often composed of limestone, volcanic rock and clay.

Central Valley

- Most of Chile's wines are made in the central area of the country, which is made up of several valleys.

- Maipo Valley, located south of Santiago, is the home of most of Chile's main wineries. The Maipo Valley produces good-quality red wines made from Cabernet Sauvignon and Merlot grapes as well as white wines made from the Chardonnay grape.

What is special about Chile's Carmenère grape?

The Carmenère grape is a grape variety that was thought to have been made extinct when phylloxera (see the top of page 23) devastated its home in Bordeaux, France. However, it was discovered in the 1990s that the Carmenère grape variety was still thriving in Chile, having been imported from France almost a century beforehand. The Carmenère grape variety produces flavorful wines that have spicy, plum-like aromas and flavors.

 What labeling restrictions does Chile place on their wines?

While winemaking regulations in Chile are not as severe as other countries, Chile does have strict laws about how its wines are labeled.

- When a region is listed on a label, at least 75 percent of the wine must originate in that region.
- When a grape variety is listed on a label, at least 75 percent of the wine must be produced from that variety.
- When a year is listed on a label, at least 75 percent of the wine must have been produced in that year.

Northern Regions

- Rapel Valley, located south of Maipo Valley, produces red wines using Cabernet Sauvignon and Merlot grapes.
- The Curico area, located south of Rapel Valley, produces mostly fruity, high-acid white wines made from Sauvignon Blanc and Chardonnay grapes.

- Maule Valley is the most southern of the central valley winemaking areas and produces good-quality red wines using Cabernet Sauvignon and Merlot grapes.

- Casablanca Valley is the coolest major wine region of Chile and produces mostly white wines made from Sauvignon Blanc and Chardonnay grapes.
- Aconcagua Valley is located north of Santiago and produces mostly red wines from Cabernet Sauvignon, Merlot and Syrah grapes.

- Limari Valley is the most northern of all of Chile's winemaking regions. This area produces good-quality red wines made from Cabernet Sauvignon and Merlot grapes, as well as fruity white wines made from the Chardonnay grape.

ARGENTINEAN WINES

Argentina is South America's largest producer of wine. This winemaking powerhouse ranks fifth in world wine production, making nearly as much wine as the United States. Although there are approximately 20 different red and white grape varieties grown in Argentina, most of the higher-quality wines produced in this country are red wines.

Despite the dry climate of Argentina, the vineyards receive plenty of water from irrigation systems that bring down water from the surrounding mountains.

About Argentinean Wines

Mendoza

- Argentina's wine regions, mostly in the western part of the country, are generally warm during the day, cool at night and very dry.

- The soils in Argentina vary, but are often composed of sand and clay.

- Although Argentina does not have laws regulating grape growing and winemaking methods, the country does dictate that if a grape variety is displayed on a wine's label, at least 80 percent of the wine must be made from the grape variety.

- The Mendoza winemaking area is located to the west of the city of Buenos Aires. Mendoza is the largest winemaking area in Argentina and produces 70 percent of the country's wine.

- Mendoza is well-known for its red wines made from the Malbec grape. Malbec red wines from Mendoza are often high in acid with plum flavors and are typically best consumed within 10 years after bottling.

Have Argentina's vineyards ever been damaged by phylloxera?

Argentina is fortunate in that phylloxera (see the top of page 23) has never been a problem. Some speculate that this is because the country is situated between the ocean and mountains in relative isolation. Since none of its vineyards have been damaged by phylloxera, many of Argentina's grapevines are quite old and produce very flavorful grapes.

 Has Argentina always produced good wines?

Until recently, the wines produced in Argentina were generally inexpensive, neutral-tasting and mostly consumed only within the country. Today, there is a lot of foreign investment in Argentina's wine industry by the French, Austrians, Americans and Chileans. This money has allowed winemakers in Argentina to make improvements to their wineries and wine-production methods, which results in higher-quality wines.

San Juan

- The San Juan area is located north of Mendoza and is the second-largest winemaking area in Argentina.
- Red wines are made in San Juan using the Shiraz, Cabernet Sauvignon and Malbec grapes.
- The pink Cereza grape is the most commonly grown grape in the San Juan area. Most of the wine made from the Cereza grape is sold to larger winemakers around the world for blending with other wines.

La Rioja

- The La Rioja area is located east of San Juan and is the oldest wine-producing region in Argentina.
- Red wines made from the Bonarda grape are produced in the La Rioja area. Bonarda is the most widely planted grape variety in Argentina.
- La Rioja is best known for its light-bodied white wines made from the Torrontés grape. Torrontés white wines are flowery with a high acid content and are typically best consumed within 3 years after bottling.

AMERICAN WINES

The United States is the world's fourth-largest wine producer, with important winemaking regions in Washington, California, Oregon and New York. This huge industry has created an extremely wide selection of American wines that are enjoyed throughout the world. The most popular wines produced in the United States are made from the Chardonnay, Cabernet Sauvignon and Merlot grape varieties. One area of note in the American winemaking scene is Washington State, the country's second-largest wine producer with more than 400 wineries.

About American Wines

- The United States of America is the fourth-largest producer of wine in the world.

- America is a vast country with many different climates and soil types. In general, however, most American grape-growing areas are located close to large lakes or oceans which help make the temperatures less extreme.

- In the United States, winemakers are not bound by laws that restrict the grape varieties they can plant or blend to make their wines. There are, however, several laws that affect wine labeling practices.

- In most states, if a grape variety, such as Chardonnay, is displayed on a wine's label, at least 75 percent of the wine must be made from the grape variety.

- If a wine's label displays the name of a winemaking region, county or state, at least 75 percent of the wine must have been made there.

TIP *What are American Viticultural Areas (AVAs)?*

American Viticultural Areas are designated as wine-growing zones in the United States. There are more than 160 AVAs in the United States. When the AVA is listed on a wine's label, 85 percent of the grapes used to make the wine must be from that winegrowing zone.

TIP *Is an American wine of higher quality if it lists "private reserve" on the label?*

No. There aren't any rules restricting the use of terms on American wine labels. For example, terms like "private reserve," "reserve," "vintner's reserve," "barrel select" and "classic" are not regulated by the government and are often only used to help market and sell a wine.

Washington State

- Washington State is the second-largest wine producing state in America.

- Most of the winemaking regions in this state are east of the Cascade Mountains, where hot, dry summers, cold winters and well-drained soil allow grapes to flourish.

- Washington has several American Viticultural Areas (AVAs), which determine the boundaries of wine regions. Two important AVAs are Columbia Valley and Yakima Valley.

Note: For more information on AVAs, see the top of this page.

Columbia Valley

- The Columbia Valley AVA produces many varieties of wines, including good-quality red wines made from Syrah grapes.

- These wines often have flavors of spice and berries and are typically best consumed within 2 years after bottling.

Yakima Valley

- The Yakima Valley AVA is well known for its high-quality red wines made from Merlot grapes.

- These wines often have ripe berry flavors and are typically best consumed within 2 years after bottling.

CONTINUED

As the country's largest wine producer, California is the engine that drives the American wine industry. The state, which is home to more than 800 wineries, has a stable climate and a winemaking tradition that goes back nearly 250 years.

California is home to over 90 AVAs, which are designated winemaking zones in the United States. More than 100 grape varieties are grown in California, with Chardonnay, Zinfandel, Cabernet Sauvignon, Merlot and Pinot Noir being the most popular.

California

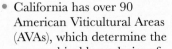

- The state of California is on the west coast of the United States and produces 90 percent of all American wines.

- The winemaking regions close to the Pacific coast and in the Coastal Mountains have the ideal climate and soil conditions for grape growing.

- California has over 90 American Viticultural Areas (AVAs), which determine the geographical boundaries of wine regions.

Note: For more information on AVAs, see the top of page 205.

Central Valley

- California's Central Valley stretches through the center of the state and includes some well-known winemaking areas, such as Lodi and Madera.

- The Central Valley produces 60 percent of all the grapes grown in California.

- The Chardonnay grape is very popular in the Central Valley.

- White wines made from the Chardonnay grape in the Central Valley often have flavors of apple and pear and are typically best consumed within 2 years after bottling.

TIP *What types of wine are made from the Zinfandel grape?*

The Zinfandel grape is an extremely popular red grape variety in California. This grape was brought to California in the mid-1800s and was planted in the Sierra Foothills to produce wine for the miners of the 1849 gold rush. While the grape is widely known for producing White Zinfandel, a light and fruity rosé wine, it is also used to produce premium red Zinfandel wines.

TIP *Are there any other wine regions of interest in California?*

California is full of wine regions that make good-quality wines. One region in particular is Mendocino County, which is slightly north of Sonoma County on California's north coast. Mendocino County has a relatively cool climate, where white grapes such as Chardonnay, Gewürztraminer and Riesling flourish and are made into high-quality wines.

Central Coast

- Santa Barbara County, in California's central coast, produces good red wines made from Pinot Noir grapes.

- These Pinot Noir wines often have flavors of berries and spice and are typically best consumed within 5 years after bottling.

- San Luis Obispo County, north of Santa Barbara County, produces good white wines made from Chardonnay grapes.

- These Chardonnay wines often have flavors of peach and butter and are typically best consumed within 2 years after bottling.

North Coast

- Napa Valley, in California's north coast, produces red wines made from Cabernet Sauvignon grapes.

- These wines often have flavors of blackcurrant and chocolate and are typically best consumed within 5 years after bottling.

- Sonoma County is east of Napa Valley and produces white wines made from Sauvignon Blanc grapes.

- These wines often have flavors of peach and grapefruit and are typically best consumed within 5 years after bottling.

CONTINUED

Oregon may not be as well known for producing wine as California, but it is home to more than 300 wineries which are producing some very good wines. Pinot Noir grapes, which are notoriously difficult to grow in many areas, grow well in Oregon and are used to make some of the state's finest and most-popular wines. Chardonnay and Pinot Gris grapes are also used to create impressive wines in Oregon.

Oregon

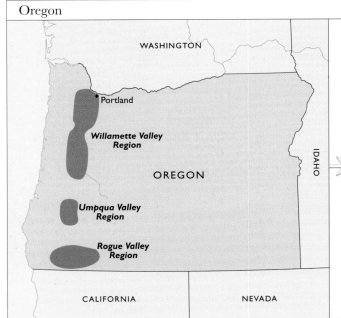

- The state of Oregon is on the west coast of the United States, just north of California.

- Most of Oregon's winemaking areas are close to the coast, where the Pacific Ocean helps cool the temperatures and provides ample rain for growing grapes.

- Oregon has 3 main American Viticultural Areas (AVAs)–Willamette Valley, Umpqua Valley and Rogue Valley. AVAs determine the geographical boundaries of wine regions.

  Note: For more information on AVAs, see the top of page 205.

Willamette Valley

- The Willamette Valley winemaking region is located just south of the city of Portland and is the home of approximately 70 percent of Oregon's wineries.

- Willamette Valley is well known for producing white wine made from the Chardonnay grape.

- Willamette Valley Chardonnay has flavors of apples and lemon and is typically best consumed within 5 years after bottling.

TIP ***Do Oregon's wine laws differ from the rest of the United States?***

Yes. If a grape variety, such as Pinot Noir, is named on the label of an Oregon wine, 90 percent of the wine must be made from that variety. Other states only require 75 percent of the wine to be made from a grape variety listed on the label. Oregon's Cabernet Sauvignon wines are an exception to the state's strict content requirements. To list Cabernet Sauvignon on the label, a wine only needs to contain 75 percent of the variety.

TIP ***Does Oregon's climate create any grape-growing challenges?***

Being in the rainy Pacific Northwest area of the United States, Oregon is sometimes short on the heat and sunshine that are so important for ripening grapes. With its somewhat unstable climate, each growing season in Oregon has the risk that the grapes will not ripen properly. When the conditions are good for grape growing, however, good-quality wines are often the result.

Umpqua Valley

- The Umpqua Valley winemaking region is located in the southwestern area of the state of Oregon.

- Umpqua Valley is renowned for its red wines made from Pinot Noir grapes, which have flavors of cherry and spice and are typically best consumed within 5 years after bottling.

- Umpqua Valley also produces fine white wines from the Chardonnay and Riesling grapes.

Rogue Valley

- The Rogue Valley winemaking region is located in the southern area of the state, just above the California border. This area's southern location provides warmer weather well suited to growing red grapes, such as Merlot.

- Rogue Valley Merlot wines have flavors of red berries and cocoa and are typically best consumed within 5 years after bottling.

- Rogue Valley also produces good-quality wines made from the red Cabernet Sauvignon grape.

CONTINUED ►

With more than 170 wineries, New York has established itself as America's third largest wine-producing state. Variety is the name of the game in New York where classic European and several North American grape varieties grow alongside a number of hybrid varieties. Since its climate is better suited to growing white grapes, 60 percent of the wines coming from New York are white. In particular, the state is noted for producing elegant, light-tasting Rieslings.

New York State

- The state of New York is located in the northeastern area of the United States.

- Most of New York State's winemaking regions are close to large bodies of water, which helps to warm the otherwise cool climate and lengthen the grape-growing season.

- New York State has several American Viticultural Areas (AVAs), which determine the geographical boundaries of wine regions, including the Finger Lakes, Long Island and the Hudson River areas.

  Note: For more information on AVAs, see the top of page 205.

Finger Lakes

- The Finger Lakes winemaking region in western New York produces approximately 80 percent of the wines in the state.

- The Finger Lakes region is best known for producing white wine made from the Riesling grape.

- Finger Lakes Riesling wines are quite dry and often have flavors of peaches and minerals.

What are hybrid grapes?

A hybrid grape is a grape variety that has been created by combining two different grape varieties. Examples include the Seyval Blanc, Vidal and Baco Noir hybrid grape varieties. Hybrids that combine classic European varieties with hardy North American varieties are ideal for growing in North America because they offer great flavor and grow well in cooler climates.

 What are Meritage wines?

Meritage wines are blended wines that use some of the classic Bordeaux grape varieties, including Cabernet Sauvignon, Merlot, Cabernet Franc, Petit Verdot and Malbec. American winemakers created the term "meritage" to indicate a wine that was similar to the wines produced in France's most prestigious region of Bordeaux. Meritage wines are made all across the United States, with a number of very good wines coming from New York.

Long Island

- The Long Island winemaking region is about 100 miles east of New York City and is divided into two separate regions—the North Fork and the Hamptons.

- The North Fork area produces white wines using Chardonnay grapes. These wines often have flavors of apple and melon.

- The Hamptons produces red wines using Merlot grapes. These wines often have flavors of cherries and spice.

Hudson River

- The Hudson River winemaking region lies along the Hudson River, just north of New York City.

- This region is a historically important area, as it is home to Benmarl, America's oldest vineyard, and Brotherhood, America's oldest winery.

- The Hudson River region is best known for producing good-quality wines using hybrid grape varieties, such as the white Seyval Blanc with crisp lemon flavors and the red Baco Noir which has flavors of blueberries and spice.

CANADIAN WINES

Canada is an up-and-coming quality wine producer that has grown significantly since the 1990s. While the Canadian climate typically provides short grape-growing seasons and cold winters, the country's winemaking regions tend to be near large lakes which have a slight warming effect on the surrounding areas.

The Canadian winter provides an ideal environment for creating the country's world-renowned ice wines. Canada is the leading producer of ice wine in the world, with the best wines coming from Ontario's Niagara region.

About Canadian Wines

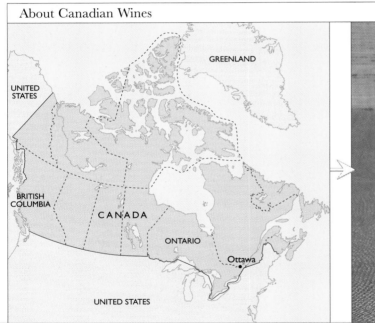

- Canada is one of the newest winemaking countries in the world.

- Canada's winemaking industry is growing rapidly and attracting attention from other countries all over the world for its high-quality wines.

- Canada has a cool climate, severe winters and a short grape-growing season. Most grape-growing areas are located close to large lakes or oceans which help make the temperatures less extreme.

- Canada's Vintner's Quality Alliance (VQA) is a system of standards and practices which typically includes the types of grapes that can be used and the methods of winemaking.

- VQA determines when a location's name, such as "Niagara Peninsula," can appear on a wine's label.

- VQA also determines the percentage of a particular grape that must be included in each wine.

- The VQA stamp on a wine label indicates a quality wine that has been tested and meets the highest standards for Canadian wines.

TIP *Are there any new types of Canadian ice wine?*

Yes. With the international success of Canadian ice wine, many Canadian winemakers are experimenting with new types of ice wine. For example, although ice wine is traditionally made from white grapes, many Canadian winemakers are producing red ice wines using red grape varieties such as Cabernet Franc, Cabernet Sauvignon and Merlot. A few winemakers are even starting to create sparkling ice wines.

TIP *What are botrytis-affected wines?*

Botrytis-affected wines are sweet wines made from grapes that have been affected by noble rot (Botrytis cinerea), a beneficial mold that grows on grapes while they are still on the vine. Canada produces a number of good-quality botrytis-affected wines. These wines usually display one of the following terms on the label: Botrytized, Botrytis Affected (B.A.), Totally Botrytized or Totally Botrytis Affected (T.B.A.).

Canadian Sweet Wines

Ice Wine

- Canada produces some of the best ice wine in the world.

- Ice wine is made from grapes that have naturally frozen on the grapevine.

- Ice wine is usually full-bodied and lusciously sweet.

- The most popular grape varieties used to make ice wine are Riesling and Vidal. The best ice wine is often made from Riesling grapes.

  Note: In Canada, ice wines are usually labeled as "Icewine."

Late Harvest Wine

- Canada produces great-quality late harvest wines, which are produced by allowing the grapes to ripen on the vines longer than normal.

- Canadian late harvest wines are sweet and lighter-bodied than ice wine.

- The most popular grape varieties used to make late harvest wine include Riesling, Vidal and Sauvignon Blanc.

CONTINUED

213

In Canada, the winemaking regions located in Ontario and British Columbia produce the majority of the country's wines. In these areas, large producers and small family-run wineries produce dry, aromatic white wines made with cool-climate grape varieties such as Riesling, Chardonnay and Sauvignon Blanc.

Given the country's relatively short grape-growing season, red grape varieties are more difficult to grow in some of Canada's regions. However, many Canadian winemakers have success at producing red wines made from Pinot Noir, Cabernet Franc, Merlot and Cabernet Sauvignon grapes.

Ontario

- Ontario, in the central-eastern part of Canada, has a cool climate which is made slightly warmer by the Great Lakes that surround the winemaking regions.

- The four major winemaking areas in Ontario include the Niagara Peninsula, Pelee Island, Lake Erie North Shore and Prince Edward County.

- Ontario's 4 main winemaking areas produce about 75 percent of Canadian wines.

- Approximately 60 percent of the wines produced in Ontario are white wines.

- Ontario's best white wines are made using the Chardonnay, Riesling, Gewürztraminer, Sauvignon Blanc, Pinot Blanc, Seyval Blanc and Vidal grapes.

- Several good-quality red wines produced in Ontario are made using the Pinot Noir, Gamay, Cabernet Sauvignon, Cabernet Franc and Merlot grapes as well as the hybrid grape varieties Maréchal Foch and Baco Noir.

TIP *What hybrid grape varieties are popular in Canada?*

A hybrid grape variety is the offspring of two different grape varieties. In Canada, several hybrid grape varieties are grown. A couple of popular examples include the Vidal grape, which is a cross of the Trebbiano and Rayon d'Or grapes, and the Maréchal Foch grape, which is a cross of the Pinot Noir and Gamay varieties.

TIP *What other areas of Canada produce wine?*

Wine is also produced in Québec and Nova Scotia. In Québec, Gamay and Riesling grapes are popular, along with hybrids like Seyval Blanc, Aurol and Vidal. There are also many good-quality wines produced in Nova Scotia. Several hybrid grape varieties are grown in Nova Scotia, including Leon Millot, Baco Noir and DeChaunac.

British Columbia

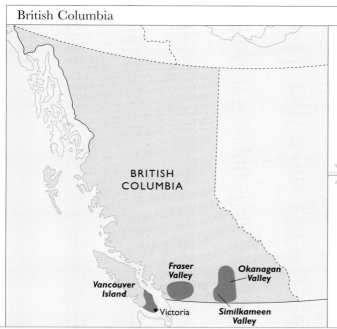

- British Columbia, on the western coast of Canada, is one of the most northern wine regions in the world, but its cool temperatures are made slightly warmer by the Pacific Ocean and coastal mountains surrounding the area.

- There are four major winemaking areas in British Columbia. These include Okanagan Valley, Similkameen Valley, Fraser Valley and Vancouver Island.

- The crisp, fruity white wines produced in British Columbia are made mostly from the Auxerrois, Chardonnay, Ehrenfelser, Gewürztraminer and Pinot Gris grapes.

- There are also many great-quality red wines being produced in British Columbia using the Pinot Noir, Cabernet Sauvignon and Merlot grapes.

Champagne and Sparkling Wines

About Champagne and Sparkling Wine

How Champagne is Made

Types of Champagne

Opening Champagne and Sparkling Wine

Serving and Storing Champagne

Evaluating Champagne and Sparkling Wine

Sparkling Wines from Around the World

ABOUT CHAMPAGNE AND SPARKLING WINE

There's no doubt that Champagne is a very special drink, closely linked with the celebrations that mark the special occasions in our lives. It is those tiny, tongue-tickling bubbles in each glass that make Champagne and other premium sparkling wines so special. While Champagne is produced exclusively in France, just about every wine-producing country makes a sparkling wine of some type. Sparkling wines produced around the world come in a wide variety of styles, different qualities and prices.

About Champagne and Sparkling Wine

Where Authentic Champagne is Made

- Unlike regular wine, Champagne and sparkling wine contain carbon dioxide gas, which adds bubbles to the wine.

- Champagne and sparkling wine ranges from dry to sweet tasting and is most often light straw in color.

- Champagne is the most famous and the best type of sparkling wine in the world.

- Although many people describe all types of sparkling wine as "Champagne," true Champagne is produced only in the Champagne region of France.

- The Champagne region is the most northern winemaking region in France and is located about an hour and a half northeast of Paris.

- The Champagne region is characterized by a cool climate and white chalky soil. This region is one of the coolest winemaking regions in the world.

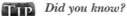

TIP *Who was Dom Pérignon?*

Dom Pérignon was a French monk and cellarmaster who lived in the seventeenth century and developed many of the techniques used to create Champagne. One of his breakthroughs was mastering the process for making white wine from red grapes. Dom Pérignon also discovered that he could create a complex wine by blending a number of different wines from different villages. Dom Pérignon Champagne is a premium brand of Champagne named in the monk's honor.

TIP *Did you know?*

✓ Champagne's signature bubbles were originally seen as a flaw by early wine producers.

✓ Up until the mid-1800s, Champagnes were all sweet wines.

✓ Only 10% of the world's sparkling wines come from the French region of Champagne.

✓ Champagnes are named for the wine producers that make them.

✓ Instead of wire cages, Champagne corks were originally held in place with string.

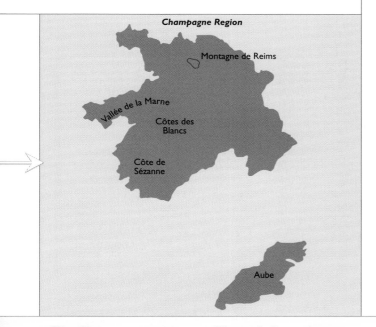

About Non-Authentic Champagne

- The Champagne region consists of five main grape-growing regions:
  ✓ Aube
  ✓ Côte de Sézanne
  ✓ Côtes des Blancs
  ✓ Montagne de Reims
  ✓ Vallée de la Marne

- The cool climate in Champagne means that the grapes are not fully ripe when picked and have a high level of acidity, which is ideal for sparkling wine.

- The Champagne region has the ideal combination of climate, soil and grapes to produce excellent sparkling wine.

- Sparkling wines produced outside of France, especially in the United States and Australia, are sometimes labeled as "Champagne" to help market the wine. These wines are usually of lower quality and should be referred to as sparkling wine.

- Most top-quality sparkling wine producers will not use the term "Champagne" on their bottles out of respect for the true Champagne producers.

219

Three main grapes—Pinot Noir, Pinot Meunier and Chardonnay—are used to create Champagne. Producers of Champagne, often referred to as Champagne houses, typically blend together separate wines made from these grapes to create complex sparkling wines. Champagne comes in unique bottles made of extra thick glass. The bottles are specially designed to handle the pressure created by the carbon dioxide in the wine. Aside from standard 750-ml bottles, Champagne comes in bottles of various other sizes, such as 375-ml half-bottles and 3-liter bottles called Jeroboams.

Grapes Used to Make Champagne

Grapes

☑ *Pinot Noir*
☑ *Pinot Meunier*
☑ *Chardonnay*

Champagne Houses

Important Champagne Houses

- Billecart-Salmon
- Bollinger
- Charles Heidsieck
- Deutz
- G.H. Mumm
- Krug
- Lanson
- Laurent-Perrier
- Louis Roederer
- Moët & Chandon
- Perrier-Jouët
- Pol Roger
- Ruinart
- Taittinger
- Veuve Clicquot

- Champagne is typically made using a blend of two or three types of grapes, which include the red Pinot Noir and Pinot Meunier grapes and the white Chardonnay grape. Most Champagne is made using all three types of grapes.

- Sparkling wines made outside of the Champagne region of France may use the same grapes used to make Champagne or local grape varieties.

- A Champagne producer is known as a Champagne house.

- Each Champagne house proudly offers a unique style of Champagne and strives to make consistent-tasting Champagne from year to year.

- The above list shows the names of some important Champagne houses.

What characteristics does each grape contribute to Champagne?

The highly-regarded red Pinot Noir grape typically gives Champagne body, texture and earthy and berry aromas. The red Pinot Meunier grape can contribute fruitiness, floral aromas and an earthy quality to the wine. The white Chardonnay grape gives the wine freshness and a delicate elegance. The more red grapes present in a Champagne or sparkling wine, the fuller the style of the wine. The more white grapes present in a Champagne or sparkling wine, the lighter the style of the wine.

 What aromas am I likely to notice when tasting Champagne?

Depending on the style of Champagne, some of the aromas you might experience include:

✓ apple	✓ pear
✓ citrus fruit	✓ spices
✓ dried fruit	✓ toast
✓ flowers	✓ walnuts
✓ hazelnuts	✓ yeast (bread dough)

Champagne and Sparkling Wine Bottles

Champagne Bottle Sizes

Common Champagne Bottle Sizes

Bottle Size	Liters	Bottles	Glasses
Half-bottle	375 ml	1/2 bottle	2 1/2 glasses
Bottle	750 ml	1 bottle	5 glasses
Magnum	1.5 L	2 bottles	10 glasses
Jeroboam	3 L	4 bottles	20 glasses

- Champagne and sparkling wine is sold in heavy bottles to prevent the bottles from exploding due to the pressure in the bottles.

- The heavier bottle used for Champagne and sparkling wine is one of the reasons why sparkling wine is more expensive than regular wine.

- Champagne and sparkling wine is available in a range of bottle sizes.

- When entertaining, the best bottle size for Champagne and sparkling wine is the magnum, which is equal to two regular-sized bottles. Champagne and sparkling wine ages more slowly in these larger bottles, which results in a more complex final wine.

HOW CHAMPAGNE IS MADE

For over three hundred years, Champagne has been made like no other type of wine in the world. The traditional method is so highly esteemed that most other quality sparkling wines are made using the same time-honored and labor-intensive techniques.

THE TRADITIONAL METHOD

All authentic Champagne and many fine sparkling wines are made by a process called the traditional method, which is also known as the Classic or Champagne Method. Champagne and sparkling wines made using this process may display the French term Méthode Traditionnelle, Méthode Classique or Méthode Champenoise on their label. Champagne and sparkling wines made using the traditional method have a smooth and creamy texture, smaller and less aggressive bubbles, tend to be less fruity and are more expensive.

STEP 1 First Fermentation

Sugar in Grapes + Yeast

⬇

Alcohol + Carbon Dioxide (CO_2)

During fermentation, yeast (microscopic organisms) consume the sugar in the grape juice and slowly convert the sugar into alcohol and carbon dioxide (CO_2) gas.

Champagne made using the traditional method goes through two fermentations. The first fermentation turns the grape juice into wine without bubbles and takes about two to three weeks. The first fermentation takes place in open containers, so the resulting carbon dioxide gas escapes into the air.

STEP 2 Blending of Wines

The blending of wines is the most important step when making Champagne. After the first fermentation, in which wines produced from different grape varieties and different vineyards are fermented separately, a Champagne producer blends the various wines. A winemaker can blend 20 to more than 100 different wines to create the final wine for the second fermentation.

THE TRADITIONAL METHOD continued

STEP 3 Second Fermentation

The second fermentation turns the still wine (without bubbles) from the first fermentation into sparkling wine (with bubbles) and takes one to three or more years. The second fermentation takes place in the sealed bottles in which the Champagne will be sold so the carbon dioxide does not escape and dissolves into the wine, creating the bubbles.

STEP 4 Aging and Sediment Removal

After the second fermentation, the bottles are aged in a cool, dark cellar. During the aging process, natural sediment, called lees, forms in each bottle. To remove the sediment, the top of each bottle is instantly frozen, the bottle caps are removed and the frozen sediment is forced out of the bottle by the carbon dioxide gas. After the sediment is removed, a sweetening mixture called a dosage is added to each bottle. The bottles are then corked for possible further aging and sale.

More Champagne-Making Facts

√ A longer second fermentation results in more complex and expensive Champagne.

√ Allowing the wine to ferment with the sediment in the bottle creates a unique texture and desirable bread-like flavors and aromas.

√ During the second fermentation, the bottles are gradually turned so that the top of each bottle is eventually facing downward and the sediment collects in the bottle's neck.

√ The sweet mixture, called the dosage, which is added to each bottle after the second fermentation determines the final level of sweetness for the Champagne.

OTHER METHODS

There is a less-expensive method for making sparkling wine in which the second fermentation step takes place in a large, refrigerated, pressurized tank rather than in each individual bottle. This process, which normally produces inexpensive sparkling wines, is called the tank method, bulk method, charmat method or cuve close. Large quantities of sparkling wine can be made in just a few weeks with this method. Aside from the Pinot Noir and Chardonnay grapes that are traditionally used for making Champagne, various other grape varieties are used for sparkling wines that are produced in this manner.

223

TYPES OF CHAMPAGNE

Champagne is available in several different types, depending on the year when the grapes used to make the Champagne were harvested. Champagne that is made from grapes that were harvested in different years is labeled non-vintage Champagne. Champagne that is made exclusively from grapes harvested in one specific year is called vintage Champagne. Prestige cuvée Champagne is made from grapes that were harvested in one year that was deemed to have produced exceptionally good grapes.

Non-Vintage Champagne

Non-Vintage Champagne

☑ *Aged 2½ to 3 years after bottling*

- Most of the Champagne produced is non-vintage (NV) Champagne.

- Non-vintage Champagne is made using a blend of grapes from two or more years and does not show a year, or vintage, on the bottle.

- Champagne producers make non-vintage Champagne so they can offer consumers a consistent-tasting Champagne year after year that reflects their unique style.

- Most non-vintage Champagne is aged for 2 ½ to 3 years after bottling, to enhance the wine's flavors and complexity, before it is released for sale.

- Non-vintage Champagne is moderately priced and lighter, fresher and less complex than vintage Champagne, but not necessarily less enjoyable.

TIP *Did you know?*

✓ Champagne producers normally produce an average of only three vintage Champagnes each decade.

✓ Prestige cuvée Champagne is also known as tête de cuvée, cuvée de prestige and crème de tête.

✓ Non-vintage Champagne is normally made from a blend of two-thirds red grapes (Pinot Noir and Pinot Meunier) and one-third white grapes (Chardonnay).

✓ A vintage or prestige cuvée Champagne is usually made from a blend of only the red Pinot Noir grape and the white Chardonnay grape.

TIP *What are the best recent-vintage Champagnes?*

Recent years have seen an unusually high number of very good vintages for Champagne. If you are looking to buy vintage Champagne, consider buying Champagne from one of the following years:

✓ 2002   ✓ 1997
✓ 2000   ✓ 1996
✓ 1999   ✓ 1995
✓ 1998   ✓ 1990

Vintage Champagne

Prestige Cuvée Champagne

- Vintage Champagne is made entirely of grapes from a single year and shows the year, or vintage, on the bottle.

- Vintage Champagne is usually only made in years when an individual Champagne producer feels the grapes are exceptional.

- Most vintage Champagne is aged for 4 to 6 years after bottling before it is released for sale to enhance the wine's flavors and complexity.

- Vintage Champagne is moderate to expensive in price and fuller, richer, creamier and more complex than non-vintage Champagne.

- Prestige cuvée Champagne is made using grapes from a single year, when a Champagne producer feels that the grapes are exceptional.

- Prestige cuvée Champagne is the most expensive, finest quality Champagne. This Champagne is made in small quantities.

- Prestige cuvée Champagne is typically aged for 4 to 6 years after bottling before it is released for sale.

- The shape of a Prestige cuvée bottle is often different from a traditional Champagne bottle.

CONTINUED

Champagne can be classified in terms of color. Rosé Champagne, which is popular for celebrating romantic occasions, comes in varying shades of pink. Blanc de blancs Champagne, which is made exclusively from white Chardonnay grapes, ranges from pale yellow to amber in color. Blanc de noirs Champagne is generally golden with a hint of pink.

The sweetness of various Champagnes can also differ dramatically. Many Champagnes are quite dry, while other Champagnes are semi-sweet or even very sweet in flavor.

Rosé Champagne

Blanc de Blancs Champagne

- Rosé Champagne is usually made from a blend of the white Chardonnay grape and the red Pinot Noir grape. The color of the Champagne comes from the skins of the red Pinot Noir grapes.

- The color of rosé Champagne ranges from pale cherry to salmon, with higher quality rosé Champagne usually having a lighter color.

- Rosé Champagne has richer flavors and is fuller, smoother, more expensive and made in smaller quantities than non-vintage Champagne.

- Blanc de blancs means "white from whites," or white wine from white grapes. This Champagne is made entirely from the white Chardonnay grape.

- Blanc de blancs Champagne ranges from a light pale-straw color to a light golden or amber color.

- This Champagne is typically lighter, more expensive and made in smaller quantities than non-vintage Champagne.

- The best blanc de blancs Champagne comes from Côte des Blancs, the best region in Champagne for growing the Chardonnay grape.

What does "Grande Marque" mean?

The term Grande Marque means "great brand" in French. Grande Marque is an unofficial term used to refer to the most highly regarded Champagne producers. Even though the term is used to identify the most well-established Champagne houses, it does not guarantee the quality of the Champagne made by these producers.

 What are the general characteristics of rosé, blanc de blancs and blanc de noirs Champagnes?

Rosé Champagnes offer ripe, red berry flavors, crisp acidity and full body. Earthy and spicy aromas are also present in some rosé Champagnes. Blanc de blancs Champagnes are normally citrusy and fresh tasting, often displaying the aromas of flowers and green apple. Blanc de noirs Champagnes often smell of white currants, raspberries and spices, with good acidity and full body.

Blanc de Noirs Champagne

CHAMPAGNE

LOUIS BEAUFORT

BLANC DE NOIRS
BRUT

PRODUCT OF FRANCE   12% alc./vol. 750ml

Sweetness Level of Champagne

Term on Bottle	Sweetness Level
Extra brut	Bone dry
Brut	Very dry
Extra dry	Dry to medium dry
Sec	Slightly sweet
Demi-sec	Sweet
Doux	Very sweet

- Blanc de noirs means "white from blacks," or white wine from red (black) grapes. This Champagne is made from a blend of the red Pinot Noir and Pinot Meunier grapes.

- Blanc de noirs Champagne is a slightly pink, golden-colored Champagne.

- Blanc de noirs Champagne is typically more expensive and made in smaller quantities than non-vintage Champagne.

- The blanc de noirs Champagne comes from the Aube region in the Champagne region.

- Champagne ranges from bone dry to very sweet tasting. The very dry, or brut, style is the most popular style.

- On a Champagne bottle, you will see an indication of the sweetness level of the wine. The above list shows the terms you will commonly see on a Champagne bottle.

OPENING CHAMPAGNE AND SPARKLING WINE

You should take special care when removing the cork from a bottle of Champagne or sparkling wine. There is so much pressure built up behind the cork that the cork could injure someone if removed improperly. The technique for opening a bottle of Champagne or sparkling wine is different from the technique used to open a regular bottle of wine. After carefully removing the wire cage that holds the cork in place, you hold the cork and gently twist the bottle of Champagne or sparkling wine.

Chill Before Serving

Opening Champagne and Sparkling Wine

- Before opening a bottle of Champagne or sparkling wine, make sure the wine is well-chilled, since this will help to reduce the pressure in the bottle.

1 Chill a Champagne or sparkling wine bottle standing upright in a refrigerator for two hours. You can also chill the wine in an ice bucket filled with one-half ice cubes and one-half water for about 30 minutes.

- Do not chill Champagne or sparkling wine in the freezer since the bottle may explode.

1 Place the Champagne or sparkling wine on a table and remove the foil that covers the top of the bottle.

- Many bottles have a tab that you can pull to help you easily remove the foil. With other bottles, you can use a knife to cut and then remove the foil.

TIP *Are there any tools I can use to open a bottle of Champagne or sparkling wine?*

There are several devices designed to grip the cork and help open a bottle of Champagne or sparkling wine—Champagne pliers, a Champagne star and a Champagne key.

TIP *What else should I know about opening a bottle of Champagne or sparkling wine?*

- If you encounter a cork that won't move, you may find it helpful to wrap a clean towel around the cork to obtain a better grip.

- A Champagne bottle that has been moved around will have extra pressure built up inside the bottle and should be left to settle for a day before opening.

- A corkscrew should never be used to open a bottle of Champagne or sparkling wine. The pressure inside the bottle could forcefully eject the cork and corkscrew, which could cause serious injury.

Steps 2 & 3   Step 4

2 Place one hand on top of the bottle's cork. Do not remove your hand until the cork comes out of the bottle.

3 With your other hand, loosen and remove the wire cage covering the cork by untwisting the wire.

4 Keeping your hand on the cork, place your other hand on the body of the bottle and hold the bottle at a 45 degree angle. Make sure you point the bottle away from other people and fragile objects.

5 Holding the cork firmly in your hand, use your other hand to gently twist the bottle toward you in order to twist the bottle off of the cork. You want to gently, not forcefully, remove the bottle from the cork.

- When the cork comes out, you should hear a sigh or hiss, rather than a loud pop.

- If you hear a loud pop when you open a bottle, the valuable carbon dioxide bubbles escape from the wine and if the wine froths out of the bottle, you will also lose some wine.

SERVING AND STORING CHAMPAGNE

Proper serving and storage of Champagne is essential for preserving the wine's delicate bubbles, aromas and flavors. Serving Champagne chilled preserves the bubbles and highlights the wine's flavors. Tall, narrow Champagne glasses are ideal for keeping the bubbles from disappearing too quickly and concentrating the wine's aromas.

When storing leftover Champagne, a specialized Champagne stopper will help keep the wine from going flat and losing its delicate flavors. Storing unopened Champagne in a cool, dark location will keep the wine at its best.

Serving Temperature

- To fully appreciate the aroma and flavor of Champagne and sparkling wine and help preserve its bubbles, serve the wine chilled, at about 45°F (7° C).

  Note: To use a wine thermometer to check a wine's temperature, see page 90.

- To chill an unopened bottle, refrigerate the bottle for about 4 hours or place the bottle in an ice bucket filled with one-half ice cubes and one-half water for about 30 minutes.

- After serving the wine, immediately place the bottle in the refrigerator or ice bucket since the wine will warm up quickly.

Champagne Glasses

Flute

Tulip

- Champagne and sparkling wine is best served in flute and tulip-shaped glasses.

- Flute and tulip-shaped glasses have a narrow opening, which helps prevent the bubbles in Champagne and sparkling wine from escaping and concentrates the aroma of the wine in the glass.

- Although the saucer-shaped Champagne glass is popular for serving Champagne and sparkling wine, you should avoid using this glass since the wine will lose its bubbles more quickly and the glass will not allow you to fully appreciate the aroma of the wine.

What should I eat with Champagne?

Champagne and other sparkling wines pair wonderfully with food because the acidity and bubbles in the wine help to refresh the taste buds. There are different styles of Champagne and each style matches well with different types of food. Lighter styles of Champagne go well with creamy cheeses, pork, poultry and seafood dishes with cream or butter sauce. Complex vintage Champagnes work better with hard, aged cheeses and roasted red meats. Sweet Champagnes go well with simple desserts.

TIP *Did you know?*

- Champagne should not be stored in the refrigerator for more than a few days to avoid prolonged exposure to the light, cold temperature and vibrations of the refrigerator.

- Traditionally, Champagne is poured with one hand. The thumb is placed in the hollow at the bottom of the bottle and the fingers are spread around the bottle's base.

- Pour only a small amount of Champagne into a glass at first. After the wine settles, fill the glass two-thirds full.

Storing Leftover Champagne

Storing Unopened Champagne

- Once you open a bottle of Champagne or sparkling wine, you can use a Champagne or sparkling wine stopper to help keep leftover wine fresh for a couple of days in the refrigerator.

- A Champagne or sparkling wine stopper helps to keep the wine from being exposed to oxygen too rapidly. Without a Champagne or sparkling wine stopper, the bubbles in the wine will escape more quickly, resulting in a flat wine and a loss of the wine's aroma and flavor.

- Store unopened Champagne and sparkling wine in a cool, dark place, at a constant temperature and on their side.

- Non-vintage Champagne and sparkling wine will not improve with age. You should drink this wine within 2 to 3 years.

- Vintage and prestige cuvée Champagne and sparkling wine improves with age. You should wait at least 8 years from the date on the bottle before drinking.

Note: For information on non-vintage, vintage and prestige cuvée Champagne, see page 224.

EVALUATING CHAMPAGNE AND SPARKLING WINE

Evaluating Champagne and sparkling wines is somewhat different from evaluating regular wines. Along with the color, aromas and flavors, the character of the bubbles in sparkling wine needs to be assessed. To help you evaluate sparkling wines, you can photocopy the Champagne and Sparkling Wine Tasting Notes on the next page. Remember that wine tasting is a very personal experience. Your individual preferences will ultimately determine whether or not you enjoy a sparkling wine.

Evaluating Champagne and Sparkling Wine

• When evaluating Champagne and sparkling wine, evaluate the appearance, nose (smell) and taste of the wine as you would for a regular wine (see page 68). You should also evaluate the bubbles in the wine.

1 Look at the number and size of the bubbles and how long the bubbles last (persistence).

• Higher quality wine has numerous, tiny bubbles that last a long time.

Note: If you do not see many bubbles in a glass, you could have a poor glass, a wine that is too old or a faulty bottle of wine.

2 Determine if the bubbles in the wine drift upward in a steady stream, indicating a higher quality wine, or if the bubbles drift upward randomly, indicating a lower quality wine.

3 When you taste the wine, determine if the wine feels soft and creamy in your mouth, indicating a higher quality wine, or if the wine feels aggressive in your mouth, like a soft drink, indicating a lower quality wine.

Champagne and Sparkling Wine Tasting Notes

Name of Taster: _____   Date: _____
Place of Tasting: _____   Time: _____
Type/Region of Wine: _____   Vintage: _____
Grape Variety: _____   Price: _____
Producer's Name: _____   Purchased From: _____

Appearance

Color: White light straw-green, straw, gold, gold-copper, copper, amber
Rosé pale cherry, soft pink, salmon

Effervescence: **Size of Bubbles** very fine, fine, large
Number of Bubbles many, few, scarce
Persistence of Bubbles very persistent, persistent, brief

Nose (Smell)

Aromas: Fruit _____   Floral _____
Herb _____   Toasted _____
Spice _____

Intensity: none, faint, delicate, medium intensity, intense, very intense
Quality: common, good, fine, excellent
Length: very short, short, medium, long, very long
Additional Comments: _____

Taste

Sweetness: very dry, dry, off-dry, sweet, very sweet
Acidity: flat, flabby, lively, vibrant, crisp, tart
Alcohol: light, medium-bodied, full-bodied, hot, alcoholic
Body: thin, light, medium, full, rich
Complexity: very simple, simple, average, complex, very complex
Balance: unbalanced, balanced, very well-balanced
Intensity: weak, faint, delicate, medium intensity, intense, very intense
Quality: common, good, fine, excellent
Length: very short, short, medium, long, very long
Finish: Intensity none, faint, delicate, medium intensity, intense, very intense
Length very short, short, medium, long, very long
Description _____
Additional Comments: _____

Final Considerations

Overall Quality: poor, fair, good, very good, outstanding
Final Comments: _____

SPARKLING WINES FROM AROUND THE WORLD

While Champagne is the best-known sparkling wine, it is certainly not the only one available. Many other countries produce good alternatives to the sparkling wines from France's Champagne region. In fact, most wine-producing countries boast a sparkling wine of some type.

When making sparkling wine, many wineries outside of the Champagne region use the traditional method for making Champagne. However, these sparkling wines are different from Champagne because the wineries use locally grown grapes, sometimes of a different variety than the grapes used to produce Champagne.

Spain

- Spain produces an affordable and good-quality sparkling wine called Cava.
- Cava sparkling wine is made using the traditional Champagne method and typically uses local Spanish grapes. The wine may also include Chardonnay and Pinot Noir grapes.
- Cava sparkling wines are typically dry and medium-bodied with earthy flavors.
- Some high-quality Cava sparkling wine producers include Segura Viudas, Codorniu and Freixenet.

France

- France produces many affordable and good-quality sparkling wines outside of the Champagne region. These sparkling wines are called vin mousseux. The finest quality sparkling wines are called Crémant.
- Crémant sparkling wines are made using the traditional Champagne method and use local French grapes.
- Crémant sparkling wines are typically dry or off-dry and light- to medium-bodied.
- Some high-quality French sparkling wine producers include Bouvet Ladubay, Gratien & Meyer and Kriter.

Do any other countries make sparkling wine?

Many countries including Argentina, Australia, Austria, Germany, New Zealand and South Africa produce sparkling wines. As wine drinkers have become more knowledgeable, the demand for high-quality sparkling wines has increased. Many winemakers outside of France's Champagne region have produced good sparkling wines to meet this demand.

 What are some other popular types of Italian sparkling wine?

Italy produces several noted sparkling wines:

- **Franciacorta** is a sparkling wine that uses Chardonnay, Pinot Noir, Pinot Gris and Pinot Blanc grapes. This wine is typically dry, medium- to full-bodied with citrus, apple, nut and toast-like flavors.

- **Moscato d'Asti** is very similar to Italy's Asti sparkling wine but it is semi-sparkling and lower in alcohol content.

- **Prosecco** is a popular Italian sparkling wine made with the Prosecco grape. This wine, which can be sparkling or semi-sparkling, is typically dry and medium-bodied, with citrus and pear flavors.

United States

Italy

- California, New York, Oregon and Washington State are the main producers of sparkling wine in the United States.

- High-quality American sparkling wine is made using the same traditional method and grapes used to make Champagne.

- American sparkling wines are typically dry, medium- to full-bodied and fruity tasting.

- Some high-quality American sparkling wine producers include Roederer Estate, Domaine Carneros and Domaine Chandon.

- Italy produces a sparkling wine called spumante and a semi-sparkling wine called frizzante.

- Asti, or Asti Spumante, is the most popular Italian sparkling wine.

- Asti is made using a cost-effective tank method and the Moscato grape. This wine is typically off-dry to sweet, light- to medium-bodied and fruity with melon and peach flavors.

- Some high-quality Asti sparkling wine producers include Cerutti, Fontanafredda and Gancia.

Fortified and Sweet Wines

About Sherry

About Port

About Madeira

About Sweet Wines

ABOUT SHERRY

Sherry is a wine that goes quietly unnoticed by many North American wine drinkers. However, authentic Sherry, produced in southwestern Spain, is considered to be one of the world's best fortified wines. In fact, many other regions from around the world have tried to duplicate the qualities of authentic Sherry and none have been truly successful. Authentic Sherries from Spain come in an extremely diverse range of styles and qualities. Fortunately, even premium Sherry is priced very affordably.

About Sherry

Where Authentic Sherry is Made

- Sherry is a type of wine, which ranges from dry to sweet tasting.

- Sherry is a fortified wine, which means that alcohol, typically a grape brandy, is added to the wine after the fermentation process. Adding alcohol to the wine increases the alcohol content of the wine to 15 to 18 percent.

- Sherry comes from the Andalusia region of southwestern Spain.

- The Sherry region is located around the towns of Jerez de la Frontera, Puerto de Santa María and Sanlúcar de Barrameda, which form a triangle in the center of the Sherry region.

- The Sherry region is characterized by hot and dry summers and the chalk-white, albariza soil.

TIP *Who are some of the best Sherry producers?*

To find the best Sherry, it is important to take note of the producer who creates the wine. The following are several of the top-quality Sherry producers:

✓ Croft
✓ Emilio Lustau
✓ González Byass
✓ Harveys
✓ Hidalgo

✓ Osborne
✓ Pedro Domecq
✓ Sandeman
✓ Savory & James
✓ Williams & Humbert

TIP *What type of glass should I use to drink Sherry?*

While Sherry is often served in small, thimble-style glasses, or Port glasses, the wine's characteristics will be better experienced when it is sipped from an elongated, tulip-shaped glass called a copita.

About Non-Authentic Sherry

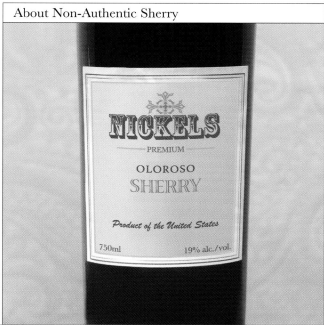

NICKELS
PREMIUM
OLOROSO
SHERRY
Product of the United States
750ml   19% alc./vol.

- Sherry produced in other countries, especially in the United States and Australia, are labeled as "Sherry" even though the wine was not produced in the Sherry region of Spain. These wines are usually of lower quality.

- Only Sherry produced in the Sherry region of Spain can be properly labeled "Sherry." Some Sherry labels display the official name Jerez-Xérès-Sherry.

Grapes Used to Make Sherry

TIO PEPE

- The Palomino grape is the main type of grape used to make Sherry. This grape is a neutral-flavored white grape that thrives only in the Sherry region.

- Most of the vineyards in the Sherry region of Spain plant the Palomino grape.

- The Pedro Ximénez and Moscatel (Muscat) grape varieties are used to turn dry Sherries into sweet Sherries.

CONTINUED

ABOUT SHERRY CONTINUED

The process for aging Sherry is different from the process used to age other wines. Instead of having each new batch of Sherry age on its own, a portion of each new batch of Sherry is added to the Sherries that were previously produced. As these wines age, they all begin to display identical characteristics.

During the winemaking process, winemakers usually prevent air from interacting with the wine. When producing Sherry, however, winemakers allow air to interact with the wine to further develop Sherry's distinct flavors.

Bodega

Flor

- After fermentation, winemakers place Sherry in wooden casks, or barrels, and place the casks in a bodega to age.

- A bodega is a large, dry, airy, aboveground building, which is a very different environment from the humid, underground cellars that are typically used to age wine.

- Winemakers fill casks containing Sherry only about two-thirds full and place the corks loosely in the casks to allow air into the casks. The air oxidizes the wine, which gives Sherry its distinctive flavor.

- Flor is a type of yeast that naturally grows in Sherry casks and creates a white layer which floats on the surface of the wine. The white layer on the surface of the wine is also known as flor.

  Note: In the above photo, Sherry has been removed from the cask and only the flor remains.

- The white layer of flor forms a physical barrier between the wine and the air, protecting the wine from contact with the air and reducing any further oxidation.

- Flor affects the flavor, aroma and character of the wine.

Where do the terms "flor" and "solera" come from?

The word flor is the Spanish term for flower. The flor, or yeast, that develops in Sherry as it ages was given this name because the flor seems to bloom on the wine's surface as it ages. The word solera comes from the Spanish word "suelo," which means floor. As wines are allowed to age in the Solera System, the Sherry that is ready for bottling is always drawn from the bottom row of barrels which is nearest to the floor.

What is Montilla?

Montilla is a wine that is very much like Sherry. This wine is produced in the Montilla-Moriles region, northeast of the Sherry region. Unlike Sherry, however, the main grape used to make Montilla is the Pedro Ximénez grape. Similar to Sherry, Montilla is made using the Solera System, but it does not typically need to have alcohol added because it naturally reaches high levels of alcohol on its own. Montilla is widely available and usually sold at a lower price than Sherry.

The Solera System

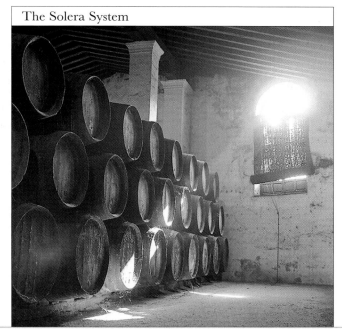

- In casks that develop flor, the wine will become Fino Sherry, which is one of the two main types of Sherry.

- In wine casks that do not develop enough flor, the wine will become Oloroso Sherry, which is the second main type of Sherry. As the wine ages in these casks, the wine is exposed to more oxygen than Fino Sherry, which results in a different flavor, aroma and character than Fino Sherry.

  Note: For more information on the types of Sherry, see page 242.

- Winemakers use the Solera System to maintain a consistent quality and style of Sherry from year to year.

- The Solera System is an aging process that involves the continuous blending of old wine with new wine to make Sherry.

- To make room for new wine, some older wine is withdrawn from casks and is added to the casks of even older wine. Over time, the younger wine mixes with the older wine to create a consistent-tasting wine from year to year.

CONTINUED ▶

Sherry is made in two different styles. Fino Sherry is pale, light-bodied and dry. Oloroso Sherry is dark-colored, full-bodied and can range from sweet to dry. Several other types of Sherry are made using these two styles, including Manzanilla, Amontillado, Cream and Pale Cream Sherries.

Delicate Fino and Manzanilla Sherries should be consumed soon after bottling. Once opened, they should be consumed within one or two days. Other Sherries can be aged for several years and will keep for two weeks after being opened.

Popular Types of Sherry

Fino

Oloroso

Manzanilla

Cream

- There are two main types of Sherry—Fino and Oloroso.

Fino—A type of Sherry that is pale in color, very dry and light bodied, with an almond aroma. Fino means "fine" in Spanish.

Oloroso—A type of Sherry that is dark gold to dark brown in color, ranging from sweet to dry, full bodied, with a walnut and raisin aroma. Oloroso has a higher alcohol content than Fino Sherry and means "scented" in Spanish.

- The following Sherries are made from Fino and Oloroso Sherry.

Manzanilla—A variety of Fino Sherry that is aged in the cooler seaside town of Sanlúcar de Barrameda, Spain. Manzanilla is pale in color, dry and delicate tasting.

Amontillado—A variety of Fino Sherry that is amber in color and dry to medium-dry.

Cream—A sweet Sherry that is deep mahogany in color and is made by sweetening Oloroso Sherry.

Pale Cream—A sweet Sherry that is pale in color and is made by sweetening Fino Sherry.

TIP *Why do Fino and Manzanilla Sherries only last for a few days after being opened?*

During aging, Fino and Manzanilla Sherries are protected from the air by a layer of yeast, called flor, which forms on the surface of the Sherry. When these Sherries are bottled, they lose the protection of the flor, so when you open a bottle of Fino or Manzanilla Sherry, the wine is exposed to oxygen which will gradually spoil the wine. Other types of Sherry have more longevity because they have a higher alcohol content and have already been exposed to oxygen.

TIP *What can I eat with Sherry?*

Dry Sherries, such as Fino and Manzanilla, make great food accompaniments. They are delicious served with hard cheeses, salted nuts and seafood. Dry Sherries should always be served at the beginning of the meal, either as an apéritif or with the first course. Sweet Sherries, such as Oloroso and Cream Sherry, can be great matches with dessert, as long as the Sherry is sweeter than the dessert. Sweet Sherries also pair well with blue cheese after a meal.

Storing and Serving Sherry

Fino and Manzanilla Sherry

- Fino and Manzanilla Sherry should be treated like white wine. Once opened, you should keep the Sherry refrigerated and drink the Sherry within one or two days.

- You can keep unopened bottles of Fino and Manzanilla Sherry for up to three months.

- Fino and Manzanilla Sherry are best served lightly chilled.

Other Sherries

- After opening a bottle of Oloroso, Amontillado or sweet Sherry, keep the Sherry refrigerated and drink the Sherry within two weeks.

- You can keep unopened bottles of Oloroso, Amontillado and sweet Sherry for several years before opening.

- Oloroso, Amontillado and sweet Sherries are best served at room temperature.

ABOUT PORT

Port is a popular fortified wine that has a colorful history. During one of its wars with France, England did not have access to French wine and was forced to look to Portugal as an alternate wine supplier. To keep the Portuguese wine from spoiling on its journey to England, a dose of brandy was added to the wine and Port was created. Port is named after the city of Oporto where the wine was, and still is, exported.

About Port

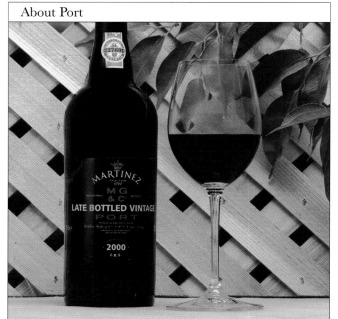

Where Authentic Port is Made

- Port is a type of sweet wine and is also known as Porto wine.

- Port is a fortified wine, which means that alcohol, in the form of grape brandy, is added to the wine during the fermentation process. Adding alcohol to the wine stops the fermentation process and increases the alcohol content of the wine to about 20 percent.

- Port is made in the mountainous Douro region in northern Portugal and is named after the city of Oporto, which is the coastal city that ships Port around the world.

- Port can be made from a selection of over 80 different types of grapes. Most of these grapes are grown only in Portugal.

TIP *What type of glass is used to drink Port?*

You can use any regular-sized wine glass to drink Port. Keep in mind that the wine glass should be big enough to swirl the Port. A portion of 2 1/2 to 3 1/2 ounces should be poured into the glass.

TIP *What is the most important type of port?*

Vintage Port is generally considered to be the finest type of Port available and is made from grapes harvested in one specific year. Vintage Ports are not usually made every year. Reputable Port producers will declare a Vintage Port year only when a year has been particularly good for producing Port. Compared to other Ports, Vintage Port is fairly expensive and rare. Some of the best recent Vintage Port years include 2003, 2000, 1997, 1994 and 1992. For more information on Vintage Ports, see page 248.

About Non-Authentic Port

- In other countries, especially in the United States and Australia, sweet red wine made in the Port style is often labeled as "Port" even though the wine was not made in Portugal. Although these wines can be good wines, they are not true Port.

- Only Port produced in the Douro region in Portugal can be properly labeled "Port."

- To stop the misuse of the name "Port," Port from Portugal was renamed "Porto." When buying Port, look for the word "Porto" on the label to identify true Port from Portugal.

Important Port Producers

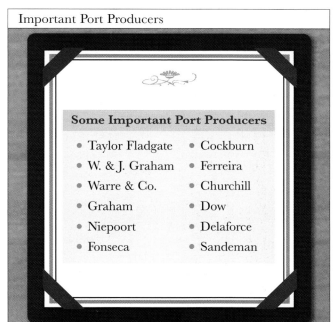

Some Important Port Producers

- Taylor Fladgate
- W. & J. Graham
- Warre & Co.
- Graham
- Niepoort
- Fonseca
- Cockburn
- Ferreira
- Churchill
- Dow
- Delaforce
- Sandeman

- When buying Port, it is important to choose a Port made by a producer with a good reputation for making quality Port.

- The above list shows the names of Port producers that are known for making quality Ports at various price levels.

CONTINUED ►

There are two main types of Port, which are made using different methods. Wood Ports are typically aged for 2 to 50 years in wooden barrels. This type of Port is ready to drink as soon as it is bottled. Bottle-aged Ports spend just a couple of years in wooden barrels before being bottled and left to age in the bottle. Bottle-aged Ports typically need to be aged in the bottle for decades before they are ready to drink.

Types of Port

- There are two main types of Port—wood Ports and bottle-aged Ports.

Wood Port

- Wood Ports age in wooden barrels for 2 to 50 years and are bottled when they are ready to drink. Once bottled, wood Ports do not improve with age.

- You can drink wood Ports immediately or store them for up to two years before opening.

- Wood Ports typically have a stopper cork, which is a cork that is attached to a bottle's cap.

Bottle-Aged Port

- Bottle-aged Ports age in wooden barrels for about 2 years and then finish their development by spending a long period of time aging in a bottle.

- Bottle-aged Ports improve with age and are usually not mature, or ready to drink, until about 20 years after they are bottled. Once bottled, the best Ports may need to age for 50 years or more.

- Bottle-aged Ports have a regular cork that requires a corkscrew to remove.

How should Port be stored?

Ports are stored differently depending on the type of Port. Wood ports should be stored in an upright position before opening. Bottle-aged ports should be stored on their sides. All Ports should be stored in a location that is cool and dark. If you plan to drink a Vintage Port, which is stored on its side, you should stand the bottle upright several days before opening so the sediment has a chance to settle to the bottom of the bottle.

 What should I eat with Port?

Ports are generally served at the end of a meal and are often matched with cheeses or desserts. A classic food-and-wine combination is Vintage Port and Stilton cheese. Tawny Port matches well with sheep's milk and blue cheeses, as well as caramel and custard dishes. Ruby Port pairs well with desserts that incorporate bittersweet chocolate. When serving Port with dessert, the dessert should be less sweet than the Port. For more information on styles of Port, see page 248.

Serving Port

- Once opened, Port can generally last longer than regular wine because of its higher alcohol content.

- Once you open a bottle of Port, you should keep the wine refrigerated. Drink wood Port within one week and bottle-aged Port within several weeks.

- Port is best served when it is at a cool room temperature.

- Before serving Port, you should aerate the wine for about one to five hours to expose the wine to oxygen, which will enhance the wine's aromas and flavors.

- Due to the long time that bottle-aged Ports spend aging in bottles, these Ports tend to accumulate sediment. Before drinking bottle-aged Ports, you should decant the Port to separate the sediment from the wine.

Note: To aerate and decant wine, see pages 94 to 96.

CONTINUED

For those who are not familiar with Port, the different styles of this unique Portuguese wine can seem overwhelming. There are several different types of Port, which differ in terms of where the grapes are grown, the quality of the wines used to produce the Port and the way the Port is aged. Fortunately, Port is a very approachable wine, which means that first-time Port drinkers are likely to enjoy their first sips, regardless of the style they decided to purchase.

STYLES OF PORT

Ruby Port

Ruby Port is a popular, inexpensive style of Port. It is generally a blend of lower-quality wines from several different years produced from grapes grown in the less prestigious section of Douro. This bright red wine tends to be simple, fruity and sweet with a slight peppery bite.

Barrel-aged: 2 or 3 years before bottling.

Ready to drink: Immediately.

Tawny Port

Tawny Port is a higher-quality blend of wines from different years that develops a brownish-yellow color and aromas of caramel and hazelnut. Bottles of good-quality Tawny Port indicate how long the wine has aged in wood—usually between 10 and 40 years.

Barrel-aged: Up to 40 years before bottling.

Ready to drink: Immediately.

Vintage Port

Vintage Port, often considered the best and most expensive type of Port, is made from grapes grown in the winemaker's best vineyards during one exceptional year, which appears on the wine's label. Vintage Port is rich, complex and deep red in color, with aromas of blackberries, mocha and spice.

Barrel-aged: About 2 years before bottling.

Ready to drink: Typically needs to be aged in the bottle for 20 years or more before drinking. The best Vintage Ports need to age for 50 years or more.

STYLES OF PORT continued

Vintage Character Port

Vintage Character Port is a higher-quality Ruby Port. Vintage Character Ports often have a deep red color and flavors of ripe fruit, spice and chocolate. Some labels do not call the wine Vintage Character Port, but use the producer's name instead, such as Taylor Fladgate's "First Estate."

Barrel-aged: 4 to 6 years before bottling.

Ready to drink: Immediately.

Single Quinta Vintage Port

Single Quinta Vintage Port is made from grapes grown in one of the winemaker's best vineyards during a good year. This rich red wine can have aromas of spice, blackcurrant and mocha and should be decanted (page 96) and aerated (page 94) before serving.

Barrel-aged: About 2 years before bottling.

Ready to drink: Needs to age in the bottle for 10 years or more before drinking.

Crusted Port

Crusted Port is a tannic Port made from grapes harvested in different years. It is generally dark red and has aromas of blackberry and tobacco. Crusted Port develops a lot of sediment, or crust, in the bottle during aging and must be decanted (page 96) before serving.

Barrel-aged: 3 or 4 years before bottling.

Ready to drink: Immediately or can age in the bottle for up to 10 years.

Late-Bottled Vintage (LBV) Port

Late-Bottled Vintage Port is a dark red Port that has rich, jam-like fruit flavors. These very good Ports are made from grapes grown in one year. LBV Port is similar to Vintage Port but is less rich and complex and does not have the same potential for aging.

Barrel-aged: 4 to 6 years before bottling.

Ready to drink: Immediately or can age in the bottle for up to 10 years.

Colheita Port

Colheita Ports are a rare and expensive type of Tawny Port made from grapes harvested in a single year. These wines offer aromas of coffee, vanilla, caramel and nuts. Like Vintage Ports, these wines display the year on the label, but Colheita Ports are not classified as Vintage Ports.

Barrel-aged: At least 7 years before bottling. Some Colheita Ports spend 30 years or more aging in barrels.

Ready to Drink: Immediately.

White Port

White Port is the least complex of all Ports. This Port is made with white grapes using the same methods that are employed to produce red Ports. White Port is generally made from grapes grown in different years. This Port is off-dry to sweet and pale amber in color, with nutty aromas.

Barrel-aged: Up to 2 years before bottling.

Ready to drink: Immediately.

ABOUT MADEIRA

Madeira is one of the world's most well-known fortified wines. It was once extremely popular and is even said to have been the wine with which the founding fathers of the United States toasted the Declaration of Independence. In the late 1800's, however, the Madeira vineyards were nearly wiped out by mildew and pests. The quality of wine was diminished, as was its popularity. Fortunately, the vineyards have since recovered. Today, high-quality Madeira wines display deep complexity and are extremely long-lasting.

About Madeira

- Madeira is a type of wine, which ranges from dry to sweet tasting.

- Madeira is amber in color, has a uniquely high level of acidity and a noticeably long finish, or aftertaste, which lingers in your mouth long after you swallow the wine.

- Madeira is a fortified wine, which means that alcohol, typically a grape brandy, is added to the wine during or after the fermentation process. Adding alcohol to the wine increases the alcohol content of the wine to 17 to 20 percent.

- Madeira is made on the small, volcanic Portuguese island of Madeira, which is located in the Atlantic Ocean.

- Madeira is the most long-lasting wine in the world. You can still find Madeira wine from the late 18th century that is still enjoyable and safe to drink.

Can I cook with Madeira?

Madeira is an excellent wine for cooking. It gives sauces and desserts great depth and an extra richness. You should consider whether you want to use a sweet or dry style of Madeira when cooking because your decision will change the flavor of the food. Another great thing about Madeira is that it lasts for a long time. Even if you only need a small amount for a recipe, the remainder will last forever as Madeira does not spoil.

 What is vintage Madeira?

At the top end of the quality scale for Madeira wines, you will find vintage Madeiras. Like other vintage wines, the grapes used to make vintage Madeira must all come from the same year. In addition, vintage Madeiras must spend at least 20 years aging in a cask. These wines are then aged two more years after being bottled. Some of the best vintage Madeira wines date back as far as the 18th century.

Madeira Winemaking Process

High-Quality Madeira

☑ Natually baked in casks for 20 years or more

Less-Expensive Madeira

☑ Placed in heated vats or tanks for 3 months or longer

- After fermentation, the wine used to make Madeira is heated, a process called estufagem, which gives Madeira a toffee-caramel flavor.

- The best Madeira wine is naturally baked in casks, or barrels, for 20 years or more on the warm upper floors of the wine lodges, which get quite hot under the Madeiran sun.

- The best Madeira wine is also exposed to oxygen since the casks are not completely filled with wine. This also contributes to the unique flavor of Madeira.

- For less-expensive Madeira wine, the wine is placed in heated vats or tanks for three months or longer to try to replicate the long heating process of the more expensive Madeira wine.

- The less-expensive Madeira wine is also exposed to oxygen since the vats or tanks are left open.

CONTINUED ►

Madeira wines are made in several different styles. The four main styles of high-quality Madeira are each made with and named after a different grape. These grapes are the Sercial, Verdelho, Bual and Malvasia varieties. Lower-quality Madeira is made with the less complex Tinta Negra Mole grape.

When serving Madeira, dry styles should be served slightly chilled, while sweeter styles should be served at room temperature. Remember that there is no rush to finish up a bottle, as Madeira wines never spoil.

Styles of Madeira

- These four best Madeira wines are named after the grape used to make the wine.

Verdelho

- Verdelho Madeira is made from the Verdelho grape. Verdelho Madeira is gold in color, medium-bodied and medium-dry with nutty, baked peach flavors.

Sercial

- Sercial Madeira is made from the Sercial grape. Sercial Madeira is pale gold in color, light-bodied and dry with nutty flavors.

Malvasia

- Malvasia, or Malmsey, Madeira is made from the Malvasia grape. Malvasia Madeira is dark amber in color and is the richest, sweetest style, with coffee, crème caramel and hazelnut flavors.

Bual

- Bual, or Boal, Madeira is made from the Bual, or Boal, grape. Bual Madeira is dark amber in color, medium-bodied and medium-sweet with almond and raisin flavors.

TIP *What kinds of food should I serve with Madeira?*

The lighter and drier styles of Madeira, Sercial and Verdelho, are fantastic with first courses such as chilled soups, pâtés and light fish dishes. They are also a perfect accompaniment for sipping alongside simple snacks, like salted nuts and dried fruits, before the start of a meal. The richer, sweeter versions of Madeira, Bual and Malvasia, are wonderful served with blue cheeses, hard dry cheeses, chocolate, coffee or caramel-flavored desserts. They are also satisfying as a dessert on their own.

 TIP *What type of glass should I use to serve Madeira?*

Madeira is best served in a wine glass that holds at least 6 ounces and tapers slightly toward the rim so that it will concentrate the wine's aromas.

Less Expensive Madeira

- Most Madeira produced is less expensive Madeira and is made using the pale-red Tinta Negra Mole grape, which is the most widely planted type of grape on the Madeira island.

- Winemakers use the Tinta Negra Mole grape to imitate the more expensive styles of Madeira. These wines are basic quality Madeira and do not show the name of the grape on the bottle.

- If a Madeira wine label says "Sercial-style" or "Verdelho-style," for example, the wine is likely made from the Tinta Negra Mole grape.

Storing and Serving Madeira

- Once opened, Madeira can last nearly forever. Madeira is extremely durable since it is subjected to heat and oxygen during the winemaking process—the two main factors that typically spoil wine.

- Drier Madeira wine, including Sercial and Verdelho, is best served slightly chilled. Sweeter Madeira wine, including Bual and Malvasia, is best served at room temperature.

ABOUT SWEET WINES

With a sweetness similar to that of a luscious dessert, it's no wonder that sweet wines are sometimes called dessert wines. Sweet wines are wines that have higher levels of both sugar and alcohol than normal white or red wines. The four main types of sweet wine—ice wine, late harvest wine, dried grape wine and noble rot wine—are made using grapes that have lower water content and higher concentrations of sugar. Most often, these sweet wines are sold in 375 milliliter bottles.

Ice Wine

- Ice wine is made from grapes that have naturally frozen on the grapevine. When the frozen grapes are pressed, the frozen water in the grapes is left behind and a sugar-rich juice is created, resulting in a sweet wine.

- The most popular grape varieties used to make ice wine include Vidal, Muscat, Riesling and Sémillon. The best ice wines are made from Riesling grapes.

- A new style of red ice wine is now made from the Cabernet Franc, Cabernet Sauvignon and Merlot grapes.

- The best ice wine is made in Canada and Germany. In Germany, ice wines are known as "Eiswein," pronounced "ice-vine."

- Ice wine is typically medium- to full-bodied with apricot, candied-lemon and spice flavors.

- Once opened, you should keep ice wine refrigerated and drink the wine within 2 to 3 days.

- You can typically keep unopened bottles of ice wine for 5 to 10 years, depending on the quality of the wine.

What type of glass should I use to drink sweet wine?

Due to their intense sweetness and richness, sweet wines are normally served in smaller amounts and in smaller glasses than normal white or red wines. A six-ounce glass that tapers to a narrow opening at the top is ideal for pouring the one- or two-ounce servings that are typical for sweet wine.

What type of food should I serve with sweet wine?

Sweet wines are typically served after a meal with a dessert, blue cheese or on their own. When drinking sweet wine with dessert, keep in mind that the wine should be sweeter than the dessert. Good desserts to enjoy with sweet wine include crème brulee, biscotti and fruit tarts. If you would like to serve sweet wine before a meal, try serving the wine with liver pâté or foie gras.

Late Harvest Wine

- Late harvest wine is made from grapes that are picked later than grapes used to make regular wine, so the grapes are overripe and very sweet, resulting in a sweet wine.

  Note: Some late harvest wine may be made from grapes that have been partially affected by a beneficial mold known as noble rot. For information on noble rot, see page 257.

- The most popular grape varieties used to make late harvest wine include Riesling, Chenin Blanc, Gewürztraminer, Muscat, Sémillon and Vidal.

- The best late harvest wines are Canadian late harvest wines, French "Vendange Tardive" wines, German and Austrian "Trockenbeerenauslese" wines and Italian "Raccolta Tardiva" wines.

- Late harvest wine is typically medium- to full-bodied with honey and apricot flavors.

- Once opened, you should keep late harvest wine refrigerated and drink the wine within 2 to 3 days.

- You can typically keep unopened bottles of late harvest wine for 3 to 8 years.

CONTINUED

Sweet wines are sometimes viewed as being less important or less interesting than normal wines. In reality, sweet wines require a great deal of skill to create. Wine producers go to great lengths to make these fine wines, often risking their crop by waiting for just the right conditions to harvest their grapes. As a result of these extraordinary efforts, high-quality sweet wines have complex aromas and flavors that are every bit as interesting as those found in normal wines.

Dried Grape Wine

- Dried grape wine is made from grapes that are picked when fully ripe and then naturally dried on straw mats in the sun or inside a winery. The grapes shrivel into near raisins, leaving sugar-rich grapes which create a sweet wine.

- The most popular grape varieties used to make dried grape wine include Aleatico, Malvasia and Muscat.

- The best dried grape wines are Italian "Vin Santo" and "Passito" wines, French "Vin de Paille" wines and German "Strohwein" wines.

- Dried grape wine is typically medium- to full-bodied with nutty, floral, honey and spice flavors.

- Once opened, you should keep dried grape wine refrigerated and drink the wine within one week.

- You can typically keep unopened bottles of dried grape wine for 3 to 10 years.

At what temperature should I serve sweet wine?

Most sweet wines are served chilled. You should serve white ice wine, late harvest wine, dried grape wine and noble rot wine chilled at a temperature of 42°F (6°C). Red ice wine should be served just a bit warmer at a slightly chilled temperature of 46°F (8°C).

 What is the most famous sweet wine?

The most renowned sweet wine in the world is most likely Sauternes, which is a noble rot wine made in the Sauternes region of Bordeaux, France. The Sauternes wine produced by Château d'Yquem is considered the most exquisite and expensive version of this type of wine. High-quality Sauternes wines, which can age for more than 60 years, can cost hundreds of dollars per bottle.

Noble Rot Wine

- Noble rot, also called *botrytis cinerea*, is a beneficial mold or fungus that dehydrates and shrivels grapes on the grapevine, leaving sugar-rich grapes which create a sweet wine.

- The most popular grape varieties used to make noble rot wine include Chenin Blanc, Gewürztraminer, Pinot Gris, Riesling, Sauvignon Blanc and Sémillon.

- Some of the best noble rot wines are Hungarian "Tokaji" wines, German and Austrian "Trockenbeerenauslese" wines and French noble rot wines.

- Noble rot wine is typically medium- to full-bodied with honey and lemon-marmalade flavors.

- Once opened, you should keep noble rot wine refrigerated and drink the wine within 2 to 3 days.

- You can typically keep unopened bottles of noble rot wine for 2 to 20 years, depending on the quality of the wine.

CHAPTER 15

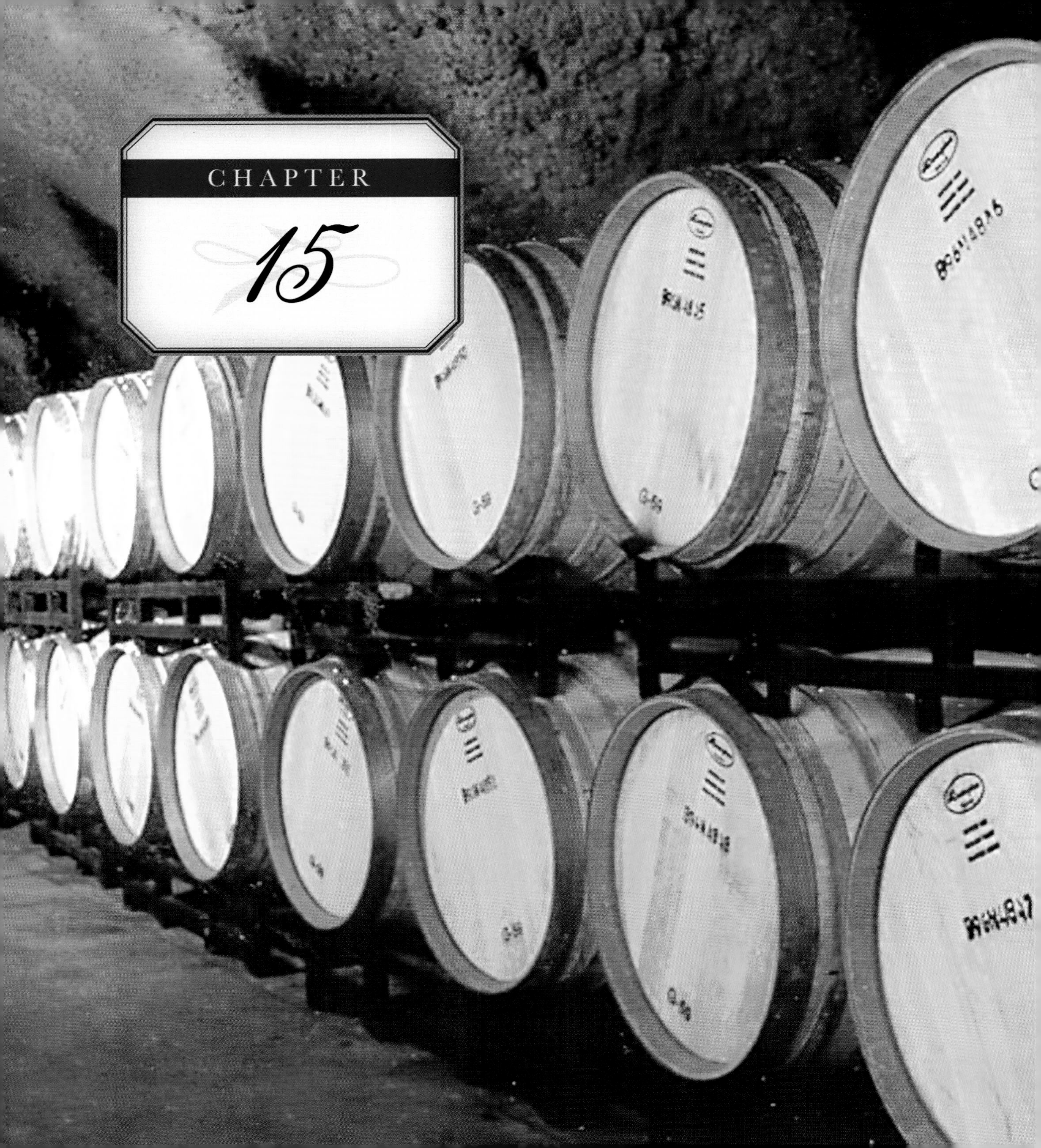

Learning More About Wine

Wine-Education Classes

Participating in Wine Tastings

Visiting Wineries

WINE-EDUCATION CLASSES

Wine-education classes are a fantastic resource for learning about wine, enhancing your appreciation of wine and meeting other individuals who are interested in wine.

These classes, which typically run for two to three hours at a time, will teach you more about appreciating and tasting wine than you could learn by yourself at home.

ABOUT WINE-EDUCATION CLASSES

Wine-education classes are a good way to learn more about wine and develop your wine-tasting skills. Wine-education classes can range from introductory wine-appreciation classes to more advanced classes that lead to professional credentials.

Introductory wine-education classes usually discuss the major styles of wine, how wines are made and how to appreciate and serve them. An introductory wine-education class should also teach you how to select wine from a restaurant wine list or wine shop.

IN-CLASS WINE TASTING

During a wine-education class, in-class wine tastings will help you learn to identify and describe the aromas and flavors of various wines. During in-class wine tastings, you can share your tasting observations with other students. Your instructor should provide guidance and feedback on your tasting observations.

Don't worry about becoming intoxicated when tasting wine in class. Most samples in a wine-education class are only one to two ounces in size. Additionally, you are not likely to sample more than five or six wines during each class. If a larger number of tastings will be served, the instructor will likely make a spittoon available. A spittoon is a cup, bottle chiller or ice bucket for spitting wine into after you have tasted the wine.

FINDING A WINE-EDUCATION CLASS

Wine-education classes are available in most cities from private instructors, wine and cheese shops and cooking schools. Adult-education or college-level classes on wine are also available.

If you do not live in an area where wine-education classes are offered, look for classes you can take on the Internet.

INSTRUCTOR QUALIFICATIONS

In a wine-education class, the instructor provides authoritative information and guidance. When investigating a wine-education class, be sure to ask about the instructor's qualifications. The instructor should be a wine authority with expert knowledge in the areas of grape growing, wine regions, the winemaking process and wine tasting.

Some instructors have earned credentials from wine-education or sommelier organizations. A sommelier is a person who specializes in restaurant wine service. Look for titles such as Certified Sommelier, Certified Wine Educator (CWE), Master Sommelier (MS) and Master of Wine (MW).

WINERY OR DISTRIBUTOR-SPONSORED CLASSES

Some wine-education classes are sponsored by specific wineries or wine distributors. The instructors are often winery representatives who are interested in promoting the wines sampled in the class. While taking a class from an independent instructor is preferable, you can still learn about wine in a sponsored wine class if the instructor has expertise beyond the wines he represents.

PARTICIPATING IN WINE TASTINGS

If you would like to sample a variety of wines, you should consider attending a wine tasting. Wine tastings are events for wine enthusiasts of all levels where participants taste a selection of wines and compare their impressions of the wines. At a wine tasting, you will likely sample many different types of wines that you would not try on your own. Wine tastings often have a theme, such as wines from a specific region, producer or grape variety.

About Wine Tastings

- Wine tastings are gatherings where wine enthusiasts sample and evaluate a variety of wines.

- Wine tastings range from relaxed get-togethers where guests mingle with one another to more formal occasions where participants are seated.

- Wine tastings are a great opportunity to taste a wide variety of wines.

- At a wine tasting, you also have the chance to learn from the observations of more experienced tasters.

- Wine tastings may be hosted by restaurants, wine shops, sommelier organizations and even wine distributors representing specific countries.

Note: A sommelier organization is an association that provides training in restaurant wine service.

- The cost of attending a wine tasting varies depending on the wines being tasted.

Why do some tasters slurp their wine?

You might notice that some wine tasters purse their lips and suck air into their mouths when they have a mouthful of wine. This action, which can sometimes produce a slurping or gurgling sound, is meant to enhance the person's ability to taste the wine. If you are hesitant about making such noises in public, you can still properly taste wine without making noisy slurping or gurgling sounds. For information on proper tasting techniques, see page 62.

 When should I share my opinion about the wines I taste?

To avoid making a social blunder, do not share your impressions of a wine until everyone else has been able to taste the wine. Experienced tasters prefer to form their own opinions about a wine before hearing other people's observations on the wine. After everyone has tasted the wine, try to keep your comments focused on the characteristics and qualities of the wine rather than general comments such as "I don't really like that wine" or "This wine is good."

About Spitting at Wine Tastings

Scented Items to Avoid

Scented Items to Avoid

- Perfume or cologne
- Scented hairsprays, deodorants and cosmetics
- Cigarettes, cigars and pipes
- Breath mints and breath fresheners
- Strongly flavored foods (consumed before the wine tasting)

- Participants at wine tastings normally spit out wine rather than swallow it. Spitting out the wine keeps the alcohol from negatively affecting a person's ability to taste and judge wine.

- Wine tasters are normally provided with a cup, bottle chiller or ice bucket for spitting out their wine. The container is called a spittoon.

- Strong odors can ruin a wine taster's ability to smell a wine.

- You should avoid using or consuming any products that may take away from your own or another taster's ability to smell and properly experience the wines offered at a wine tasting.

- When you attend a wine tasting, you should avoid strongly scented items, including the items displayed in the above list.

VISITING WINERIES

There are few better places to learn about wine than at a winery. Whether you are close to home or abroad, you will find that both small and large wineries alike are generally welcoming to visitors. During a visit, you will typically have the opportunity to take a tour of the facilities, taste the wines and talk to the people who make the wine. A winery visit is a thoroughly enjoyable way to expand your understanding and appreciation of wine.

About Visiting Wineries

- Visiting wineries allows you to see how wine is produced and is a great way to further your wine education.

- A visit to a winery may be as simple as a day trip by car or may involve traveling to a foreign country.

- When you visit a winery, you can also experience the climate, geography, local food and history that may have influenced the development of wines made at the winery.

Winery Sizes

- Wineries around the world range in both size and the complexity of their operations.

- Some wineries are large operations that use the latest technologies to create their wines.

- Other wineries are very small operations that often take a more traditional approach to producing their wines.

What is a winemaker dinner?

A winemaker dinner is an event typically hosted at a local hotel, restaurant or social club where the wines of a specific winery are sampled. At these multi-course meals, each course of the meal is created to complement a different wine from the winery. High-quality wines and older wines that are no longer available in stores may also be featured.

Winemaker dinners can be quite interesting and may give you the opportunity to ask questions of the winemaker directly—a big bonus if you are not able to visit the winery in person. Announcements of winemaker dinners can often be found on winery Web sites.

Winery Tours and Tastings

- Many larger wineries have been designed to accommodate visitors. These wineries generally offer daily tours and tastings all year round.

- Smaller wineries normally also welcome visitors, but the availability of tours and tastings may be more limited, depending on the season.

- You should contact a winery before you plan to visit to ensure it will be open when you arrive.

- During a winery tour, you will usually see how the wines are made and where the wines are aged.

- Most wineries allow you to sample and purchase their wines, including some wines that may not be available elsewhere.

- When visiting a winery, you may also have a chance to talk to the winemaker or winery owner about his approach to winemaking.

Glossary

Glossary

A

Acidity

A characteristic of wine you can taste. The acid in a wine provides a crisp and lively taste. Too little acidity creates a flat and lifeless tasting wine, whereas too much acidity creates a sour tasting wine.

Aerate

Exposing wine to oxygen, by pouring the wine into a container or wine glass before serving the wine. Aeration can help enhance the aromas and flavors of young, tannic red wines, as well as full-bodied red wines. Sometimes referred to as letting wine breathe.

Aging

The process of storing wine for a number of years to allow the wine's aromas and flavors to develop and mature. Aging softens wines with high levels of tannin, resulting in a smoother, more balanced wine. Less than one percent of all wines are meant to be aged longer than five years.

Albariño

A variety of white grape found mostly in Spain and Portugal. This grape often produces dry white wines with flavors of peaches, spice and minerals.

Alcohol

A characteristic of wine you can taste. Wines with higher levels of alcohol are rounder (smoother), feel heavier and produce a warm or hot sensation at the back of your throat.

Appellation

A government-registered winemaking region in which winemakers must follow the standards and practices defined by the local government, often including the types of grapes grown and the winemaking and grape-growing methods.

Aroma

The smell of a wine. Also called bouquet or nose.

B

Balance

The relationship between each component in a wine, including sweetness, acidity, tannin and alcohol. A wine is balanced when you can notice each component in the wine, and one component does not overpower the other components.

Barrel

A container made of wood in which wine is aged or fermented.

Blending

Mixing together two or more types of wine. The wines may be made from different grape varieties, different vineyards or both.

Body

The weight of a wine on your tongue. A wine's body is primarily determined by the amount of alcohol and extract (minerals, sugars and other trace elements) in the wine.

Botrytis Cinerea

See noble rot.

Bottle Aging

Storing a wine in its bottle for a period of time to enhance the aromas and flavors of the wine, soften tannins and increase the complexity of the final wine. Bottle aging may be done by the winery or by the consumer at home.

C

Cabernet Sauvignon

A variety of red grape found throughout the warmer winemaking regions of the world. One of the world's most important red grapes, this grape often produces full-bodied red wines with flavors of blackcurrants and chocolate.

Canopy

The leaves and shoots, or new stems, of a grapevine.

Canopy Management

The techniques used to manipulate a grapevine's canopy, including pruning, leaf removal and attaching the grapevine to a trellis, which is a structure that supports the grapevine. Canopy management is done to optimize the quality of the grapes, resulting in a higher-quality wine.

Carbonic Maceration

A method of fermentation in which whole, uncrushed grapes are allowed to ferment in a closed tank where the air has been replaced by carbon dioxide. Carbonic maceration creates fruity, light red wines such as the renowned wines from France's Beaujolais region.

Champagne

Sparkling wine produced in the Champagne region of France.

Chardonnay

A variety of white grape found throughout the winemaking regions of the world. One of the world's most important white grapes, this grape often produces dry white wines with varying flavors, from green apple to tropical fruit.

Chenin Blanc

A variety of white grape that grows well in the Loire Valley of France, South Africa and California and Washington State in the United States. This grape can produce wines ranging from very sweet to bone dry with flavors of lime, white flowers and honey.

Complex

A term used to describe a wine that has many characteristics, aromas and flavors which are all well balanced.

Corked

A term used to describe a bottle of wine that has been spoiled by a defective cork. A corked wine can only be detected by smelling or tasting the wine.

D

Decant

The process of pouring a bottle of wine into a glass or crystal container before serving the wine. Many full-bodied red wines should be decanted to remove the sediment that has accumulated at the bottom of a bottle as the wine has aged.

Dry

A characteristic of wine you can taste. Dry wine has very little to no sugar, or sweetness.

E

Estate-bottled

The phrase "estate-bottled" appears on a wine's label when the company that made and bottled the wine also grew the grapes used to make the wine.

F

Fermentation

A natural process that turns grape juice into wine. During fermentation, microscopic organisms, known as yeast, consume the sugar in the grape juice and slowly convert the sugar into alcohol as well as carbon dioxide gas which evaporates into the air.

Finish

The flavors and sensations that linger in your mouth after you swallow or spit out the wine. Also known as aftertaste.

Flavors

A characteristic of wine you can taste. There are hundreds of different flavors that you can identify in wine, such as fruits, vegetables, herbs and spices.

Fortified Wine

A type of wine that has had alcohol added during or after the fermentation process. Popular types of fortified wines include Port, Sherry and Vermouth. Also known as liqueur wines.

GLOSSARY

G

Gewürztraminer
A variety of white grape that is most often found in Germany, Austria and the Alsace region of France. This grape produces dry, aromatic white wines that often have aromas of lychee and roses.

H

Hybrid
A grape variety that is the result of pairing two different grape varieties. For example, the Maréchal Foch grape variety is a hybrid formed from the Pinot Noir grape and the Gamay grape.

I

Ice Wine
A type of sweet wine produced from grapes that have naturally frozen on the grapevine. Ice wine is most commonly produced in Germany, Austria and Canada and is usually full-bodied and lusciously sweet.

L

Late Harvest Wine
A type of sweet wine produced by allowing the grapes to ripen on the vines longer than normal. Late harvest wines are often sweet and medium to full bodied.

Lees
Sediment that forms in wine after the fermentation process. This sediment is normally filtered out of a wine, but a winemaker may choose to keep the lees in the wine for a period of time to give the wine a somewhat richer texture, a slight nutty flavor and often more complexity.

Legs
The drops of wine that run down the inside of a glass after the wine is swirled in the glass. The legs indicate the thickness, or viscosity, of the wine. If the wine runs quickly down the glass, the wine has a lighter style and may have a lower alcohol content. If the wine runs more slowly down the glass, the wine has a thicker style and may have a higher alcohol content, sugar content, or both.

M

Maceration
The process of soaking grape skins, seeds and pulp in wine for a period of time. This is done to add the color, tannin, aroma and flavor from the grape skins to the wine.

Madeira
A fortified wine made on the small Portuguese island of Madeira. The wine is amber in color, has a uniquely high level of acidity and a noticeably long finish, or aftertaste. Madeira ranges from dry to sweet tasting.

Magnum
A 1.5-liter bottle of wine. A magnum is the equivalent of two 750 ml bottles and holds about 10 glasses of wine.

Malolactic Fermentation
A natural process in which naturally-occurring bacteria in the wine converts sharp malic acid to lactic acid, which is softer and less tart. This process is typically used in the production of red wines and full-bodied white wines, such as Chardonnay.

Merlot
A variety of red grape that is most commonly found in the Bordeaux region of France, Chile, the United States, Italy and Australia. This grape often produces a medium-bodied red wine with flavors of plums and blackberries.

Microclimate
Refers to an area that has a climate within a climate, caused by factors such as exposure to wind or the slope of the land. For example, a single vineyard may have a warmer climate than the rest of the surrounding winemaking region.

Muscat

A variety of white grape that is found in many countries throughout the world. This grape is very versatile and is used to make fragrant wines ranging from dry to sweet. Muscat has flavors of white flowers, musk and ripe grapes.

Must

The juice of freshly-crushed grapes that will become wine.

N

Nebbiolo

A variety of red grape that is grown mostly in the Piedmont region of Italy. This grape produces fine, full-bodied red wines that often have flavors of strawberries, dried tea and roses.

New World

Refers to winemaking regions outside of Europe, such as in Australia, South Africa and North and South America, where technology and innovation are often the keys to making good wine.

Noble Grapes

Grape varieties that produce the world's finest wines. Noble grapes that produce white wines include Chardonnay, Chenin Blanc and Riesling. Noble grapes that produce red wines include Cabernet Sauvignon, Pinot Noir and Syrah.

Noble Rot

A beneficial fungus, or mold, that grows on grapes when they are still on the vines. The mold dehydrates the grapes leaving them very concentrated in flavor. These grapes are used for sweet wines.

O

Oak

The wood used for barrels in which fermenting or aging takes place. The oak for wine barrels usually comes from France, America or Slovenia. Oak barrels make wine more complex, fuller, sweeter and richer tasting and add tannin to wine.

Off-dry

A characteristic of wine which refers to its taste. Off-dry wines are not fully dry and have a light taste of sweetness.

Old Vines

Vines that have been producing grapes for many years. Old vines usually yield smaller amounts of good-quality, concentrated grapes resulting in higher quality wines. The term "old vines" or "vieilles vignes" on a wine's label often indicates a concentrated, flavorful wine.

Old World

Refers to winemaking regions in Europe, such as in France, Italy, Germany and Austria, where tradition and old-fashioned methods are often the basis of winemaking.

Oxidation

The effect of oxygen on wine. If wine comes in contact with oxygen for too long, the aromas of the wine will fade and a nutty smell may develop.

P

Phylloxera

Tiny, parasitic lice which infect the roots of the widely used *Vitis vinifera* grape vines.

Pinot Gris

A variety of white grape found mostly in Germany and Northeastern Italy. This grape produces white wines that often have flavors of peaches and almonds. Also called Pinot Grigio.

Pinot Noir

A variety of red grape that is most often found in the Burgundy region of France, New Zealand and Oregon in the United States. This grape produces medium-bodied red wines with flavors of mushrooms, earth and cherry.

R

Port

A type of sweet, fortified wine made in the mountainous Douro region in northern Portugal. Also known as Porto wine.

Region

A winemaking area, usually legally defined and having particular guidelines and standards by which wines must be made. See also appellation.

Residual Sugar

The sugar that remains in wine after fermentation has occurred.

Riesling

A variety of white grape found mostly in cool winemaking regions, such as Germany, Canada and New York State. This grape can produce wines ranging from dry to sweet, often with flavors of lime blossoms, grapefruit and minerals.

Rootstock

The roots of a grapevine.

Rosé Wine

A type of wine that is pink in color and tastes more like white wine than red wine. Rosé wines are generally light and fruity tasting and can be sweet. Also called blush wine.

S

Sangiovese

A variety of red grape found mostly in the Tuscany region of Italy. This grape can produce a variety of wines from light- to full-bodied with flavors of cherry, herbs and nuts.

Sauvignon Blanc

A variety of white grape most often found in the Bordeaux and Loire regions of France, Northeastern Italy and New Zealand. This grape produces dry white wines that often have flavors of citrus fruit, minerals and herbs. Also called Fumé Blanc.

Sediment

The grainy deposits at the bottom of a wine bottle which have formed after a wine has aged.

Sherry

Sherry is a fortified wine produced in the Andalusia region of southwestern Spain. Sherry is made in two styles. Fino Sherry is pale in color, is very dry and light-bodied and has an almond aroma. Oloroso Sherry is dark in color, ranges from sweet to dry, is full-bodied and has a walnut and raisin aroma.

Shiraz

See Syrah.

Sommelier

A person who specializes in restaurant wine service.

Sparkling Wine

A type of wine that contains carbon dioxide bubbles. Sparkling wine is most often white or pink in color, with some versions being red in color.

Structure

Refers to the wine's form and includes the wine's alcohol level, acid, tannin and sugar.

Style

The characteristics found in a wine, such as full-bodied or tannic.

Sulfites

Most U.S. wine labels display the phrase "contains sulfites," which refers to the presence of sulfur dioxide in a wine. Small amounts of sulfur dioxide develop naturally in some wines during the winemaking process. Many winemakers also add sulfur dioxide to their wine to help stabilize and preserve the wine.

Super Tuscan

Refers to some expensive, high-quality Tuscan wines which do not conform to regional regulations and incorporate French varieties of grapes, such as Cabernet Sauvignon and Merlot. Super Tuscan wines usually have special brand names, such as Tignanello and Sassicaia.

Sweet Wine

A type of wine made from grapes with a higher concentration of sugar or wine that has had sugar added during or after the fermentation process. A popular type of sweet wine is ice wine. Also known as dessert wine.

Sweetness

A characteristic of wine you can taste. The sweetness of a wine is determined by the amount of sugar left in the wine after the fermentation process is complete.

Syrah

A variety of red grape that is most often found in the Rhône winemaking region of France, South Africa and Australia. This grape often produces full-bodied red wines with flavors of spice, black pepper and berries. Also called Shiraz.

T

Table Wine

A generic category of wine. Table wine includes white, red and rosé wine.

Tannin

A characteristic of wine you can taste. Tannin is found mainly in the skins and pips (seeds) of grapes as well as in oak barrels used to store wine. When a wine has a high level of tannin, the wine gives you a drying, mouth-puckering sensation and can taste bitter.

Tempranillo

A variety of red grape that is grown mostly in Spain and in the Douro region of Portugal. This grape often produces medium- to full-bodied wines with flavors of raspberries and spice.

Terroir

A French word used to describe the overall growing environment of a vineyard, which influences the taste of a wine. Terroir encompasses factors such as the soil, altitude, climate and physical features of the land. Pronounced ter-wahr.

U

Unoaked

A term used to describe wine that has not been fermented or aged in oak barrels.

V

Varietal Wine

Describes a wine that is named according to the main grape used to make the wine. For example, a varietal wine made from Riesling grapes is called Riesling.

Viniculture

The process of making wine from grapes.

Vintage

The year in which grapes are harvested for wine.

Viticulture

The grape-growing process in a vineyard.

Y

Yeast

Microscopic organisms that consume the sugar in the grape juice during the winemaking process and convert the sugar into alcohol and carbon dioxide gas which evaporates into the air.

Yield

The amount of grapes a grapevine or vineyard produces. Most of the best wines in the world are made from low-yielding grapevines and vineyards.

Z

Zinfandel

A variety of red grape that is most commonly found in Italy and California. This grape often produces a wide variety of wines, from light pink rosé wines to rich, full-bodied red wines. Also called Primitivo.

Index

A

AC, classification, France, 41, 139
acid level, consideration, pairing wine with food, 130
acidity, 268
    tasting in wine, 63
aerate, 94-95, 268
aftertaste, 269
age-worthy wines, 108-109
    collecting, 110-111
aged wines, combining with food, 131
aging, 268
    and winemaking, 52
    Champagne, 223
    Sherry, 240-241
    wine. *See also* storing
        how long, 16, 108-109
Aglianico, grapes, 27
ah-so, cork removal tool, 87
air pumps, 99
Albariño, grapes, 30, 268
alcohol, 268
    content
        and body of wine, 39
        consideration, pairing wine with food, 130
        on wine labels, 38
    tasting in wine, 64
Aligoté, grapes, 145
Alsace, France, 152-153
altitude, and grape development, 49
Alvarinho, grapes. *See* Albariño
America
    California, 206-207
    New York State, 210-211
    Oregon, 208-209
    overview, 204
    sparkling wine, 235
    Washington State, 205
Amontillado Sherry, 242
Andalusia, Spain, 238
AOC, classification, France, 41, 139
appearance, of a wine, 58
appellations, 268. *See also* winemaking regions
    in France, 138-139
Argentina, 202-203
aromas, 268
    in Champagne, 221, 227
    in wine

        determining, 60-61
        unpleasant, 70-71
auctions, and wine buying, 76-77
Australia, 192-195
Austria, 184-185
AVA, classification, America, 41, 205

B

Bairrada, Portugal, 179
balance, 268
    tasting in wine, 66
balloon-shaped, wine glasses, 92-93
barrel-aged wine, 55
barrel-fermented wine, 54
barrels, 54-55, 268, 271
base, of wine glass, 92
Beaujolais Nouveau, France, 147
blanc de blancs, Champagne, 226
blanc de noirs, Champagne, 227
blending, 268
    and Australian wines, 195
    and Bordeaux wines, 141
    and making Champagne, 222
    and winemaking, 53
blush wine. *See* rosé wine
bodegas, Sherry, 240
body, 268
    tasting in wine, 65
Bordeaux, France, 140-143
botrytis cinerea, 268
    wine, 213, 257
bottle aging, 268
bottle-aged, Port, 246
bottles, for Champagne, 221
bottling, and winemaking, 53
bouquet, 60, 268. *See also* aromas
Bourgogne. *See* Burgundy
bowl, of wine glass, 92
brand-names, wine, 35
British Columbia, Canada, 215
Bual Madeira, 252
Burgenland, Austria, 185
Burgundy, France, 144-147
butler's friend, cork removal tool, 87
buying wine,
    by the case, 115
    strategies for, 80-81
    where to, 74-77

C

Cabernet Franc, grapes, 27
Cabernet Sauvignon, grapes, 24, 268
California, USA, 206-207
calories, in wine, 16
Campania, Italy, 171
Canada, 212-215
candles, and decanting wine, 96-97
Cannonau, grapes. *See* Grenache
canopy, 46, 268
    management, 46, 269
Cape Peninsula, South Africa, 199
capsule, 88
carbonic maceration, 53, 269
Carmenère, grapes, 201
catalogs, wine, 75
Cava, Spain, 175, 234
Certified Sommelier, 261
Certified Wine Educator (CWE), 261
Champagne, 269. *See also* sparkling wine
    and food, 231
    buying, amount, 101
    evaluating, 232-233
    glasses, 230
    opening, 228-229
    overview, 17, 20, 218-221
    serving, 230
    storing, 231
    types, 224-227
    winemaking process, 222-223
chaptalization, 181
Chardonnay, grapes, 28, 269
charmat method, for making Champagne, 223
château, 142
Châteauneuf-du-Pape, France, 148
cheeses, pairing with wine, 134
Chenin Blanc, grapes, 30, 269
Chile, 200-201
chilling
    Champagne and sparkling wine, 228
    wine, 91
classes, wine-education, 260-261
classification, of European wine, 40-41
climate, and grape development, 48-49
Colheita Port, 249
collecting, wine, 110-111
    strategies, 112-115
color, of wine, determining, 58-59

commune, distinction, Burgundy, 144
complex, 269
complexity, tasting in wine, 66
computers, and wine collections, 115
cork retriever, 89
corked wine, 70-71, 269
corks
    inspecting, 123
    pieces in wine bottles, 89
    removing
        from Champagne and sparkling wine, 228-229
        from wine, 88-89
    smelling, 89, 123
    tools for removing, 86-87
Côtes du Rhône, France, 149
country of origin, on wine labels, 36
Cream Sherry, 242
Crémant, sparkling wine, France, 234
Crete, Greece, 189
cru classé, 143
crushing, grapes, to make wine, 50
Crusted Port, 249
cuve close, for making Champagne, 223

D

Dão, Portugal, 179
darkness, for storing wine, 105
decant, 96, 269
decanting, 96-97
    and aerating wine, 95
descriptions, on wine labels, 37
dessert wine. *See also* sweet wines
    in Greece, 189
desserts, pairing with wine, 135
destemming, grapes, to make wine, 50
DO, classification
    Portugal, 41
    Spain, 41, 174
DOC, classification
    Italy, 41, 159
    Portugal, 41, 178
    Spain, 41, 174
DOCG, classification, Italy, 41, 159
Dom Pérignon, 219
Douro, Portugal, 179, 244
dried grape wine, 256
dry, 269
dryness, consideration, pairing wine with food, 131

Index

E

Eiswein. *See* ice wine
environment, and grape growing, 44-45
estate-bottled, on wine labels, 39, 269
estufagem, Madeira, 251
European wine, classification, 40-41
everyday wines, collecting, 110-111

F

fermentation, 269
    malolactic, and winemaking, 51, 270
    to make Champagne, 222-223
    to make wine, 50-51
filling, wine glasses, 58
filtering, and winemaking, 52
fining, and winemaking, 52
finish, 269
    tasting in wine, 67
Fino Sherry, 242
flavors, 269
    tasting in wine, 65
        unpleasant, 70-71
flawed, wine, 70-71
flor, Sherry, 240-241
flute, glasses, 230
foil cutter, 87
food
    and Champagne, 231
    and Madeira, 253
    and Port, 247
    and Sherry, 243
    and sweet wine, 255
    and wine, 128-135
fortified wine, 21, 269. *See also specific wine type*
France
    Alsace, 152-153
    Bordeaux, 140-143
    Burgundy, 144-147
    Champagne, 218-219
    Languedoc-Roussillon, 155
    Loire, 150-151
    Provence, 154
    Rhône, 148-149
    sparkling wine, 234
    wines, overview, 138-139
Franciacorta, Italy, 235
free-run wine, 51
Friuli-Venezia Giulia, Italy, 169

frizzante, Italy, 235
frost, and grape development, 49
Fumé Blanc, grapes. *See* Sauvignon Blanc
Furmint, grapes, 31

G

Gamay, grapes, 27
garigue, 155
Garnacha, grapes. *See* Grenache
gas preservatives, 99
generic wine names, 34
Germany
    Mosel-Saar-Ruwer, 182
    Nahe, 183
    Pfalz, 182
    Rheingau, 183
    Rheinhessen, 183
    wines, overview, 180-181
Gewürztraminer, grapes, 29, 153, 270
GI, classification, Australia, 41
glasses
    Champagne, 230
    Madeira, 253
    Port, 245
    Sherry, 239
    sweet wine, 255
    wine
        and aerating wine, 95
        filling, 58
        holding, 58
        types, 59, 92-93
grand cru
    classé, 143
    distinction, Burgundy, 144
Grande Marque, Champagne, 227
grapes
    and climate, 48-49
    crushing, to make wine, 50
    destemming, to make wine, 50
    how grown, 44-47
    hybrid, 211, 215, 270
    transporting to wineries, 47
    varieties. *See also specific grape variety*
        and environmental factors, 44-45
        noble, 23
        on wine labels, 37
        overview, 22-23
        red, 19, 24-27
        regional names, 23

used in Champagne, 220
white, 19, 28-31
Greece, wines, 188-189
Grenache, grapes, 27
growing season, and grape development, 49
Grüner Veltliner, grapes, 31, 184

H

harvest, and grape growing, 47
holding, wine glasses, 58
house wine, in restaurants, 119
humidity
        and grape development, 49
        for storing wine, 104
Hungary, 186-187
hybrid, grape varieties, 211, 215, 270

I

ice wine, 21, 213, 254, 270
Internet, and wine buying, 77
IPR, classification, Portugal, 178
Italy
        Campania, 171
        Friuli-Venezia Giulia, 169
        Northeastern, 168-169
        Piedmont, 160-163
        Sicily, 170
        sparkling wine, 235
        Trentino-Alto Adige, 169
        Tuscany, 164-167
        Umbria, 171
        Veneto, 168
        wines, overview, 158-159

L

La Rioja, Argentina, 203
labels, terms, 36-39
Languedoc-Roussillon, France, 155
late harvest wine, 21, 153, 213, 255, 270
Late-Bottled Vintage Port, 249
lees, 53, 270
legs, 270
Liebfraumilch, Germany, 183
liqueur wines, 269
lists, wine, organization, 120-121
Loire, France, 150-151
Lower Austria, Austria, 184

M

Macedonia, Greece, 188
maceration, 51, 270
        carbonic, 53, 269
Madeira, Portugal, 250-253, 270
magnum, 111, 270
Malbec, grapes, 27
malolactic fermentation, 51, 270
Malvasia Madeira, 252
Manzanilla Sherry, 242
Marsala, Sicily, Italy, 170
Marsanne, grapes, 31
Master of Wine (MW), 261
Master Sommelier (MS), 261
maturation, 52. *See also* aging
Mendoza, Argentina, 202
Meritage, wines, 211
Merlot, grapes, 25, 270
microclimates, 48, 270
Montilla, 241
Mortagua. *See* Touriga Nacional
Moscato d'Asti, Italy, 235
Mosel-Saar-Ruwer, Germany, 182
movement, and storing wine, 105
Muscadet, grapes, 151
Muscat, grapes, 30, 153, 271
must, 50, 271

N

Nahe, Germany, 183
naming, wines, 17, 32-35
Naoussa, Greece, 188
Navarra, Spain, 175
Nebbiolo, grapes, 25, 271
négociant, 145
New South Wales, Australia, 195
New World wines, overview, 17, 271
New York State, USA, 210-211
New Zealand, 196-197
noble
        grapes, 23, 271
        rot, 271
                wine, 21, 257
non-vintage
        Champagne, 224
        wines, 38
nose, 268. *See also* aromas
nosing wine, 60
notes, tasting, writing, 68-69

Index

O

oak, 271
    barrels, 54-55
oaked wines, 55
off-dry, 271
old vines, 271
Old World wines, overview, 17, 271
Oloroso Sherry, 242
Ontario, Canada, 214
open
    Champagne, 228-229
    wine, 88-89
        sparkling, 228-229
Oregon, USA, 208-209
orientation, for storing wine, 105
oxidation, 271

P

Pale Cream Sherry, 242
particles, in wine. See sediment
passito wines, 169, 256
Peloponnese, Greece, 189
Pfalz, Germany, 182
phylloxera, 23, 271
Piedmont, Italy, 160-163
Piemonte. See Piedmont
Pinot
    Blanc, grapes, 31
    Grigio, grapes. See Pinot Gris
    Gris, grapes, 29, 153, 271
    Noir, grapes, 24, 271
Port, 244-249, 272
Porto. See Port
Portugal, wines, 178-179
    Madeira, 250
    Port, 244
Prädikat, Germany, 181
premier cru, distinction, Burgundy, 144
press wine, 51
pressing, 51
Prestige cuvée, Champagne, 225
Primitivo, grapes, 26. See also Zinfandel
Priorat, Spain, 177
producer name, on wine labels, 36
proprietary wine names, 35
Prosecco, Italy, 235
Provence, France, 154

Q

QbA, classification, Germany, 41, 180
QmP, classification, Germany, 41, 180
quality wine, Europe, 40-41

R

raccolta tardiva, 255
rainfall, and grape development, 49
ratings, wine, 82-83
recorking, wine, 98-99
red
    grape varieties, 19, 24-27
    meat, pairing with wine, 132
    wine. See also specific red wine
        in Bordeaux, France, 141
        in Burgundy, France, 145
        overview, 19
        sparkling, in Loire, France, 151
refilling, wine glasses, 101
refrigerators, and storing wine, 105
regional wines, 33
regions, winemaking, 33, 272. See also specific region
    on wine labels, 37
removing
    corks, 88-89, 228-229
        tools for, 86-87
    sediment, from wine, 96-97
reserve, on wine labels, 39
residual sugar, 272
restaurants, wine
    buying in, 118-119
    lists
        organization, 120-121
        wine names on, 35
    service, 122-125
retailers, and wine buying, 74
retsina, Greece, 189
Rheingau, Germany, 183
Rheinhessen, Germany, 183
Rhône, France, 148-149
Rías Baixas, Spain, 177
Ribera del Duero, Spain, 176
Riesling, grapes, 28, 153, 272
rim, of wine glass, 92
Rioja, Spain, 175
rootstock, 272
rosé
    Champagne, 226
    wine, 19, 272

Ruby Port, 248
Rueda, Spain, 176
Ruländer, grapes. *See* Pinot Gris

S

Samos, Greece, 189
San Juan, Argentina, 203
Sangiovese, grapes, 26, 272
Sauternes, 143, 257
Sauvignon Blanc, grapes, 29, 272
screw caps, 193
seafood, pairing with wine, 133
second label, wine, 143
sediment, 53, 59, 272
   removing
      during Champagne making, 223
      from wine, 96-97
sélection de grains nobles (SGN), wine, 153
Sémillon, grapes, 31
Sercial Madeira, 252
serving
   Champagne, 230
   Madeira, 253
   Port, 247
   Sherry, 243
   wine, 100-101
      at correct temperature, 90-91
      sparkling, 230
      sweet, 257
shape, of wine glass, 92
shelf-talkers, 75
Sherry, 238-243, 272
shipping wine, 77
Shiraz, grapes, 25. *See also* Syrah
Sicily, Italy, 170
Single Quinta Vintage Port, 249
size, of wine glass, 93
slurping, and wine tastings, 263
smelling
   corks, 89, 123
   wine, 60-61
smells, and storing wine, 105
soil, and grape growing, 45
Solera System, Sherry, 241
sommelier, 272
South Africa, 198-199
South Australia, Australia, 193
Spain, 174-177
   Sherry, 238

sparkling wine, 175, 234
sparkling wine. *See also* Champagne
   evaluating, 232-233
   France, 151, 234
   Italy, 162, 235
   opening, 228-229
   overview, 20, 218-221, 272
   serving, 230
   Spain, 175, 234
   storing, 231
   United States, 235
spitting, and wine tastings, 263
spumante, Italy, 235
Steen, grapes. *See* Chenin Blanc
stem, of wine glass, 92
storage space, renting, for storing wine, 107
storing
   Champagne, 231
   leftover wine, 16, 21, 98-99
   Madeira, 253
   Port, 247
   Sherry, 243
   wine, 104-105. *See also* aging
      how long, 16, 108-109
      sparkling, 231
      where, 106-107
Strohwein, 256
structure, 272
style, 272
sulfites, and wine labels, 37, 272
sunshine, and grape development, 48
Super Tuscans, 166-167, 273
supermarkets, and wine buying, 74
sur lie, 141
Süssreserve, 183
sweet wines. *See also specific wine type*
   and food, 131, 255
   Austria, 185
   Canada, 213
   glasses, 255
   Greece, 189
   overview, 21, 254-257, 273
   temperature for serving, 257
sweetness, 273
   and Champagne, 227
   consideration, pairing wine with food, 131
   tasting in wine, 63
swirl, wine, in glass, 60
Syrah, grapes, 25, 273

Index

T

table wine
 Europe, 40-41
 overview, 18-19, 273
 United States, 41
tank method, for making Champagne, 223
tannin, 19, 65, 273
 consideration, pairing wine with food, 130
 tasting in wine, 64
tasting
 Champagne and sparkling wine, 232-233
 notes, writing, 68-69
 wine
  how to, 62-67
  order, 71
  tips, 70-71
tastings, wine, 262-263
 at wineries, 264-265
 in classes, 260
Tawny Port, 248
temperatures
 and grape development, 48, 49
 for serving wine, 18-19, 90-91
 for storing wine, 104
Tempranillo, grapes, 26, 273
terroir, 44, 273
thermometers, wine, 91
thickness
 of wine, determining, 59
 of wine glass, 93
Tinta Roriz, grapes, 26. See also Tempranillo
Tokaji Aszú, Hungary, 187, 257
tools, for removing corks, 86-87
Touriga Nacional, grapes, 27
tours, wineries, 264-265
Trentino-Alto Adige, Italy, 169
Trockenbeerenauslese, 185, 255, 257
tulip-shaped, glasses, 92-93, 230
Tuscany, Italy, 164-167
twist-style cork remover, 86
type of wine, on wine labels, 36
typicity, of wine, 67

U

Umbria, Italy, 171
Unico, Spain, 176
United States. See America
unoaked, 273

V

varietal wines, 32-33, 273
VDQS, classification, France, 41, 139
vendange tardive (VT), wine, 153, 255
Veneto, Italy, 168
Verdelho Madeira, 252
vibration, and storing wine, 105
Victoria, Australia, 194
Vieilles Vignes, 139
Vienna, Austria, 185
village, distinction, Burgundy, 144
vin de paille, 256
vin mousseux, France, 234
vin santo, 167, 256
vineyard, on wine labels, 39
Vinho Verde, Portugal, 179
viniculture, 45, 273
vinification. See winemaking
Vintage Character Port, 249
Vintage Madeira, 251
Vintage Port, 245, 248
vintages, 17, 273
 Champagne, 225
 on wine labels, 38
Viognier, grapes, 31
viticulture, 45, 273
Vitis, grape genus, 23
volume, on wine labels, 39
VQA, classification, Canada, 41, 212
VQPRD, classification, Europe, 41

W

waiter's corkscrew, 86
 using to remove corks, 88-89
waiter's friend, 86
Washington State, USA, 205
Web sites, and wine buying, 77
Western Australia, Australia, 195
white
 grape varieties, 19, 28-31
 meat, pairing with wine, 133
 wine, 18. See also specific white wine
  in Bordeaux, France, 141
  in Burgundy, France, 145
  sparkling, Asti region, Italy 162
White Port, 249
wind, and grape development, 49

wine. *See also specific wine type*
    aerating, 94-95, 268
    aging. *See* aging
    and food, combining. *See* food
    bring your own, to restaurants, 119
    buying
        amount, 101
        by the case, 115
        in restaurants, 119
        strategies, 80-81
        where to, 74-77
    cabinets, 107
    calories, 16
    catalogs, 75
    cellars, 106
    chilling, 91
    clubs, and wine buying, 77
    collecting, 110-111
        strategies, 112-115
    color, determining, 58-59
    decanting, 96-97
    education, classes, 260-261
    entertaining with, 100-101
    fermenting, 50-51
    freshness, determining, 99
    glasses
        and aerating wine, 95
        filling, 58, 101
        holding, 58
        number to use when entertaining, 101
        types, 59, 92-93
    how it is made, 50-53
    how it is named, 17, 32-35
    in restaurants, 118-119, 122-125
    lists, organization, 120-121
    New World, 17, 271
    Old World, 17, 271
    older
        buying, 81
        when to drink, 113
    pressing, 51
    ratings, 82-83
    recorking, 98-99
    refrigerators, 107
    sediment, 59
    serving, at correct temperature, 90-91
    shipping, 77
    shops, 75
    choosing, 78-79
    smelling, 60-61
    storage units, 107
    storing, 104-105
        how long, 16, 108-109
        leftover, 16, 21, 98-99
        where, 106-107
    swirl, in glass, 60
    tasting
        how to, 62-67
        notes, writing, 68-69
        tips, 70-71
    tastings, 262-263
        at wineries, 264-265
        in classes, 260
    thermometers, 91
    thickness, determining, 59
    types, overview, 18-21, 36. *See also specific wine type*
    typicity, 67
    where to buy, 74-77
winemaker dinner, 265
winemaking, 50-53
    and oak barrels, 54-55
    Champagne, traditional method, 222-223
    regions, 33, 41, 272. *See also specific region*
        on wine labels, 37
    styles, 161, 175
wineries
    and wine buying, 76
    visiting, 264-265
wing-type cork remover, 87
WO, classification, South Africa, 41, 198
wood Port, 246
wooden crates, and storing wine, 107
writing, tasting notes, 68-69

Y

yeast, 50, 273
yields, and grape growing, 46-47, 273

Z

Zinfandel, grapes, 26, 207, 273

Did you like this book? MARAN ILLUSTRATED™ also offers books on the most popular computer topics, using the same easy-to-use format of this book. We always say that if you like one of our books, you'll love the rest of our books too!

Here's a list of some of our best-selling computer titles:

Guided Tour Series - 240 pages, Full Color

MARAN ILLUSTRATED's Guided Tour series features a friendly disk character that walks you through each task step by step. The full-color screen shots are larger than in any of our other series and are accompanied by clear, concise instructions.

	ISBN	Price
MARAN ILLUSTRATED™ Computers Guided Tour	1-59200-880-1	$24.99 US/$33.95 CDN
MARAN ILLUSTRATED™ Windows XP Guided Tour	1-59200-886-0	$24.99 US/$33.95 CDN

MARAN ILLUSTRATED™ Series - 320 pages, Full Color

This series covers 30% more content than our Guided Tour series. Learn new software fast using our step-by-step approach and easy-to-understand text. Learning programs has never been this easy!

	ISBN	Price
MARAN ILLUSTRATED™ Access 2003	1-59200-872-0	$24.99 US/$33.95 CDN
MARAN ILLUSTRATED™ Computers	1-59200-874-7	$24.99 US/$33.95 CDN
MARAN ILLUSTRATED™ Excel 2003	1-59200-876-3	$24.99 US/$33.95 CDN
MARAN ILLUSTRATED™ Mac OS® X v.10.4 Tiger™	1-59200-878-X	$24.99 US/$33.95 CDN
MARAN ILLUSTRATED™ Office 2003	1-59200-890-9	$29.99 US/$39.95 CDN
MARAN ILLUSTRATED™ Windows XP	1-59200-870-4	$24.99 US/$33.95 CDN

101 Hot Tips Series - 240 pages, Full Color

Progress beyond the basics with MARAN ILLUSTRATED's 101 Hot Tips series. This series features 101 of the coolest shortcuts, tricks and tips that will help you work faster and easier.

	ISBN	Price
MARAN ILLUSTRATED™ Windows XP 101 Hot Tips	1-59200-882-8	$19.99 US/$26.95 CDN

 PIANO

MARAN ILLUSTRATED™ **Piano** is an information-packed resource for people who want to learn to play the piano, as well as current musicians looking to hone their skills. Combining full-color photographs and easy-to-follow instructions, this guide covers everything from the basics of piano playing to more advanced techniques. Not only does MARAN ILLUSTRATED™ Piano show you how to read music, play scales and chords and improvise while playing with other musicians, it also provides you with helpful information for purchasing and caring for your piano.

ISBN: 1-59200-864-X

Price: $24.99 US; $33.95 CDN

Page count: 304

illustrated DOG TRAINING

MARAN ILLUSTRATED™ **Dog Training** is an excellent guide for both current dog owners and people considering making a dog part of their family. Using clear, step-by-step instructions accompanied by over 400 full-color photographs, MARAN ILLUSTRATED™ Dog Training is perfect for any visual learner who prefers seeing what to do rather than reading lengthy explanations.

Beginning with insights into popular dog breeds and puppy development, this book emphasizes positive training methods to guide you through socializing, housetraining and teaching your dog many commands. You will also learn how to work with problem behaviors, such as destructive chewing.

ISBN: 1-59200-858-5

Price: $19.99 US; $26.95 CDN

Page count: 256

MARAN ILLUSTRATED™ **Knitting & Crocheting** contains a wealth of information about these two increasingly popular crafts. Whether you are just starting out or you are an experienced knitter or crocheter interested in picking up new tips and techniques, this information-packed resource will take you from the basics, such as how to hold the knitting needles or crochet hook, to more advanced skills, such as how to add decorative touches to your projects. The easy-to-follow information is communicated through clear, step-by-step instructions and accompanied by over 600 full-color photographs—perfect for any visual learner.

ISBN: 1-59200-862-3
Price: $24.99 US; $33.95 CDN
Page count: 304

MARAN ILLUSTRATED™ **Yoga** provides a wealth of simplified, easy-to-follow information about the increasingly popular practice of Yoga. This easy-to-use guide is a must for visual learners who prefer to see and do without having to read lengthy explanations.

Using clear, step-by-step instructions accompanied by over 500 full-color photographs, this book includes all the information you need to get started with yoga or to enhance your technique if you have already made yoga a part of your life. MARAN ILLUSTRATED™ Yoga shows you how to safely and effectively perform a variety of yoga poses at various skill levels, how to breathe more efficiently and much more.

ISBN: 1-59200-868-2
Price: $24.99 US; $33.95 CDN
Page count: 320

MARAN ILLUSTRATED™ Weight Training is an information-packed guide that covers all the basics of weight training, as well as more advanced techniques and exercises.

MARAN ILLUSTRATED™ Weight Training contains more than 500 full-color photographs of exercises for every major muscle group, along with clear, step-by-step instructions for performing the exercises. Useful tips provide additional information and advice to help enhance your weight training experience.

MARAN ILLUSTRATED™ Weight Training provides all the information you need to start weight training or to refresh your technique if you have been weight training for some time.

ISBN: 1-59200-866-6

Price: $24.99 US; $33.95 CDN

Page count: 320

MARAN ILLUSTRATED™ Cooking Basics is an information-packed resource that covers all the basics of cooking. Novices and experienced cooks alike will find useful information about setting up and stocking your kitchen as well as food preparation and cooking techniques. With over 500 full-color photographs illustrating the easy-to-follow, step-by-step instructions, this book is a must-have for anyone who prefers seeing what to do rather than reading long explanations.

MARAN ILLUSTRATED™ Cooking Basics also provides over 40 recipes from starters, salads and side-dishes to main course dishes and baked goods. Each recipe uses only 10 ingredients or less, and is complete with nutritional information and tips covering tasty variations and commonly asked questions.

ISBN: 1-59863-234-5

Price: $19.99 US; $26.95 CDN

Page count: 240

maran illustrated PUPPIES

MARAN ILLUSTRATED™ Puppies is a valuable resource to a wide range of readers—from individuals picking out their first puppy to those who are looking to correct their new puppy's most challenging behaviors.

This full-color guide, containing over 400 photographs, walks you step by step through finding a breeder and choosing your puppy from the litter. You will then learn how to use positive training methods to work with your puppy on housetraining, socialization and many obedience commands. MARAN ILLUSTRATED™ Puppies will also show you how to use tricks and games to teach your puppy good manners and prevent problem behaviors before they start.

ISBN: 1-59863-283-3
Price: $19.99 US; $26.95 CDN
Page count: 240

maran illustrated GUITAR

MARAN ILLUSTRATED™ Guitar is an excellent resource for people who want to learn to play the guitar, as well as for current musicians who want to fine tune their technique. This full-color guide includes over 500 photographs, accompanied by step-by-step instructions that teach you the basics of playing the guitar and reading music, as well as advanced guitar techniques. You will also learn what to look for when purchasing a guitar or accessories, how to maintain and repair your guitar, and much more.

Whether you want to learn to strum your favorite tunes or play professionally, MARAN ILLUSTRATED™ Guitar provides all the information you need to become a proficient guitarist.

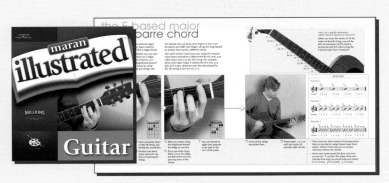

ISBN: 1-59200-860-7
Price: $24.99 US; $33.95 CDN
Page count: 320

MARAN ILLUSTRATED™ Effortless Algebra is an indispensable resource packed with crucial concepts and step-by-step instructions that make learning algebra simple. This easy-to-use guide is perfect for those who wish to gain a thorough understanding of algebra's concepts, from the most basic calculations to more complex operations.

Clear instructions thoroughly explain every topic and each concept is accompanied by helpful illustrations. This book provides all of the information you will need to fully grasp algebra, whether you are new to the subject or have been solving quadratic equations for years. MARAN ILLUSTRATED™ Effortless Algebra also provides an abundance of practice examples and tests so that you can put your knowledge into practice. This book is a must-have resource for any student of algebra.

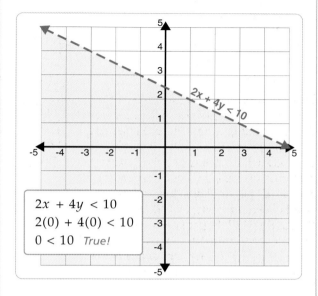

$$2x + 4y < 10$$
$$2(0) + 4(0) < 10$$
$$0 < 10 \quad \textit{True!}$$

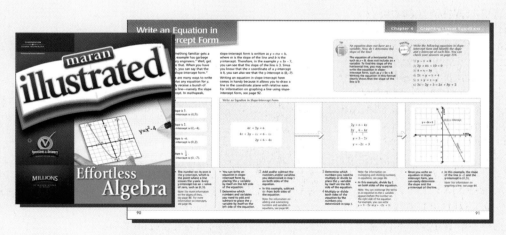

ISBN: 1-59200-942-5
Price: $24.99 US; $33.95 CDN
Page count: 304

illustrated BARTENDING

MARAN ILLUSTRATED™ Bartending
is the perfect book for those who want to
impress their guests with cocktails that are
both eye-catching and delicious. This
indispensable guide explains everything
you need to know about bartending in
the most simple and easy-to-follow terms.
Maran Illustrated™ Bartending has recipes,
step-by-step instructions and over 400
full-color photographs of all the hottest
martinis, shooters, blended drinks and
warmers. This guide also includes a
section on wine, beer and alcohol-free
cocktails as well as information on all
of the tools, liquor and other supplies
you will need to start creating drinks
right away!

ISBN: 1-59200-944-1
Price: $19.99 US; $26.95 CDN
Page count: 256